T0330025

The Ecological Footprint

New Developments in Policy and Practice

Andrea Collins

Lecturer, Cardiff University, UK

Andrew Flynn

Reader in Environmental Policy and Planning, Cardiff University, UK

Edward Elgar
PUBLISHING

Cheltenham, UK • Northampton, MA, USA

Published by
Edward Elgar Publishing Limited
The Lypiatts
15 Lansdown Road
Cheltenham
Glos GL50 2JA
UK

Edward Elgar Publishing, Inc.
William Pratt House
9 Dewey Court
Northampton
Massachusetts 01060
USA

A catalogue record for this book
is available from the British Library

Library of Congress Control Number: 2014957093

This book is available electronically in the **Elgar**online
Social and Political Science subject collection
DOI 10.4337/9780857936967

ISBN 978 0 85793 695 0 (cased)
ISBN 978 0 85793 696 7 (eBook)

Typeset by Columns Design XML Ltd, Reading
Printed and bound in Great Britain by T.J. International Ltd, Padstow

Contents

Acknowledgements

During the course of researching the Ecological Footprint and writing this book a number of people have helped us. A very sincere thank you goes to all who have supported us.

We would especially like to thank the late Morgan Parry who played such a key role in promoting the Ecological Footprint in Wales. Morgan was always a stimulating colleague and is much missed. We would also like to thank Alan Netherwood who was involved with us from the outset in debates on the Ecological Footprint in Wales. Without Alan, we would not have been able to undertake our work with Cardiff Council, and he has provided many stimulating insights. His friendship and support are greatly appreciated. Richard Cowell and Max Munday (Cardiff University) have also contributed much to our thinking on the Ecological Footprint and are highly valued colleagues.

We would also like to thank those who have been so helpful to us in our work. These include Susan Burns and Mathis Wackernagel (Global Footprint Network), John Barrett, Tommy Weidman and Rachel Birch (SEI–York), Nicky Chambers and Craig Simmons (Best Foot Forward), Jim Poole (Environment Agency Wales – now Natural Resources Wales), and staff in WWF Cymru, WWF UK, the Welsh Government, Cardiff Council and the Environment Protection Authority Victoria (Australia).

Many thanks to those who have funded our work on the Ecological Footprint, including Biffa Award and the ESRC-funded BRASS Research Centre at Cardiff University. In particular, we would like to thank Professors Ken Peattie, Bob Lee and Terry Marsden for their support and encouragement. We would also like to thank our colleagues in the School of Planning and Geography at Cardiff University for their support.

We also wish to acknowledge the following for giving permission to reproduce material in Chapter 3:

- *Local Environment*, 2007, copyright Taylor & Francis, available online: http://www.tandfonline.com, DOI:10.1080/1354 9830601183339.
- *Journal of Industrial Ecology*, 2006, copyright John Wiley & Sons, available online: http://onlinelibrary.wiley.com, DOI: 10.1162/jiec.2006.10.3.9.

Finally, we would like to give very special thanks to our families. Andrea would like to thank John and Jake. Andrew would like to thank Suki, Jake, Laura and Holly.

Abbreviations

ACCA	Association of Chartered Certified Accountants
ACF	Australian Conservation Foundation
ACORN	A Classification Of Residential Neighbourhoods
AGEDI	Abu Dhabi Global Environment Data Initiative
BFF	Best Foot Forward
BOS	Bristol Online Survey
BRASS	Centre for Business Relationships, Accountability, Sustainability and Society
CCW	Countryside Council for Wales
CO_2	carbon dioxide
COICOP	Classification of Individual Consumption According to Purpose
CSIRO	Commonwealth Scientific and Industrial Research Organisation
CURE	Centre for Urban and Regional Ecology
EEA	European Environment Agency
EF	Ecological Footprint
EIA	environmental impact assessment
EMS	environmental management system
EPA Victoria	Environment Protection Authority Victoria
ESRC	Economic and Social Research Council
EU	European Union
EUSA	Environmental Utilisation of Space
EWS-WWF	Emirates Wildlife Society – World Wide Fund for Nature
FoE	Friends of the Earth
GDP	gross domestic product
GFN	Global Footprint Network
gha	global hectare
GHG	greenhouse gas
GVA	gross value added
ISA	Centre for Integrated Sustainability Analysis

ISEW	Index of Sustainable Economic Welfare
ISI	Institute for Scientific Information
ISO	International Organization for Standardization
LBAP	Local Biodiversity Action Plan
LCA	life cycle analysis
LDP	Local Development Plans
LPR	*Living Planet Report*
METI	Ministry of Economy, Trade and Industry
MRIO	multiregional input–output
MSF	Multiple Streams Framework
NEF	New Economics Foundation
NFAs	National Footprint Accounts
NGO	non-governmental organisation
OPEN	One Planet Economy Network
REAP	Resources and Energy Analysis Programme
RIVM	National Institute for Public Health and the Environment
SA	sustainability appraisal
SCP	sustainable consumption and production
SDU	Sustainable Development Unit
SEA	strategic environmental assessment
SEI	Stockholm Environment Institute
SEI–York	Stockholm Environment Institute – York
TBL	triple bottom line
UAE	United Arab Emirates
UK	United Kingdom
UNDP	United Nations Development Programme
USA	United States of America
WWF	World Wide Fund for Nature
WWF Cymru	World Wide Fund for Nature Cymru (Wales)

1. Origins, diffusion and development of the Ecological Footprint

THE ORIGINS OF THE ECOLOGICAL FOOTPRINT

The Ecological Footprint has stimulated an enormous amount of academic and policy attention since its initial inception in the early 1990s. Van den Bergh and Grazi (2010) report that the Institute for Scientific Information (ISI) Web of Knowledge delivered over 500 journal articles for 'ecological footprint', with an increasing trend from 2001 to 2008, while the Google search engine delivered more than 2 million hits and Google Scholar more than 14 000 hits for 'ecological footprint'. This is an impressive rate of activity since the first academic article on the concept of the Ecological Footprint was published in 1992 (Rees 1992). Initially Professor William (Bill) Rees, who along with Mathis Wackernagel (his former PhD student) is most frequently associated with the Ecological Footprint, did not use the term but instead referred to 'regional capsule' and 'appropriated carrying capacity' (Rees 1992). It was only later that Rees coined the term 'Ecological Footprint' when critiquing economic models of resource use, arguing that more attention should be paid to the land area required by urban areas to sustain themselves.

Rees has described how he drew upon the biological notion of carrying capacity when developing the idea of an Ecological Footprint (see Gismondi 2000). Carrying capacity is typically defined as the maximum population size that can be supported indefinitely by a given environment (Hixon 2008). The term 'carrying capacity' is however problematic because empirically it is not a constant but will vary, for example, due to fluctuations in the climate. For this reason, carrying capacity has a greater theoretical utility value than practical value for ecologists (Hixon 2008,

p. 530). For Rees, though, it was not so much the practical challenge of trying to interpret human resource use in the language of carrying capacity that was problematic, it was the critique of economists who pointed out that the term had little value for the analysis of human consumption. This was for two reasons. First was the possibility of trade between areas: if an area is experiencing a shortage of one product this means that it can then be imported from another area, whilst a surplus can be exported to an area that demands it. The other challenge from an economic perspective to basing a resource tool on carrying capacity was that it failed to account for technology: when goods or services, whether these be man-made or natural, are in scarce supply it creates an ever greater incentive to provide a substitute. Technological innovations can overcome resource scarcity by enabling more efficient use of those resources or delivering a substitute for them. To meet the objections of economists, Rees reformulated the question of carrying capacity. Instead of asking the ecological question of 'What are the number of organisms per unit area?' he asked the Ecological Footprint question of 'How much area is needed per organism per population?' (Gismondi 2000).

By posing the question of how much land is needed to meet the consumption demands of individuals, or a defined population or activity, the advocates of the Ecological Footprint reframe environmental policy debates away from those predicated upon growth, such as weak forms of sustainable development, Factor Four (von Weizsacker et al. 1997) or ecological modernisation (see Hajer 1995; Mol 1995, 2001; Mol and Sonnenfeld 2000), to one where environmental limits are to the fore. This is because Rees and other advocates of the Ecological Footprint estimate that globally there are less than 2 hectares per capita of productive land and water area, and according to the World Wide Fund for Nature's (WWF's) *Living Planet Report* (LPR) those who live in the wealthier countries use between 4 and 12 hectares per capita per year (see WWF 2014). With those living in the developing world seeking to improve their standard of living towards that of the West, and as the world's population continues to grow, then the demands placed on the Earth's resources will continue to increase. Rees clearly expressed the problem as: 'you can't bring 9 billion people to the same material standards that we enjoy with anything like the kinds of technologies that we are using or are likely to emerge or be made available particularly in the developing world in the next 40 years' (Gismondi 2000). Similar sentiments are echoed from an ecological perspective, where it is recognised that 'the carrying capacity concept is clearly of heuristic value given the fundamental truth that no population can grow without limit, and especially given the fact that many human societies have behaved as if no limits exist' (Hixon 2008, p. 530).

THE RISE TO PROMINENCE OF THE ECOLOGICAL FOOTPRINT

In this section, we briefly introduce two key concepts that have frequently been presented as alternatives to the Ecological Footprint, namely Environmental Space and the Ecological Rucksack. Neither has gained the popularity of the Ecological Footprint. Interestingly the Ecological Footprint emerged onto the international stage at a similar time to that of the concept of Environmental Space (Opschoor and Reijinders 1991; Carley and Spapens 1998), but their fortunes have subsequently diverged markedly. Both the Ecological Footprint and Environmental Space, and related terms such as the Ecological Rucksack, have been devised to link consumption to resource use (Carley and Spapens 1998, p. 70). Within these different methods there is a desire to ask whether current patterns of resource use are sustainable and equitable. For these approaches the answer is clearly no, but they arrive at their conclusions in different ways. According to McLaren et al. (1998, p. 6): 'Environmental space is the share of the planet and its resources that the human race can sustainably take. Or in other words, the share of the Earth's resources that humanity can use without depriving future generations of the resources that they will need'.

Environmental Space identifies a number of resources that are key for production and consumption, including energy, strategic non-renewable resources (for example, pig iron for steel, cement), fresh water, woodlands, land use providing living space and a source of renewable resources (for example, food production) (Carley and Spapens 1998, p. 61). For each of these resources an assessment is then made of their exploitation (usually over a year) by humans without harming the quantity and quality that can be used by future generations. So, whereas the Ecological Footprint converts the impacts of resource use into a single unit (the global hectare) (gha), the Environmental Space method provides a separate measure of each of the key resources. As the advocates of Environmental Space admit, 'it is the more complex approach ... it is also probably more difficult to understand and communicate' (Carley and Spapens 1998, p. 70).

The concept of Environmental Space was most widely discussed in the Netherlands (see Hille 1997). The term gained much broader international currency with the publication in English of the Action Plan for a Sustainable Netherlands (Buitenkamp et al. 1992) by Friends of the Earth (FoE) Netherlands. The Action Plan is an effort to quantify the amount of Environmental Space for some major resources that will be available to each Dutch resident in 2010. The Action Plan prompted similar efforts in other countries, most notably a pan-European perspective, *Towards Sustainable Europe* (Spangenberg 1995), carried out by the Wuppertal Institute in cooperation with Friends of the Earth Europe. There is perhaps only one significant example of the application of the Environmental Space approach in the UK, that of McLaren et al. (1998). Part of the reason for the different experiences of the Ecological Footprint and Environmental Space approaches is that the latter is targeted at national government, whereas the former has most often been promoted to local government where there can be more sympathy for innovative tools, and it has much more flexibility in its application.

The idea of Environmental Space is operationalised through the measurement of material inputs. These are the sum of problems associated with materials consumption (for example, physical disturbance, pollution, waste disposal) and can be roughly related to the total amount of materials moved in the course of economic activity (Hille 1997). Materials include the earth that must be moved to get to resources and the extraction of those resources to make products. Finally, material input analysis includes the economically worthless materials that have to be moved in the course of construction activities, and materials unintentionally moved in the course of economic activity. In a further refinement of the materials input approach is the Ecological Rucksack. The Rucksack calculates what would normally be hidden behind our material inputs as it includes all of the resources used in our consumption of a particular material (Hille 1997). Rather like a more sophisticated and comprehensive form of life cycle analysis, research on the Ecological Rucksack has concentrated on products but has also gone further to compare different ways of consuming foods, for example ready meals versus home-prepared food (Sonesson et al. 2005), and been used to critique the Carbon Footprint (Burger et al. 2009; Giljum et al. 2011).

Although Environmental Space and the Ecological Rucksack have their advocates and show considerable methodological sophistication, they have not gained the same prominence as the Ecological Footprint (see Table 1A.1 in the Appendix to this chapter for a timeline of key events in the Ecological Footprint storyline). In part this is because, as the case of the UK shows, the Ecological Footprint has had a number of applications, including products, organisations, services, and at different levels of government (Chambers and Lewis 2001; BFF 2002a; Barrett and Scott 2003; Barrett et al. 2005c; Collins et al. 2005). More than that, though, the Ecological Footprint has had policy entrepreneurs who have championed its case. These entrepreneurs have been able to promote the Ecological Footprint to a wide range of policy audiences and to promote it as a way of helping to improve the quality of decision making by ensuring that more attention is given to the environmental consequences of policies. In the section below we briefly review Kingdon's (1984) policy model and its usefulness in helping to understand the rise to prominence (and subsequent demise) in public policy agendas of the Ecological Footprint.

POLICY CHANGE AND THE ECOLOGICAL FOOTPRINT

Kingdon (1984) proposed a Multiple Streams Framework (MSF) to explain how agenda-setting occurs. Policies change (or remain stable) according to the extent to which a series of independent streams conceived of as problems, policies (solutions) and politics come together. Boezman et al. (2010) have also drawn upon Kingdon's work to explore the waxing and waning of the Ecological Footprint in Dutch policy making. The MSF theorises that the coupling of these streams at critical junctures results in the greatest potential for public policy agenda change. The MSF is helpful for understanding how the Ecological Footprint has become legitimised in public policy because it attaches problems to policies. Policy agendas do not change because of an objective and rational search for solutions to policy problems. Rather, solutions compete with one another, and much depends on how problems and their solutions are constructed in policy arenas. As Boezman et al. (2010, p. 1757) note, 'Policy processes are as much structured by ideas, causal stories and beliefs as they are structured by institutions'. Moreover, the MSF is helpful because it highlights the part that may be played by key organisations who advocate the Ecological Footprint such as WWF and Global Footprint Network (GFN) and policy entrepreneurs such as Mathis Wackernagel in promoting policy change.

Policy entrepreneurs play a key part in the MSF model as they are able to bring together policies, problems and politics to advance their favoured policy option. Kingdon (1984) recognised that a small number of highly motivated actors exercise a significant ability to build coalitions of support for their ideas and secure policy change. These policy entrepreneurs tend to share a number of characteristics, including the identification of an alternative policy or approach and a drive to promote change; an assertion of legitimacy, such as scientific expertise (the Ecological Footprint is promoted as a technically sophisticated model) or the ability to speak on behalf of others (Wackernagel is the leading figure and founder of GFN, the network organisation that promotes the use of the Ecological Footprint and standardises its methodology; see Chapter 6); and, because of their credibility, policy entrepreneurs often have access to political and policy elites (for instance, Wackernagel has worked with the Environment Protection Authority Victoria in Australia (EPA Victoria); see Chapter 4), and with the United Arab Emirates (UAE) Ministry of Environment and Water (see Chapter 3); and the work of policy entrepreneurs can be linked to organisations that wish to show that they can provide leadership. For example, the Welsh Government, a devolved governmental body in the UK (created in 1998), has from the outset wanted to show that its legislative responsibility to promote sustainable development in all of its activities has made it different from other legislative bodies. It has thus been sympathetic to using the Ecological Footprint as one of its headline indicators for measuring progress towards sustainability (Flynn 2010). Similarly, in Australia the Environment Protection Authority Victoria (EPA Victoria) has made much use of the Ecological Footprint (see Chapter 4). Finally, policy entrepreneurs are successful at defining problems, highlighting problem attributes and formulating credible policy solutions; what Kingdon calls a policy stream. Policy streams are the way in which issues become topics of public policy concern, and the way in which they are defined.

The Ecological Footprint has further reinforced the concerns raised by environmentalists and scientists regarding the extent of environmental degradation. WWF's biennial LPRs, the most recent one being published in 2014 (WWF 2014), provide an overview of the biocapacity and resource use of countries and how that has changed over time. The message that emerges is that biocapacity is declining and resource use increasing, but that it is doing so in a highly differentiated way. Some countries are major users of resources, such as Qatar and the UAE; whilst industrialisation, urbanisation and a growing middle class are fuelling enormous increases in consumption in China, so that although China has a low Ecological Footprint per capita, at a national level it is large and on an upward trajectory. In 2008, China's Ecological Footprint per capita was 2.1 gha, lower than the global average of 2.7 gha, but its total Ecological Footprint was 2.9 billion gha due to its total population and per capita footprint (WWF China 2012). The use of data over time and between countries enables comparisons to be made, questions to be raised, and for the nature of continuing on current development paths to be problematised. Thus, a major environmental problem becomes defined as one that demands action from governments.

So far in this chapter we have explored how policy entrepreneurs identify policy problems and provide policy solutions. In Kingdon's model, how problems are defined is also important. The timing of the rise of the Ecological Footprint to public policy prominence in the 1990s, and then its demise from the mid-2000s onwards (see Chapter 5), is tied into wider environmental and sustainability debates. Through the 1980s and particularly in the 1990s a series of high-profile summits, such as the United Nations Conference on Environment and Development in Rio (1992) and the World Summit on Sustainable Development in Johannesburg (2002), and growing concern with climate change, such as the United Nations

Environment Programme and the World Meteorological Organization establishing the Intergovernmental Panel on Climate Change (1998), and the adoption of the Kyoto Protocol (1997), meant that there was widespread recognition of the scale and significance of environmental change. Debates on sustainable development, which often sought to connect local consumption with global impacts, could combine with climate change debates that drew attention to resource limits in the Ecological Footprint. Here was an indicator which was based upon the finiteness of the Earth's resources and could show how individuals, cities or countries were consuming or overconsuming their share.

According to Boezman et al. (2010, p. 1757), policy actors are engaged in a process of continuous communicative interaction in which ideas and arguments are being tested and reformulated. Drawing upon the work of Kingdon (1984), Boezman and his colleagues point out that experts, bureaucrats, academics and advisors rework scientific insights into new policy concepts, of which the Ecological Footprint and its variants such as the Carbon Footprint and Water Footprint make good examples. Those involved in the policy process spend a considerable amount of time and resources promoting their favoured concepts, so that when a policy window or opportunity opens up they can manoeuvre their concept into a leading position as a policy solution.

In their work on the transfer of the Ecological Footprint into Dutch environmental policy, Boezman et al. (2010) also point out that the way in which a policy issue is framed may impact upon its use. They distinguish a number of features that a policy concept may hold. First, and perhaps one of the most important for our purposes, is the quality of the scientific knowledge behind the concept. GFN has recognised the importance of scientific validity and has sought to demonstrate the robustness of the Ecological Footprint through publications in peer-reviewed scientific journals (see Chapter 5) and standardising the methodology (see Chapter 6). Critics of the Ecological Footprint have similarly recognised the claims that can be made by a scientifically valid concept, and have sought to undermine its method (see, for example, Van den Bergh and Verbruggen 1999; Lenzen and Murray 2001; Ferng 2002; Van Vurren and Smeets 2001; McDonald and Patterson 2004; Moffatt 2000; van Kooten and Butle 1999; Ayres 2000; Herendeen 2000; McGregor et al. 2004). Second, there is the fit between the normative claims made by a concept, and existing value systems. Central to the Ecological Footprint are claims of resource limits and fair share of the Earth's resources. At a time of widespread prosperity in the West, rethinking models of economic growth (see, for example, Anderson and M'Gonigle 2012; Beder 2011; Illge and Schwarze 2009) can have some appeal. The onset of recession in 2008 makes more traditional models of growth more attractive, and arguments for 'sustainable growth' move to the fore. A third feature is the rhetorical quality of a concept (Hannigan 2006). The Ecological Footprint strikes a resonant chord with the public and policy makers; it makes complex problems understandable and communicates the scale of the environmental challenge. As we argue below, the Footprint has considerable metaphorical power.

By applying Kingdon's (1984) MSF, Boezman et al. (2010) compare the fates of the Ecological Footprint and Environmental Space (Boezman et al. call it the Environmental Utilisation of Space, EUSA) in Dutch environmental policy. Both concepts portray natural systems as providing a boundary condition for societal development. EUSA measures material flows that an economy can extract from the environment and return as waste. EUSA disaggregates its data by sector, whilst the Ecological Footprint turns all resource usage into a single measure, the hypothetical global hectare. EUSA was championed by an academic entrepreneur, J.B. Opschoor (Opschoor and Weterings 1994), but never received the recognition of the Ecological Footprint. In explaining the rise of the Ecological Footprint to policy prominence in the Dutch environmental policy between 1998 and 2006, Boezman et al. (2010, p. 1762) draw upon three contextual factors. The first of these is the way in which wider environmental policy debates were focusing upon resource depletion. Second, there was a set of agency variables which involved the lobbying practices of non-governmental organisations (NGOs) and the importing of expertise from GFN. As Boezman et al. (2010, p. 1762) explain:

> NGOs invited Wackernagel to the Netherlands (1999) and gave him the opportunity to present the Ecological Footprint repeatedly to audiences of experts, civil servants, scientists and others involved in the environmental policy and advisory field. The involvement of Wackernagel himself and the echoes of his involvement in the RIVM [National

Institute for Public Health and the Environment] publications decisively endorsed the Ecological Footprint's scientific credibility.

A further boost to the legitimacy of the Ecological Footprinting in the Netherlands was its endorsement by the Environment Minister Pronk. Third, there was a set of issue-specific factors, particularly related to the Ecological Footprint's rhetorical qualities and the imagery that it conjured up. The Footprint was considered to have had widespread appeal in the Netherlands (and elsewhere) because it 'succeeded in bridging the gap from scientific ecological knowledge to the (policy) public in what initially appeared to be a consistent and easy-to-understand way' (Boezman et al. 2010, p. 1762).

In the demise of the Ecological Footprint it was agency variables that proved to be of major importance. For instance, from early on there were robust critiques of the Ecological Footprint by well-respected scientists such as Van den Bergh and Verbruggen (1999). Official environmental advisory committees also pointed to weaknesses in the methodology (Boezman et al. 2010). In a similar way to that of the UK, the Ecological Footprint was only able to temporarily 'fix' itself to the mainstream Dutch environmental policy agenda. The reasons why the Ecological Footprint may not become firmly fixed on policy agendas can be complex, and this is discussed in more detail in Chapter 4 when we explore how the Ecological Footprint has developed in the UK, and bring together local and national agendas and the roles of different professional interests.

THE ECOLOGICAL FOOTPRINT AND POLICY DEVELOPMENT

Having looked at how the rise of the Ecological Footprint can be linked to the way in which the policy process works, in this section we explore in more detail how the Footprint may contribute to policy development. First, we assess the ways in which knowledge and expertise can contribute to policy making; and second, we examine how environmental indicators may help to shape policy, but also how expert-led systems, which typifies the Footprint experience, can quickly become marginal to policy development.

Knowledge, Expertise and Policy

There is widespread recognition that environmental issues tend to be marginalised in decision making (Hertin et al. 2009). A prime motivation of those involved in promoting the Ecological Footprint is that it should inform the policy process, and therefore bring knowledge on the scale of environmental change to the attention of decision makers. In their thinking on how they may contribute to policy development, Ecological Footprint practitioners are engaging in debates on how environmental knowledge is used, and as discussed below, working with a very particular view of the policy process.

Rayner (2003, p. 164) has characterised contemporary policy making as taking place in the 'age of assessment'. He notes (ibid.) that there is a '[g]rowth in the reliance on … assessment techniques has been accompanied by an expansion of expertise to design, operate and interpret such tools'. This is certainly true of the Ecological Footprint, where interest in its use grew dramatically (see, for example, Chapters 3, 4 and 5). At the same time there was the emergence of a set of elite actors able to undertake sophisticated Ecological Footprint analyses (in the UK this included Best Foot Forward, BFF; and the Stockholm Environment Institute – York, SEI–York) and to bestow legitimacy on Ecological Footprint studies (for instance GFN; see Chapter 6).

Appraisal, or a tool like the Ecological Footprint, is presented by its proponents as an objective practice, 'valued for its scientific authority' (Clark and Majone 1985, p. 16). Drawing on the work of Owens et al. (2004), Adelle et al. (2012) describe traditional forms of appraisal in which a 'technical-rational model' is based on a positivist epistemology. Here an 'objective appraisal' leads straightforwardly to 'better' decisions via instrumental forms of learning. Instrumental learning is that in which knowledge directly informs decisions because it provides specific information (that is, information that is relevant to a particular time and place). This can be contrasted with conceptual learning, in which knowledge gradually challenges existing belief systems or identifies new ideas; and strategic learning, in which knowledge is used in a more overtly political way to support or challenge existing positions. For the latter, knowledge can often have a symbolic value and a power to legitimate actions (see Waylen and Young 2014; Hertin et al. 2009).

A common argument for the adoption of assessment techniques is their transparency: that it becomes clearer how decisions have been made and how judgements have been formed. An interviewee[1] commented:

> My key clients are who I would call decision makers or people who help, decision support officers I suppose ... So my idea is that the position that the person ... is not important ... [W]e see council officers, civil servants, we see that we are offering them help in formulating policy and offering support to provide numbers to the policies which they may or may not put forward to [politicians].

There is, though, an alternative and more critical perspective on the Ecological Footprint. Key data is the preserve of consultancies and they protect it. This enables consultants to gain repeat business through new Footprint studies but can make it difficult for analysts to understand how the Ecological Footprint results have been derived. As one critical commentator pointed out: 'By offering no transparency in how it [the Ecological Footprint] is calculated, how it's done, offering no explanation of the assumptions behind it, you can't even tell where the data has come from, and so people have to go to them [consultants] again if they want an update'.

Nevertheless, the belief is that by providing information to decision makers that they would not otherwise have had, a fuller picture is provided of the implications of any decision. However, what may count as a more comprehensive data set to help inform decisions is not straightforward. At a normative level, Footprint advocates wish to increase the information on offer to decision makers but are also able to recognise that in practice information can be used selectively. As one practitioner interviewee explained:

> What we highlight is its [the Ecological Footprint] use as a decision support tool and that's what we sell it as more than anything. We have also tried to suggest that it is organic and dynamic in its approach ... to give the user the ability to identify with the tool on their own personal terms; they can add their own perspective into the tool, where they got the data from, what they think of the components ... So it's about the user being able to identify with the tool and have some sense of ownership over it and this was so important to us.

Most commentators argue that the rational–technical model sits alongside more deliberative policy styles in which actors pursue multiple goals and policy appraisal becomes a means to support arguments or deflect critical attention. Information arising from an appraisal or an Ecological Footprint study would not be expected to directly transfer into policy or decision making (Owens et al. 2004; Adelle et al. 2012).

Ecological Footprint practitioners recognise that they are working in a complex policy arena. When one consultant was asked what difference their Ecological Footprint studies had made, the response was very cautious:

> For its [the Footprint's] impact on policy and strategy, there may be someone in the council who likes it, who tries to use it on something or quoted it to a politician. But I don't think it actually changed policy. In [name of another local council] it is going to be included in the strategy [but] that doesn't really mean anything unless you're going to act on it, but the foundation is there as they are not frightened of it. And in the future, when they come to recalculate they'll be ready for the idea. I have no knowledge at all that [name of local council] are going to use it as an indicator. [Whilst for another council the] Ecological Footprint is an indicator that [name of local council] have got it on their list.

To put the Ecological Footprint on an environmental indicator list was, however, dismissed by the interviewee as a minimal commitment.

In addition, as Hertin et al. (2009, p. 1197) have pointed out, often an assessment report is used to justify a specific measure on the basis of its superiority to alternative courses of action. For the Ecological Footprint this is a major challenge. This is because the Footprint questions the basis of existing policy since it assumes the existence of environmental limits and economic constraints. This means that in pro-growth political systems the Ecological Footprint as a tool to analyse policy or contribute to policy development will often find itself on the margin. Footprint practitioners recognise the dilemma that they face, and as one explained:

> We try to be as objective as we can but at the same time we had to make changes in [name of] report because we were told they were too controversial. Now you may say 'oh you may sell out if you make those changes' but the response from the Steering Group was if you don't make those changes then the credibility [of the overall report will suffer], people will turn off because they will see this as too radical.

Advocates of the Ecological Footprint believe passionately in the value of the Footprint as a tool to aid better decisions, and also of the need to raise the status of the environment in decision making. To cope with a situation in which their findings can be marginalised, practitioners act as policy entrepreneurs, seeking to change policy where they think that they can. The interviewee continued:

> So it is a case of its [*sic*] better to say something rather than nothing? I kind of twist it in a way. I do try and say things which the results say to me, because we do analysis as well as showing the results. We do highlight what the reduction [in the Footprint] would be if you take on certain policy options. We don't just stop at 'there's your report, good luck'. I'd be a bit bored if I didn't do that to tell you the truth.

In the following chapters, we explore in more detail how ideas and arguments shape policy, particularly at the local level where some of the most innovative work on the Ecological Footprint has taken place. Whilst the rational model is empirically weak it continues to hold a fascination for Footprint practitioners and those they seek to influence in government. In practice, though, knowledge is not simply used to help solve problems; it is also used strategically to help structure problems and solutions (Hertin et al. 2009). Chapter 2 argues that the Cardiff Ecological Footprint was partially successful in making use of data in an instrumental fashion as it tried to address contemporary policy issues. In Chapters 3 and 4 we explore the broader, more strategic context in which knowledge was being used. In these two chapters we look at the numerous local Ecological Footprint studies, all of which began to add to the credibility to the tool. At the same time, there was growing academic interest in the Footprint, and we chart the rise and fall of Footprint papers in academic journals. Together these practitioner and academic knowledge bases reinforced one another and could combine with other ideas (for example, the Carbon Footprints, debates on environmental limits) to help shape the policy environment (Dunlop 2014; Weiss 1995; Haines-Young and Potschin 2014).

Ecological Footprint and Sustainability Indicators

The Ecological Footprint has become increasingly popular as an indicator of environmental sustainability. As previously discussed, the Footprint has been adopted by the Welsh Government as one of its headline sustainability indicators. The literature on sustainability indicators has blossomed in recent years. Policy makers, researchers, citizens and environmental groups have all been keenly interested in finding out whether or not units of government or organisations are becoming more or less sustainable over time. As the UK Sustainable Development Commission (2008) has noted: 'Indicators are an effective means of quantifying and measuring progress towards sustainable development'. Whilst it is undoubtedly true that indicators can help to measure progress, their use in practice is more complex. The Ecological Footprint provides a good example of the multifaceted nature of some indicators: the Footprint can serve different purposes for different audiences. At times, both the purpose of the Ecological Footprint and the interpretation of the data which it produces can be contested, and so our perspective on the Footprint is unlikely to remain constant. Indeed, it is one of the reasons why in this book we have analysed the Ecological Footprint in an organisational context (see Chapter 2).

For their proponents, environmental or sustainability indicators can 'measure, simplify and communicate important issues and trends' (Department of the Environment, Transport and the Regions 2000, p. 5). Their development has been called for at all levels of government, from the international stage, through Agenda 21 to national and local governments. In recent years there has been a proliferation of work on sustainability indicators and its reporting. The debate about sustainability indicators has involved many disciplines, for example ecological economics (Hezri and Dovers 2006). However, it has also been noted that when put into practice, sustainability indicators are 'socially constructed policy instruments' (Astleithner and Hamedinger 2003).

There are many different types of indicator. A useful and widely noticed classification has been offered by (Brugmann 1997):

● Integrating indicators or indexes, to portray linkages between economic, social and environmental phenomena.
● Trend indicators, linked to targets and thresholds.
● Predictive indicators, relying upon mathematical forecasting models or, alternatively, conditional indicators using 'if–then' scenarios to estimate future conditions.

- Distributional indicators, measuring intergenerational equity and specifying local, upstream and downstream effects through the use of highly disaggregated data.
- Depending upon the framework applied, condition–stress–response indicators that provide simple causal models for local conditions. (Brugmann 1997, p. 62; based on Maclaren 1996, p. 186)

The growth of sustainability indicators has reflected a wider concern to measure performance. Trends in the organisation of national, regional and local governments to contract out services or to work with external bodies has led to much greater attention being given to the setting of targets, measuring performance and providing rewards (or penalties). So a sustainability indicator, like any other indicator, is 'a policy-relevant variable that is specified and defined in such a way as to be measurable over time and/or space … [T]he key feature of an indicator is that measurement can take place and this, in turn, allows comparison' (Astleithner et al. 2004, p. 8).

In addition, indicators have been seen by some as a 'green herring', signifying a focus on measurement rather than action (MacGillivray 1998, p. 93). Despite this, the view that 'at the local level, indicators are ideally suited for performance measurement' (Brugmann 1997, p. 59) is becoming increasing popular (Hemphill et al. 2004, p. 726). Whilst such indicators 'are not themselves "the answer" … they can lead us to better answers if they provide trustworthy information about those things in life that we value' (Lawrence 1998, p. 68).

Within the literature on indicators there is widespread awareness that indicators are not neutral. The information that they provide can help to make more informed policy decisions, but assessment requires the selection and weighing of criteria. There is, thus, much discussion of the methodologies to be used in the development of indicators, technical debates around what is (or is not) being measured, and how indicators can best be used in the decision making process. We follow the approach outlined in the literature, but towards the end add two important caveats that should be borne in mind in what follows. First, indicators are social constructs in that they indicate what key groups regard as important features of sustainable development. Second, indicators are used in real-life contexts and so their development, interpretation and implications for action will be intertwined with patterns of urban culture and governance (Astleithner et al. 2004).

Indicators can also be used for educative purposes, to guide policy or assess performance; however, these uses often have contradictory objectives which can result in confusion (Brugmann 1997, p. 59). For example, some local governments in the UK have sought to use the Ecological Footprint as a means to guide policy development, as it appears to show the environmental pressures arising from different development strategies, and at the same time to use the Footprint to communicate with their citizens about the scale of their resource use. Whilst the Ecological Footprint may have multiple functions, its use for different purposes can be confusing since it means that data has to be presented and interpreted in different ways for diverse audiences.

However, as sustainability is a contested concept with a proliferation of operational definitions, the choice of measure will never be wholly objective or value-neutral. Consequently, there tends to be a lack of consensus about the indicators that should be used and how they should be considered (Hemphill et al. 2004, p. 726). As Owens and Cowell (2002, p. 29) have pointed out, decisions about what is 'sustainable' are inseparable from moral and political choices. Taking on board the injunction from Owens and Cowell in itself presents a range of issues about desirable ends and the ways of measuring progress towards them. It is therefore essential to remember that 'those developing indicators need to be deliberate in their choice of sources, and accept that reasonable people can disagree' (Lawrence 1998, p. 70).

From a process perceptive, it is important to keep in mind that the use of sustainability indicators can generate outcomes in many ways. These can be divided into three groups (Gahin et al. 2003, p. 662):

1. through the process of developing the indicators;
2. by communicating (publishing and distributing) the indicators;
3. by action arising from the development of the indicators.

Table 1.1 provides a summary of the different areas of applicability of sustainability indicators.

Table 1.1   Areas of applicability of sustainability indicators

Administrative context	Type of analysis	Practical application
Information and debate	Individual/household evaluation	In education As an element of environmental protection work Publication on municipal home page
Political guidance	National benchmarking Trend analysis Identifying priorities across sectors Performance measurement	In annual reports In municipal planning reports Community strategies
Administrative guidance	Impact assessment	Incorporation in existing systems of impact assessment in administrative procedure

Sources: Based on Aall and Norland (2005, p. 33), Bond (2002), Brugmann (1997).

THE ECOLOGICAL FOOTPRINT AS A METAPHOR

Cohen (2011) has argued that discursive entrepreneurs invoke new imagery that reframes challenges. The Ecological Footprint brings together two unrelated terms: (1) 'ecological', with its suggestion of biodiversity, management and fragility; and (2) the 'Footprint' – a human mobility activity – to give an impression of how people's actions have ecological consequences. For instance, at the launch of Wales's second Ecological Footprint report in Cardiff (May 2005) one of the keynote speakers vividly illustrated the power of the Footprint as a metaphor: 'I like the Footprint (stamps the floor repetitively), because that's exactly what we're doing to the Earth every day' (environmental NGO; quoted in Collins et al. 2009, p. 1709). Here the Ecological Footprint is being used as a conceptual metaphor: 'a simple set of relationships ... [that helps in] communicating more complex analogous concepts' (Raymond et al. 2013, p. 537).

By symbolically asserting that our ecological resource use is a Footprint, we begin to think of how our decisions on consumption – our Footprint – can have environmental impacts. In doing so, we begin to make connections between the ways in which we live our lives and the environmental consequences that arise from our lifestyle decisions. At a political level, metaphors work by bringing together what may otherwise have been diverse constituencies and fostering a collective understanding of potential courses of action (Cohen 2011). Similarly Larson (2011) reminds us that metaphors are performative; they do something. As Larson (2011, p. 8) goes on to explain:

> [metaphors] influence our conception of the world, they catalyze particular outcomes. They dramatically affect our world views, which is not just our view of the world but also our way of living within it. Thus, the metaphors we select have very real outcomes in the constitution of culture and the political realm.

One reason why the Ecological Footprint works well as a metaphor is that the multiple meanings that can be attached to it provide a variety of messages for action. For example, the Ecological Footprint may enable us to think about inequalities of consumption as some individuals and nations have much higher Ecological Footprints than others, and so proposals to promote greater equity become attractive. Alternatively the Ecological Footprint can provide connections to how consumption in one place may have environmental consequences in another, so that a connection is made between local consumption and the global environment. Or the Ecological Footprint may suggest the finiteness of resource availability on the Earth so that the focus moves to efforts to reduce demands upon the Earth's resources. Throughout any discussions of the Ecological Footprint it is anthropocentric (the image is of a human footprint) and the interest is in human resource demand and the impacts of depleting resources upon human welfare. These different interpretations of the Ecological Footprint show how metaphors 'both highlight and hide' (Larson 2011, p. 209). Metaphors provide only partial understandings (Raymond et al. 2013, p. 537) and the Ecological Footprint privileges some features of environmental management such as resource consumption, whilst marginalising others such as social welfare.

Metaphors can be particularly powerful in environmental policy as they help to interpret the natural world. As we have seen in the discussion above on the MSF, the Ecological Footprint rose quickly to public policy prominence, and one of the reasons why it was able to do so is because of its wide-ranging appeal. Larsson (2011, p. 7) has argued that:

A metaphor must be both accurate and comprehensible if people are to understand and embrace it. And because scientists and non-scientists live in a similar bodily and cultural context, well chosen metaphors appeal to both audiences. Whether from embodied or cultural sources, metaphors provide a remarkable way for scientists to describe their findings to others, including colleagues, scientists in other disciplines, and even non-scientists.

As the Ecological Footprint moved up public policy agendas in central and local governments, it inevitably marginalised other ideas such as Environmental Space. Whilst the Ecological Footprint may not have been as conceptually or methodologically robust as Environmental Space (see Hille 1997), it proved to be the politically more attractive. This is at least partly due to its power as a metaphor (Raymond et al. 2013).

Interest in analysing metaphors and their meaning has grown markedly in recent years. According to Low et al. (2010, pp. vii–viii), there is now widespread agreement that metaphors are important for the communication of abstract ideas, and that they have an ideological role; they help privilege some ideas over others. For metaphor researchers, much attention is now being given to how people use metaphors, such as the way in which advocates of the Ecological Footprint can use it to communicate scientific knowledge about resource consumption. Clearly, claims to scientific knowledge still count for much in policy arenas, and certainly in the environmental field where claims for problems and solutions are based on scientific expertise. For the Ecological Footprint to be able to make scientific claims enhances its credibility and the way in which it can contribute to policy debates. Work on the Ecological Footprint, particularly by its advocates, makes much of the science behind the concept (see, for example, Barrett 2001; Barrett et al. 2005a; Borucke et al. 2013; Galli et al. 2007; Lenzen et al. 2007; Wackernagel et al. 1999, 2004b). Raymond et al. (2013) claim that the Ecological Footprint is a less scientific metaphor than, say, 'the war against invasive species', because it originates outside of environmental science. Nevertheless, as a metaphor to communicate the scale of resource consumption and to persuade a variety of actors, from citizens to NGOs, officials and politicians, of the need for action, the Ecological Footprint has proved remarkably effective. Indeed, an indication of the Footprint's effectiveness as a metaphor is that it has been applied to a number of other environmental tools to give them legitimacy. So we now have Carbon Footprints and Water Footprints.

BOOK STRUCTURE

We have been fortunate to be both participants and observers of developments in the Ecological Footprint. We first became involved in research on the Ecological Footprint in the early 2000s. There was much interest in the Ecological Footprint in Wales and we were then given the opportunity to work on a project investigating Cardiff's Ecological Footprint. From that time on we have been involved in thinking about new applications for the Ecological Footprint, such as for major sports events and festivals, exploring how the Ecological Footprint may or may not become embedded in an organisation (Cardiff Council), and been involved in a number of Ecological Footprint conferences. During this time we have taken the opportunity to talk to fellow academics, government officials, Ecological Footprint practitioners, NGOs and GFN staff. Many of these have been involved in multiple interviews or discussions. This has allowed us to build up a rich data source of key person interviewees. We have made use of these discussions and interviews throughout the book, as they have assisted enormously in our understanding of the Ecological Footprint. The Ecological Footprint community at a national and international level is relatively small. All of our interviewees have been anonymised. As well as interviews and discussions, Chapter 6 also makes use of an online survey that we conducted of GFN partners. The survey was conducted at a time of growth in Ecological Footprint studies. The survey provides a valuable insight into how those who work at a national level come together in an international network to further their interest in policy applications and methodological improvements.

We regard the Ecological Footprint as multifaceted – it has a policy development dimension, it is a communication tool and helps to frame environmental knowledge, and it has witnessed a number of methodological developments and novel applications – and throughout the book have sought to portray it in that way. In this chapter we have set the political and institutional context for the Ecological Footprint.

In Chapter 2, we take these ideas forward and examine how the Ecological Footprint has contributed to policy development. Our analysis concentrates on Cardiff, where we can draw upon our longitudinal data. This enables us to provide detailed insights into how the Ecological Footprint fares in an organisational setting. The approach to Ecological Footprinting in Cardiff has often been acclaimed for its efforts to mainstream environmental thinking.

Chapter 3 critically reviews the process developed to measure Cardiff's Ecological Footprint and the results that arose. Information on the size of Cardiff's Footprint led to further work on how that should be interpreted and what implications it may have for future policy development. To provide further context for the Cardiff study, its results are compared to other cities. Cardiff, like a number of other UK cities, has shown itself keen to engage with the Ecological Footprint.

In Chapter 4 we explore the reasons behind the UK's interest in Ecological Footprint studies. Key factors that we consider include funding opportunities which enabled the growth of consultancies and academic institutes, as well as the efforts of environmental NGOs such as WWF. The UK experience is contrasted with that of Australia, where with a much less favourable funding environment there have nevertheless been important initiatives undertaken to promote the Ecological Footprint. One of the more remarkable features of the Ecological Footprint has been the way in which academics and practitioners have promoted innovative applications.

In Chapter 5, we critically examine some of the key novel applications, such as Footprint calculators, and how the Ecological Footprint has been used to communicate environmental information. These innovations in the use of the Footprint have done much to ensure that debates on the Ecological Footprint have been so vibrant.

Chapter 6 provides an analysis of GFN, the key body that brings together Footprint producers and users and seeks to establish a standard that can be applied to Ecological Footprint studies. Standard-setting emerges as a key means to establish the credibility of the Ecological Footprint. The chapter also reports on a survey of GFN partners and shows that they have diverse interests in the Ecological Footprint, and that once attention begins to wane in the Ecological Footprint some partners also lose interest, which begins to undermine the credibility of the Footprint.

Finally, in Chapter 7 we cover three themes: the changing status of the Ecological Footprint; the growth of other Footprint tools, especially that for carbon; and how the Footprint contributes to our understanding of environmental knowledge.

NOTE

1. Our data collection strategy and reporting of interview material is discussed later in the chapter.

APPENDIX

Table 1A.1   *Timeline of key Ecological Footprint events, activities and publications*

Year	Events, activities, publications
1992	Professor William (Bill) Rees, School of Community and Regional Planning at the University of British Columbia, publishes first academic article 'Ecological footprints and appropriated carrying capacity: what urban economics leaves out', in the journal *Environment and Urbanisation*.
1994	Mathis Wackernagel, PhD student at University of British Columbia (under the supervision of Professor Rees) defends his PhD thesis, 'Ecological Footprint and appropriated carrying capacity: a tool for planning toward sustainability'.
1996	Wackernagel and Rees co-author first book on the Ecological Footprint, *Our Ecological Footprint: Reducing Human Impact on the Earth*.
	UK Ecological Footprint consultants Best Foot Forward (BFF), develops EcoCal™, the first computer based calculator to measure personal and household Ecological Footprints.
1999	BFF develops Regional Stepwise, the first regional Ecological Footprint calculator and undertakes the first Footprint study of a local government area in the UK (Isle of Wight).
2000	WWF publishes its first *Living Planet Report* on the planet's available biocapacity and Ecological Footprint.
	Wackernagel co-authors book with Chambers and Simmons (co-founders of BFF): *Sharing Nature's Interest: Ecological Footprints as an Indicator of Sustainability* (Chambers et al. 2000).
	Australian Conservation Foundation (ACF) publishes *Natural Advantage. A Blueprint for a Sustainable Australia* (Krokenberger et al. 2000), outlining 32 reforms needed for a sustainable environment and to reduce Australia's Ecological Footprint.
2001	World Wide Fund for Nature (WWF) Cymru (Wales) commissions first Ecological Footprint study of Wales. **Wales** adopts the Ecological Footprint as one of five headline indicators for sustainability, and is the first country to formally monitor and report on changes.
	UK Ecological Footprint consultant Stockholm Environment Institute – York (SEI-York), undertakes its first Ecological Footprint studies (Liverpool and York).
2002	Global Footprint Network (GFN) is launched, and formally established as a non-profit organisation in 2003.
	WWF publishes *Living Planet Report 2002*.
	WWF UK publishes *Ecological Footprints: A Guide for Local Authorities* (Bond 2002), explaining what an Ecological Footprint is, its calculation and value as a policy and environmental awareness tool.

Year	Events, activities, publications

The Environmental Protection Authority Victoria (EPA Victoria), Australia, invites Mathis Wackernagel, Executive Director of GFN, to the state of Victoria to facilitate training workshops and meetings in Melbourne and Sydney to help promote the Ecological Footprint. Two further visits are arranged between 2002 and 2007.

The Scottish Executive (UK) commissions Ecological Footprint study of Scotland's five main cities.

2003   WWF UK secures funding from Biffa Award to undertake Ecological Footprint studies in Wales and Scotland.

BIFFA Award publishes with SEI-York and WWF, the first material flow analysis and Ecological Footprint study of a UK region (South East of England) (Barrett et al. 2003).

2004   30+ organisations join the GFN Partner Network.

Wackernagel and Rees's book, *Our Ecological Footprint: Reducing Human Impact on the Earth*, is published in Japanese.

GFN collaborates with WWF on WWF's *Living Planet Report 2004*.

2005   50+ organisations are now part of the GFN Partner Network.

GFN establishes two committees (National Accounts and Standards), comprised of members from the network's partner organisations. Standards are drafted and made available for public comment.

GFN launches its Ten-in-Ten campaign to institutionalise the Ecological Footprint in at least ten nations by 2015. GFN is in active dialogue with 24 countries likely to be early adopters of the Ecological Footprint.

GFN develops the first set of Footprint Standards for Ecological Footprint applications and its communication.

GFN collaborates with WWF on:
Europe 2005: The Ecological Footprint (Wackernagel et al. 2005b), the first Ecological Footprint study of Europe's 25 nations. The Ecological Footprint was subsequently included in Europe's Sustainable Development Strategy;
Asia-Pacific 2005: The Ecological Footprint and Natural Wealth (Wackernagel et al. 2005a), which reports on the Ecological Footprints of more than 20 countries.

GFN with the International Institute for Sustainable Development (IISD) conducts an Ecoloigcal Footprint study of Canadian Provinces as part of the Canadian Index of Well-Being.

GFN with support from the European Environment Agency (EEA) completes a major update of the *National Footprint Accounts* (2005 edition).

EEA publishes its report (with contributions by GFN partners, SEI-York and New Economics Foundation), *The European Environment – State and Outlook 2005* (European Environment Agency 2005), which features the Ecological Footprint.

Year	Events, activities, publications
	GFN with WWF-UK, BFF and SEI-York collaborate on a One Planet Business project that measures the ecological footprint of major business sectors.
	EPA Victoria (Australia) commissions GFN and ISA at the University of Sydney to undertake the first Ecological Footprint study of the Australian state of Victoria, EPA Victoria (2005), *The Ecological Footprint of Victoria: Assessing Victoria's Demand on Nature.*
	EPA Victoria with GFN and VicUrban (an urban development agency), and the Centre for Design at RMIT, assesses the Ecological Footprint of a 'green development' in the state of Victoria.
	CSIRO (Australia) publishes *Balancing Act,* the first triple bottom-line analysis of Australian economy (study undertaken by ISA at the University of Sydney). CSIRO also funds the development of triple bottom line (TBL^3) software tool later marketed as 'BottomLine^3'.
2006	75+ organisations are now part of the GFN Partner Network.
	Biffa Award commissions SEI-York and others to undertake the Ecological Budget UK project. Project outputs include: a material flow analysis and Ecological Footprint study of the UK and several UK regions, the policy software tool REAP, a Sustainable Production and Consumption network, and a website. SEI-York also develops a suite of REAP tools for specific economic sectors (education, health, tourism).
	WWF UK publishes two reports: *Ecological Footprints: Taking the First Step, A 'How to' Guide for Local Authorities* (Bond and Matthews 2006), a guide for local authorities on how to undertake an Ecological Footprint study; *Ecological Footprints: The Journey so Far, Lesson Sharing and Case Studies of Local Authorities in the United Kingdom* (Ross 2006), which provides a summary of key lessons learnt from eight UK Ecological Footprint projects.
	GFN launches its own online personal Ecological Footprint calculator.
	GFN organises first Footprint Forum, a conference event for GFN partner organisations at Siena (Italy) which is attended by 200 Ecological Footprint practitioners and supporters. GFN launches first approved Footprint Standards at the Forum.
	GFN collaborates with WWF on *Africa's Ecological Footprint: Human Well-Being and Biological Capacity* (GFN 2006c).
	GFN collaborates with WWF on WWF's *Living Planet Report 2006.*
	GFN launches its Earth Overshoot Day campaign. In 2006, Earth Overshoot Day was estimated to be 6 October.
	Japan's Ministry of the Environment incorporates the Ecological Footprint into its Basic Environment Plan, and agrees to work with GFN to conduct a review of Japan's National Footprint Accounts.

Year	Events, activities, publications
2007	80+ organisations are now part of the GFN Partner Network.

The ESRC BRASS Research Centre at Cardiff University (UK) with GFN organises and hosts the first academic conference on the Ecological Footprint in Cardiff. Over 200 participants attend from 112 organisations in 23 countries.

Wales pledges to reduce its per capita Ecological Footprint to the global average available within one generation as part of its One Planet: One Wales campaign.

Scotland includes the Ecological Footprint in its National Performance Framework.

UK Ecological Footprint consultants, BFF, develops Footprinter, a Carbon and Ecological Footprint calculation and management tool for businesses. Specialised versions are developed for different service and business sectors.

WWF UK publishes Ecological Footprint results for 60 British cities, *Ecological Footprint of British City Residents* (Calcott and Bull 2007).

UAE launches Al Basma Al Beeiyah Initiative, its Ecological Footprint initiative, and commissions GFN to undertake an in-depth study to better understand its Ecological Footprint and improve the accuracy of its calculation.

ACF and ISA at the University of Sydney, launch first interactive Consumption Atlas showing household GHG emissions and Ecological Footprints for various geographical areas across Australia.

ISA, University of Sydney launches its TBL[3] sustainability reporting tool which incorporates Ecological Footprint data.

GFN collaborates with WWF on:
Canadian Living Planet Report 2007 (WWF and GFN 2007);
Europe 2007: Gross Domestic Product and Ecological Footprint (WWF 2007).

2008	100+ organisations are now part of the GFN Partner Network.

Welsh Assembly Government with SEI-York publishes the results from its third Ecological Footprint study of Wales, *Wales' Ecological Footprint: Scenarios to 2020* (Dawkins et al. 2008).

EPA Victoria commissions second Ecological Footprint study of Victoria.

GFN and EPA Victoria are signatories to a Sustainability Covenant to further promote the Ecological Footprint in Victoria and Australia. The Ecological Footprint is used as an indicator in Victoria's first comprehensive State of the Environment Report (Commissioner Environmental Sustainability Victoria 2008). Australia's first personal Ecological Footprint calculator is launched.

GFN collaborates with WWF on:
2010 and Beyond: Rising to the Biodiversity Challenge (WWF and GFN 2008a);
Report on the Ecological Footprint of China (WWF and GFN 2008c);
Africa: Ecological Footprint: and Human Well-being (second report) (WWF and GFN 2008b);

Year	Events, activities, publications
	Hong Kong Ecological Footprint Report 2008: Living Beyond our Means (Hong Kong's first Ecological Footprint report) (WWF Hong Kong 2008).
	GFN collaborates with WWF on WWF's *Living Planet Report 2008*.
	GFN publishes with Confederation of Indian Industry, *India's Ecological Footprint: A Business Perspective*.
	GFN publishes *The Ecological Footprint Atlas 2008*, a summary of the Ecological Footprint and biocapacity from the 2008 Edition of National Footprint Accounts (covering 201 countries).
	GFN Partners, BFF, SERI Ecologic, Envirocentre publish *Potential of the Ecological Footprint for Monitoring Environmental Impacts from Natural Resource Use* (Best et al. 2008).
	Switzerland adopts the Ecological Footprint as an indicator, and incorporates it into its Sustainability Development Plan.
	Finland includes the Ecological Footprint in its suite of sustainability indicators, and collaborates with GFN to improve its national footprint accounts.
2009	EUREAPA software developed through One Planet Economy Network (EU 7th Framework Programme for Research and Development. Project involved eight international partners (including SEI-York, WWF UK and GFN), and involves developing a 'Footprint family' of footprint indicators: Ecological, Carbon and Water.
	Ecuador incorporates the Ecological Footprint into its National Plan for Good Living and commits to reversing its ecological deficit by 2015.
	UAE as part of the Al Basma Al Beeiyah Initiative, its Ecological Footprint initiative, collaborates with GFN to develop a policy scenario to test various energy policies.
	GFN publishes: *Africa FactBook 2009*; *The Ecological Footprint Atlas 2009*, a summary of the Ecological Footprint and biocapacity from the 2009 Edition of National Footprint Accounts (covering 201 countries).
	GFN publishes with WWF, *Japan Ecological Footprint Report 2009: Maintaining Well-being in a Resource Constrained World* (Wada et al. 2009), Japan's first Ecological Footprint report.
2010	90+ organisations are now part of the GFN Partner Network.
	GFN publishes: *The Ecological Footprint Atlas 2010*, a summary of the Ecological Footprint and biocapacity from the 2010 Edition of National Footprint Accounts (covering 201 countries); *The Ecological Wealth of the Nations* report. GFN collaborates with WWF on WWF Hong Kong's *Hong Kong Ecological Footprint Report 2010*.

Year	Events, activities, publications
	GFN collaborates with WWF on WWF China's *China Ecological Footprint Report 2010*.
	GFN collaborates with WWF on WWF's *Living Planet Report 2010*.
	GFN collaborates with GIZ (Germany) WWF and others on *A Big Foot on a Small Planet?* (Amend et al. 2010).
	The **UN Development Programme** includes the Ecological Footprint as an indicator for assessing lasting human progress.
	Sao Paulo adopts the Ecological Footprint as a key sustainability indicator.
	Luxembourg's Council for Sustainable Development and the Foreign Ministry adopt the Ecological Footprint.
	Wackernagel and Beyers publish *Der Ecological Footprint: Die Walt neu Vermessen* (German), *The Ecological Footprint: The World Re-measured* (English).
2011	79+organisations are now part of the GFN Partner Network.
	GFN collaborates with Landcare Research and Massey University (New Zealand) on *An Analysis of New Zealand's Ecological Footprint as Estimated by the Global Footprint Network: An Update* (Andrew and Forgie 2011);
	GFN collaborates with San Francisco Planning & Urban Research Association on *Ecological Footprint Analysis: Francisco – Oakland-Fremont, CA Metropolitan Statistical Area* (Moore, 2011);
	GFN collaborates with UNDP on *Resource Constraints and Economic Performance in Eastern Europe and Central Asia* (GFN 2011).
	Costa Rica features the Ecological Footprint in its annual State of Nation report.
	Switzerland adopts the Ecological Footprint as an indicator in its *Sustainable Development Report 2012* (Willi et al. 2011).
2012	GFN collaborates with WWF on: *Türkiya'nin Ekolojik Ayak İzi Raporu* (Turkey Ecological Footprint Report) (WWF Türkiye); the first Ecological Footprint study of a Brazilian city, *The Ecological Footprint of Camp Grande and its Family Footprint* (Becker et al. 2012); *The Ecological Footprint of São Paulo – State and Capital and the Footprint Family* (WWF Brazil 2012); *Japan Ecological Footprint Report 2012* (Poblete et al. 2012); WWF's *Living Planet Report 2012*; WWF China's *China Ecological Footprint Report 2012*.
	GFN publishes: *Mediterranean Ecological Footprint Trends* (Galli et al. 2012b); *A Measure for Resilience 2012 Report on the Ecological Footprint of the Philippines*.

Year	Events, activities, publications
	GFN publishes with the Arab Forum for Environment and Development, *Arab Environment: 5 Survival Options Ecological Footprint of Arab Countries* (Saab 2012).
	The **Philippines** is the first country in Southeast Asia to adopt the Ecological Footprint.
	Indonesia officially adopts the Ecological Footprint.
	GFN's Ten-in-Ten campaign reaches its goal three years ahead of schedule.
2013	68+ organisations (from across six continents) are now part of the GFN partner network.
	GFN collaborates with US Environmental Protection Agency on *The Ecological Footprint and Biocapacity of California* (Moore et al. 2013).
	GFN collaborates with WWF on *Hong Kong Ecological Footprint Report 2013* (WWF Hong Kong 2013).
	GFN collaborates with Laguna Lake Development Authority on *Philippines 2013 Ecological Footprint Report: Resorting Balance in Laguna Lake Region* (GFN 2013b).

Note: Countries in bold are part of the Global Footprint Network's Ten-in-Ten campaign.

2. Government and the Ecological Footprint

INTRODUCTION

In this chapter we explore two key themes. First, we examine how the Ecological Footprint has contributed to policy development. We concentrate our analysis on Wales and its capital city Cardiff. The Welsh Government has shown itself to be an innovative institution in the way in which it seeks to tackle sustainability, and was an early adopter of the Ecological Footprint as one of its headline indicators for sustainability. Meanwhile, Cardiff Council was also early to engage in debates on the Ecological Footprint and participated in a major Footprint study (see Chapter 3). Cardiff Council also adopted a systematic effort to promote the Footprint within the organisation, which has since been promoted as a model of good practice (Ross 2006). Through a detailed examination of the fate of the Ecological Footprint in organisational settings, particularly that of Cardiff Council, we are able to throw light on how policy tools to promote environmental management fare. In the second theme of the chapter, we explore the use of the Ecological Footprint as a sustainability indicator in Wales.

In our brief review of Kingdon's (1984) model of policy change in Chapter 1, we explained how the rise of the Ecological Footprint fitted into a window of opportunity, or policy window. Policy entrepreneurs are able to link together problems and solutions, and gather momentum for change. Kingdon (1984) argued that it is often an extreme event that creates the forces necessary to drive through policy change, and this is when a policy window opens to allow for policy change. Policy windows are usually open only for a short period of time, but proposals and alternatives must be 'advocated for a long period of time before a short run opportunity presents itself on the agenda' (Kingdon 1995, p. 215). The policy

process is, therefore, much messier, contested and more compli-
cated than technical–rational models would portray (see Chapter 1).
However, as we have also seen the Ecological Footprint is often
constructed as a technical–rational model (see Collins et al. 2009).
So, how may it gain traction in decision making? Here we are
interested in understanding the ways in which the Footprint may
gain legitimacy, which is the extent to which decision makers must
consider the results of Ecological Footprint studies. To do this, we
analyse the way in which the Ecological Footprint emerged onto the
public policy agenda in Wales. We then explore how the commitment to the Footprint indicator has varied over time. The national
context for Ecological Footprinting provides the essential context
for the subsequent analysis of the use of the Footprint in Cardiff,
the capital city of Wales. The question, then, is how this concept
travels through – and reshapes – decision making processes. At one
level, the potential connections to ecological 'limits' and equal
entitlements means that the Ecological Footprint could be used to
challenge dominant interests (see Dobson 2003). Indeed, commentators often emphasise its persuasive value as an intuitive communication device (Risk and Policy Analysis Ltd 2007; WWF Scotland
et al. 2007). Others, though, downplay any radical, transformative
implications, preferring to stress instead the Footprint's practical
merits. A commonly espoused benefit is that the Ecological Footprint 'makes sustainability concrete' for individual and collective
decision making (Buhrs 2004, p. 431), and provides a 'credible
measure' for the evaluation of policies (WWF Scotland et al. 2007,
p. 2).

Whilst the Ecological Footprint may make the communication of
limits or the meaning of sustainability to decision makers easier, it
is by no means clear how they may then use the information. A
common belief is that to be useful in informing policy decisions,
then the rigour, reliability and comparability to other studies (see
Chapter 6) of the Ecological Footprint should be emphasised.
Footprint theoreticians and proponents locate the conditions
required for the Ecological Footprint to be useful to decision
makers predominantly in the 'internal', methodological, properties
of the concept. In practice, though, many applications have focused
on raising public awareness and education, suggesting greater
dependence on the metaphorical content and communicative power
of the Ecological Footprint than on the nuances of methodology.

Yet analysts have only just begun to explore the difficulties of translating the burgeoning number of Ecological Footprint measurements into practice in policy spheres. In doing so, they reveal interesting connections between technical content and social contexts (Shove 1998). A key variable affecting the accommodation of Ecological Footprint measures is the extent to which proponents secure the commitment of key corporate decision makers and technicians. As Collins and Flynn (2007) observed, where an analysis of the Ecological Footprint of a local council was parachuted in from an external consultancy, or from the 'green ghetto' (Young 1996) of the council's sustainability office, the results generally proved unpersuasive, as unsympathetic and mistrustful officers picked apart the methodology and challenged data anomalies.

POLICY COMMITMENTS: THE WELSH GOVERNMENT AND THE ECOLOGICAL FOOTPRINT

The Welsh Government was an early adopter of the Ecological Footprint as a headline sustainability indicator. It therefore became part of GFN's Ten-in-Ten campaign in which it sought to encourage within a ten-year time frame ten governments to adopt the Ecological Footprint as an indicator of progress and sustainability. The story of the Welsh Government's[1] innovative approach to sustainability indicators is bound up in the process of devolution that began in the late 1990s. Under the Government of Wales Act 1998, Wales was given limited powers across a range of policy areas (for example, health and education). There was, though, one exception in relation to sustainability: the National Assembly for Wales was given a unique duty amongst legislatures in the European Union (EU) to promote sustainable development in all of its activities. Adoption of the Ecological Footprint as an indicator is a considerable source of pride to the Assembly and marks it out as a leader on sustainability. As the Assembly's first report on its sustainability performance commented: 'We believe that this makes Wales the first country in the world to adopt the Ecological Footprint as an official indicator' (National Assembly for Wales 2000–2001). The

rise to prominence of the Ecological Footprint indicator came as
something of a surprise as work on environmental indicators in
Wales had, according to one civil servant interviewee, generally
'run into the sand'.

At the time of the National Assembly's commitment to the
Ecological Footprint, the UK Government had a list of 15 headline
indicators for sustainable development (see Department of the
Environment, Transport and the Regions 2000). These indicators
are intended to comprise a 'quality of life' barometer which can be
used to measure progress (or lack of it) over time in moving
towards a more sustainable way of life. In 2000, the Assembly
published a consultation paper on its approach to sustainability
indicators. As a matter of principle the Assembly expected to follow
the lead of the UK Government and for its indicators to be
consistent with those for the UK to allow comparison:

> At the same time, we need our indicators to support Welsh vision and
> priorities, which will in some cases, imply a different emphasis to the
> rest of the UK. Therefore we propose to adopt the UK indicators in
> *Quality of Life Counts*, but with changes where necessary to make them
> relevant in Wales. (National Assembly for Wales 2000, para. 21)

For the sake of consistency, changes would only be made for good
reasons, or if measurements were impossible in Wales. The consultation paper identified several questions to address in adapting the
UK indicator set to a Welsh context:

1.   Are the underlying aims appropriate in Wales, and compatible
      with the Assembly's vision?
2.   Are the UK indicators chosen to reflect those aims also
      relevant in Wales?
3.   Are the same measurements possible and cost-effective in
      Wales? (National Assembly for Wales 2000, para. 21)

The consultation paper (para. 24) identified several areas where the
UK indicators may not be adequate for Welsh purposes, and one of
these hinted at the need for developing a Footprint indicator:

> The UK indicators cover what we do and produce within the UK. They
> do not measure the environmental, social and economic costs incurred
> in producing the goods and services that we consume, including those

we import. Do we want measures of the impact of what we consume in Wales? (National Assembly for Wales 2000, para. 24)

Intriguingly, the consultation paper did not make any explicit reference to the use of an Ecological Footprint as an indicator.

Since the publication of the consultation paper, work on developing a full set of indicators for Wales has often been side-tracked, much to the annoyance of environmental non-governmental organisations (NGOs) such as the Royal Society for the Protection of Birds (RSPB) and official bodies like the Countryside Council for Wales (CCW) (now merged into Natural Resources Wales with other environmental protection bodies in Wales). The period of the early 2000s is illustrative of the way in which indicators have been developed in Wales. In March 2001 in its Action Plan to operationalise its sustainable development responsibilities, the Assembly adopted a shortened set of 12 headline indicators for Wales. Nine of these were also headline indicators for the UK. One of the three distinctively Welsh indicators was the Ecological Footprint. The other two relate to the use of the Welsh language, and energy generation from renewable sources; the latter was a UK core indicator but not a headline one.

The construction of environmental indicators and the dominance of some indicators over others is part of a political process in which some issues are recognised as worthy of the attention of public policy and others are not (Yearley 1991). Within Wales, the construction of composite indicators has taken place in an atmosphere of (political) competition. The Index of Sustainable Economic Welfare (ISEW) was championed by the CCW, a publicly funded body dominated by nature conservation interests. Its promotion of the ISEW has been based on a twofold calculation. First, it was designed to show that there is an economic and social value to protecting the natural environment. Second, as a body the CCW can engage in economic and social debates and so need not continually be pushed to the policy fringes of mainstream development debates. The adoption of the ISEW as an indicator by the National Assembly for Wales would add to the credibility of the CCW.

The Ecological Footprint was championed by World Wide Fund for Nature Cymru (Wales) (WWF Cymru). WWF Cymru's parent organisation had earlier produced the highly regarded *Living Planet Report* (LPR) (WWF 2000) that had calculated Footprints for 152 countries and also a global Footprint. Although a well-established environment NGO, WWF Cymru as a Welsh-based organisation was in the early 2000s a relatively new organisation and used the Ecological Footprint as a means of positioning itself both in relation to other environment groups in Wales and with policy makers in the Assembly. In short, the Ecological Footprint provided WWF Cymru with a profile, something that made it distinctive, amongst other NGOs, and gave it credibility with policy makers as it showed itself willing to engage in a partnership programme to deliver a sustainability indicator. The fact that the Assembly adopted the Footprint as one of its sustainability indicators is both a testament to the trustworthiness with which the wider organisation is regarded and also to the lobbying prowess of WWF Cymru. As the then Environment Minister, Sue Essex, commented when presenting the Action Plan on the Sustainable Development Scheme to the Assembly on 1 March 2001:

> we had good discussions with World Wildlife Fund Cymru [*sic*] about the principle of trying to use the ecological footprint as a headline indicator. That is an interesting element. This is easy for the Isle of White [*sic*] because it is a self-contained unit. It would be interesting to develop and work on the footprint ideas in Wales as an indicator. I would like to explore that further.

To provide further data on the Ecological Footprint the Assembly helped support a project to produce a Footprint for Wales (see BFF 2002a). It had been expected that the Assembly's commitment to the indicator would ensure its promotion in novel ways, such as contributing to decision making. Until the middle of 2003 that expectation seemed to be well founded, but then in a statement to the Assembly on 24 June 2003 the new Minister for the Environment, Carwyn Jones, set out his sustainable development agenda for the next four years. He outlined six themes and including issues such as exploring the opportunities for a low carbon economy and making the planning system more proactive. He also stated that he wanted to see 'the ecological footprint [used] as a means of raising public awareness of sustainable development issues'. This marked a considerable dilution from earlier expectations of the part that the Ecological Footprint may play in the Assembly. For example, in 2002 in reporting on its sustainability performance against its 12 indicators, the Assembly's Statistical Bulletin had noted in relation to the Ecological Footprint that it would:

- show how Wales is performing, including in comparison with the UK and Europe;
- guide and monitor the Assembly's policies and programmes; and
- help provide a lead to others in Wales, by clarifying common aims, increasing understanding and promoting action. (Welsh Assembly Government 2002, para 20)

At a stroke the Minister's statement had moved the Ecological Footprint from a potential decision making tool within the Assembly to a communication tool for the Welsh public with an unclear role for the Assembly. As one informed commentator pointed out in an interview:

> I think that people initially did [Footprint studies] for awareness raising and I think they do that because it's easy, it's the cushy comfortable side of sustainability isn't it? ... Nothing wrong with awareness raising and trying to change attitudes and soft policy measures, but they're useless unless you are going to combine them with hard policy decisions. So I think it's the easy way out really. (Interviewee)

In reflecting on the experience of efforts to promote the Ecological Footprint as a sustainability indicator in Wales, its ineffectiveness is rooted in two factors: an expert-led indicator that failed to sufficiently engage with senior politicians or officials; and an institutional context that failed to sufficiently understand how indicators might be used in practice. Below we consider each of these points in more detail.

Expert-Driven and Participatory Indicator Systems

Traditionally, the development of environmental indicators has been the preserve of experts (Feindt and Flynn 2009). In expert-driven indicator systems, managers select what they believe to be the most relevant indicators. Yet as Bell and Morse (2001) point out, despite the likely coincidence in views between experts and managers there are very few examples to show that indicators routinely influence policy. For some, the reason why top-down indicators fail to make much of an impact is because experts have been more concerned with improving their measurements than considering their use (Pinfield 1996). This certainly strikes a resonant chord with work on the Ecological Footprint, where research has been dominated by methodological refinements or specific applications (Collins and Flynn 2007) with scant evidence of specific policy outcomes being formed by Ecological Footprint studies (see Moore et al. 2007). An overly technocratic approach to indicators has meant that experts can often be divorced from the communities to which indicators are to apply. For example, the first Ecological Footprint produced in Wales led to much discussion amongst stakeholders within and outside of government about how the results should be interpreted. Nearly all stakeholders agreed that the Ecological Footprint data was technically sophisticated, but it was not clear to the policy community as to what type of actions might follow from the results. Whilst the results showed the need for change, quite what the implications were for future policies or for trade-offs between policies was opaque. In part, therefore, expert-led or top-down indicator systems (usually highly aggregated indexes) have been challenged because they have encountered problems in engaging with communities, whether they be geographically or policy-based. As a result, there has been much greater interest in including communities in the formulation of indicators, particularly as this may provide them with a greater sense of ownership of their environment (see Bell and Morse 1999, 2001).

More participatory forms of indicator development are much more likely to be relevant to local circumstances than those prescribed by external experts. Locally based indicators may also be more adaptable to changing circumstances. In a test of whether participatory-led indicators do realise the benefits that their advocates claim, and to see how they mesh with expert-led indicators, Fraser et al. (2006) analysed three diverse case studies (rangeland management in Botswana, forest management in Canada, and economic transition in the United Kingdom's Channel Islands). The evidence from the case studies shows that to create a hybrid of knowledge and indicator ownership there needs to be a process of integrating local knowledge (bottom-up) and scientific research (top-down). In the case of the Channel Islands, Fraser et al. (2006, p. 122) show how the initial development of indicators by experts provided the impetus to create a community response, and there then followed a series of iterations so that the '[indicator] list has evolved incrementally, slowly involving an increasing number of stakeholders'.

The work of Fraser et al. (2006) shows that for practitioners there is a difficult balancing act to be performed in terms of blending expert-driven and participatory indicators. Expert-led indicators systems retain value but on their own are likely to be inadequate (Feindt and Flynn 2009). Expert-based systems, because they are much more likely to have standard indicators, will allow a government to compare its performance over time and with others. Comparison and the opportunities that it provides for learning are important features of indicator systems. Meanwhile, the much greater variety of indicators that emerge from bottom-up processes of indicator formulation provide a much richer insight into what issues and values are important to a community. This is likely to facilitate a much greater sense of ownership of community resources (Fraser et al. 2006). In practice, there are potential trade-offs in the development of indicators between simplicity and participation on the one hand, and complexity and depth of understanding on the other (Brugmann 1997, p. 63).

Governance and Indicators

Lawrence (1998, p. 70) points out that '[i]ndicators will only be as good as the data that supports them'. As a consequence, the availability of robust and comparable data is often a significant factor in indicator selection. There will often be a pragmatic choice to be made between, on the one side, an indicator that would be an important measure of environmental performance but is data-poor, and on the other side, an indicator that provides a partial or ambiguous measure of performance but is data-rich (Feindt and Flynn 2009). In many instances, organisations that use indicators rely upon data collected by other bodies or use secondary data and then seek to apply it to their own circumstances, and both can be problematic. For example, 'official statistics do not simply exist independent of the actions of those who compile them' (May 2011, p. 91), and 'statistics do not, in some mysterious way, emanate directly from the social conditions they appear to describe' (Government Statisticians' Collective 1993 [1979], p. 163 in May 2011, p. 89). The index of multiple deprivation, for instance, is a particular social construction of a problem, and subsequently a particular handling of the data. Similarly data used in air quality measures will depend on the location of monitoring stations and judgements will then need to be made on air quality.

In one of the rare studies of the relationship between governance and sustainability indicators, Astleithner et al. (2004) have pointed to the importance of understanding the local context when analysing indicator development and interpretation. They argue that indicators must be understood as being part of local cultures and governance structures, and that the meanings attributed to indicators will inevitably be context-specific. Astleithner et al. (2004) conceive of indicators as being social constructs able to tell us something about what key actors and networks within organisations mean by sustainable development. As they explain, to understand indicators means 'understanding the networks of relationships between key policy actors and how ... [indicators] may fit into or disrupt these relationships' (Astleithner et al. 2004, p. 10).

Drawing upon case studies in London (of a regeneration project) and Vienna (of a climate protection programme), Astleithner et al. (2004) show how institutions can shape indicators. In Vienna they found:

> [a] political-administrative system consisting of strong hierarchies and exhibiting a lack of co-operation and communication across departments. In addition, technicians have the key role in defining and producing indicators ... Indicators are ... seen as instruments to support political decision making via the production of 'objective' and measurable facts ... [There is an] ecological bias in the definition of sustainability. (Astleithner et al. 2004, p. 18)

Meanwhile, in the London Borough of Southwark:

> decision making [was opened] up to a wider range of influences with more flux in the roles between actors, less potential for a group of experts to dominate and a corresponding lesser emphasis on objective facts and technical expertise ... [The] use of indicators led to an emphasis on the social side of sustainability indicators, here expressed in terms of 'quality of life'. (Astleithner et al. 2004, pp. 18–19)

Whilst it might be tempting to link models of institutional arrangements with particular types of sustainability indicators, to draw such a conclusion based upon two case studies would be dangerous. Rather, what we can point to is that institutional context is important in the development and use of indicators (Feindt and Flynn 2009), and this is what we explore below and in the following chapter.

CARDIFF COUNCIL AND THE ECOLOGICAL FOOTPRINT

A key variable affecting the fate of Ecological Footprint measures is the extent to which proponents secure the commitment of key, corporate decision makers and technicians. In Cardiff Council, the Sustainable Development Unit (SDU), which had lead responsibility for implementing the Footprint, made every effort to ensure that it would be mainstreamed across the Council's activities. The background and process to preparing the Ecological Footprint and the results for Cardiff are reviewed in the following chapter (Chapter 3).

Cardiff Council made the initial decision to embrace the Ecological Footprint in 2000 and it was regarded by staff within the SDU as a device to bolster the Council's emerging Sustainability Strategy (Collins et al. 2009). Incorporating the Ecological Footprint into the Sustainability Strategy proved to be a vital step, even though to begin with officers had no capacity to measure the city's Footprint, as it led to Cardiff Council being drawn into wider networks that were seeking to utilise the Ecological Footprint. As Cardiff was the only Welsh council at that time to have considered the Ecological Footprint, it was approached informally by WWF Cymru in 2001 about the prospect of participating in a project. Officers in the SDU were keen to participate, partly because of interest in a new environmental tool and partly as a way of raising the profile of their unit within a strongly pro-development authority (Hooper and Punter 2006). Highlighting the work of the SDU and ensuring the effective participation of the wider Council meant aligning a wider array of actors around the project. Of both symbolic and practical significance was securing the Council's matched funding for participation in the project. Officers presented to the Cabinet a case for the Council's involvement in the study, and received a positive response: 'I went to see the deputy leader to talk her through it. She said fine, seems very sensible; exciting

piece of work – you have got my authority to involve the sustainability advocates and to work across chief officers and directorates'
(Interview with staff member of SDU, Cardiff Council).
At this stage, processes of securing institutional support proved
mutually reinforcing. By being able to represent the WWF Cymru
study as 'a high-profile, corporate project that the Council is
committed to' (Interview SDU, Cardiff Council), it provided
legitimacy to officers from the SDU when seeking the involvement
of other departments, and securing greater access to senior officers
than they had previously enjoyed. It helped also that SDU officers
were supported by their Senior Director – 'the footprint is one of
[his] favourite babies' (Interview SDU, Cardiff Council). This in
turn assisted in getting the Ecological Footprint written into the
Council's Policy Action Plan, a key corporate document.

Once the Ecological Footprint was embedded in the Council's
corporate strategy, SDU officers then organised numerous meetings
and seminars at which staff could learn about, and question, the
Ecological Footprint study. Across the Council staff were also
enlisted to provide data to the Ecological Footprint project. This
had the twin benefit of providing more robust data to populate the
Footprint model and ensuring that across the Council there was
buy-in to the project. As a consequence, the Ecological Footprint
was not perceived as something to do with the environment or the
preserve of the SDU, but as a Council-wide initiative.

The skilful and assiduous deployment of organisational knowledge by SDU officers was evident in the initial successful institutionalisation of the Ecological Footprint. Their engagement of
senior politicians and officers increased the likelihood that the
results of the Ecological Footprint study, when they emerged,
would become positive features on which commitment to action
might be based (Collins et al. 2009). The reality, though, proved
much more complex.

When Cardiff's initial Ecological Footprint results were released
at a series of internal workshops and scrutiny meetings during
2004, SDU officers realised quickly that it was 'not a good news
story' for the Council's dominant development agendas (Collins et
al. 2009, pp. 1715–1716). The results highlighted that in 2001
Cardiff residents had a higher Ecological Footprint (5.59 gha/
capita) than that for Wales (5.25 gha/capita) or the UK average
(5.35 gha/capita) (Barrett et al. 2005c); moreover, in almost all

sectors, Cardiff's Ecological Footprint was increasing. That the Ecological Footprint seems to increase with income (Wiedmann et al. 2006) undermined comfy win–win conceptions of sustainable development. For example, Cardiff's waste Footprint per capita was found to be 17 per cent larger than that for Wales and the UK, and this difference has been attributed to the city's relative prosperity and also the increase in executive and single-occupancy dwellings which have resulted from the Council's regeneration strategies, whose occupants tend to have higher levels of disposable income and therefore consume more (Collins and Flynn 2005). These were all troubling results for a local council committed to pro-development discourses of international competitiveness (Hooper and Punter 2006).

It quickly became apparent that sustaining support for the Ecological Footprint across the Council had come to depend on how the results, the model and any consequences were represented. So, rather than suggesting that business-as-usual was implicated in environmental crises, SDU officers stressed the importance of presenting the Ecological Footprint results in ways that were 'non-threatening'. This meant that in meetings with other officers and in more open Council debates, the managerial value of the Ecological Footprint was emphasised – showing how more efficient use of resources could help to realise Council objectives – rather than its more challenging implications for policy goals. As a result, between 2002 and 2007 advocates of the Ecological Footprint within the Council were able to ensure that commitments to it became embedded in a series of corporate documents.

For external Ecological Footprint practitioners there was a sense of frustration at the use of the Footprint data within the Council. Amongst consultants and some researchers there remains a belief in the technical–rational model of policy making, and that public policy decisions fail to take sufficient account of the environment. As one interviewee explained:

> I like the idea that they [policy makers] can make an informed decision for the first time almost, and at this stage I don't even mind if the Footprint increases with that policy decision, at least I like to know that they made the decision based on the grounds that they knew it would increase the Footprint but that they decided at this particular point in time that it was not the right time to make that policy.

The interviewee argued that, 'When we highlight the tool to people we think it focuses their mind on how it can be used'.

The more managerialist emphasis on interpretation of the Ecological Footprint within the Council meant that results were not being translated into pressures for policy change. Moreover, whilst many staff were sympathetic to the Ecological Footprint, officers believed it had little relevance for them. There is little evidence to suggest that officers were using Ecological Footprint data to provide evidence in policy debates. Departmental managers saw commitments to 'measure and use' the Ecological Footprint as symbolic, and insufficient to displace attention from those key performance indicators or financial constraints which actually constrained day-to-day decisions. The mismatch in perceptions between the policy data 'needs' of officers in the Council and what was offered by the Ecological Footprint was vividly illustrated by the perspective of one advocate of the Ecological Footprint. The interviewee argued that the use of numbers in analysis matters because it helps to gain traction in thinking about change: 'This [the use of the Ecological Footprint] is a whole changing in the processes of ... government about how we formulate policy, how we use information, how we use quantitative figures to drive policy'.

Owens et al. (2004, p. 1953) have similarly noted that 'techniques that produce numbers ... have a particularly powerful fascination for decision makers, proving difficult to dislodge even when inadequacies are repeatedly exposed'. The practice of appraisal is, therefore, heavily influenced by the ideal of the rational–technical model (Adelle et al. 2012). Even when the Ecological Footprint is seen to have little impact, the suggestion from some practitioners is for a deepening of the rational–technical approach. When asked why it is so difficult for the Footprint to influence policy, one practitioner responded:

> I think the main reason why is because it's such a cultural shift in the way that quantitative data can be used to formulate policy. I think that's such a huge shift within local authorities ... I think that is a huge fundamental shift which people have had to adopt and take and they can't quite see how the impact of the ecological footprint [study] can lead through to a policy change.

The SDU has not found it easy to provide either a strategic level input to the Council or more tactical guidance and support for middle managers (Collins et al. 2009, p. 1718). In practical terms, the prospects of extending the Ecological Footprint across the Council became dependent on a technology: REAP (Resources and Energy Analysis Programme), a computer-based programme. REAP was developed by the Stockholm Environment Institute at the University of York (SEI–York) to enable the comparison of the sustainability consequences of policy choices. SDU staff put a lot of work into developing REAP but felt that it yielded little. According to one Council member of staff, 'REAP is not viable. The input does not give the appropriate amount of output'. For staff this is particularly frustrating as they had wanted to show the benefits of REAP to their host department, land use planning. According to SDU staff, 'REAP did not say anything that was not common sense. The Ecological Footprint increases if housing is located away from a transport hub. REAP data is simply too coarse'. Disillusionment with REAP is spreading to the Ecological Footprint more generally and SDU staff attention has shifted towards other environmental tools such as Strategic Environmental Assessment (SEA) rules.

MOVING FORWARD: THE ECOLOGICAL FOOTPRINT IN PRACTICE

Despite the difficulties that Cardiff Council has encountered in making greater use of the Ecological Footprint, and its limited role as a national-level sustainability indicator, it would be a mistake to simply dismiss the Ecological Footprint. Rather, as Kingdon (1995) suggested, those who advocate change must do so over a longer time frame. What we can now see is a series of narratives emerging that in some cases are sympathetic to the Ecological Footprint and in other cases are more resistant. So, for instance, amongst those responsible for sustainability in Cardiff Council and who had sympathy for the Ecological Footprint there was a narrative of responsible resource consumption. Officers resisted the urge to promote a message that the results showed we were consuming too much. This was for three reasons. First, to do so might have linked the Ecological Footprint findings to that of the Club of Rome and 'limits to growth' discussions. To become entangled in debates on resource depletion would dilute the Footprint findings. Second, messages on the overuse of resources tend to be negative and do not fit easily with a more positive framework of searching for sustainability solutions that would allow SDU staff to work with others across the Council. Third, it is not always apparent to people that resources are scarce, and so to get that message across can be challenging. Instead, the starting point was to ask: 'How many resources are Cardiff residents consuming?' It was then possible to go on to ask: 'Why are they consuming so much?' In answering this question it enabled an important comparative dimension to be introduced: 'How does Cardiff compare to other areas?' Or, 'How does one policy area compare to another?' Increasingly, as discussed, this narrative became mainstreamed within the Council.

In other policy areas there was a range of responses. Waste is a key policy area and the growth of waste in Cardiff is higher than for a number of areas of Wales. Cardiff faces particular challenges because the changing social profile (rise in the number of small households), and increase in prosperity are linked to changes in the development strategy within the city. Most notably there has been an increase in apartments and a decline in traditional three-bedroom houses, and this affects the patterns of waste production. Moreover, the traditional form of waste disposal – a major landfill site – was becoming a less practicable option because it was coming to the end of its life. From the early 2000s onwards, the Ecological Footprint data provided valuable supplementary data to show the pressing need for additional resourcing for waste management and the need for new policy thinking. By 2014 a new privately run energy-from-waste plant had been commissioned to help the Council dispose of its waste.

Tourism and development highlights a different response to the Ecological Footprint. The city and key partners (for example, Wales Tourist Board, now Visit Wales) have promoted Cardiff as a major urban tourism and leisure location. Whereas the environmental impacts of coastal and rural tourism are now recognised, they are ignored in urban areas. The Footprint highlighted the environmental pressures that arise from urban tourism, particularly from high-profile events (see Chapter 5). To highlight the negative impacts of tourism was regarded by leading politicians as 'anti-development' and unsympathetic to the City's economic strategy.

Transport showed a further response to the Footprint findings. Cardiff is a relatively compact city and has good public transport services and infrastructure. However, car use is, surprisingly, higher than for rural Gwynedd (in North Wales). Car use was linked not simply to commuting but also to a number of other uses (for example, the school run, shopping, and leisure). Whilst transport planning officers might have been surprised at the results of the comparison between Cardiff and an area of rural Wales, they did not feel that the Ecological Footprint could help them with policy development. They provided sophisticated critiques of the Footprint methodology and of the data used to populate the model. They also argued that the policy scenarios developed from the Ecological Footprint (for example, the Footprint impacts of alternative modes of transport) provided inferior data to their own transport models.

Given these alternative perspectives on the Ecological Footprint within Cardiff Council, it is perhaps surprising that the Council should continue to show sympathy for the Ecological Footprint. One aspect to understanding this ongoing commitment is to see how the process to develop the Ecological Footprint created deliberative spaces (see Chapter 3 for more information) such as cross-departmental Task and Finish groups. These allowed officers to develop links with one another, and developed further through a network of Sustainability Champions to be found across all Council departments. The Footprint study helped to nurture a more deliberative form of policy development in which it is possible for staff who are sympathetic to the Footprint to persuade both middle-ranking and senior staff of the merits of the Council committing itself to managing its resource consumption. This is a message that goes beyond what it had been deemed possible to voice in the mid-2000s. In a report to Cardiff Council's Cabinet in July 2013, the Corporate Director for Operations recommended that the Council adopt a One Planet Cardiff Vision which had at its heart a key Ecological Footprint point:

> Cardiff today is a three planet city. If everyone in the world consumed natural resources and generated carbon dioxide at the rate we do in Cardiff, we would need three planets to support us. Our aspiration is for Cardiff to be a one planet city by 2050. (Cardiff Council 2013)

At the national level there are also signs that there are sympathies for the Ecological Footprint, with efforts to embed it in land use planning practices. Land use planning is governed at a strategic level by the Welsh Government but delivery takes place through local governments. In its approach to sustainable development the Welsh Assembly Government identifies the planning system as one of four key themes that underpin the approach to reducing the country's Ecological Footprint. The overall aim of the planning system within the scheme is to provide for homes, infrastructure, investment and jobs in a way that helps reduce the Ecological Footprint. So, what actions is the Assembly Government taking to ensure that the Ecological Footprint can be reduced? Here we can point to three topics:

1. High-level policy guidance.
2. Promoting the Ecological Footprint in land use plan development.
3. Using the Ecological Footprint to monitor land use plan practice.

High-Level Policy Guidance

In *Planning Policy Wales* (Welsh Assembly Government 2010a), the key document that sets out the strategic context for land use planning, the Assembly Government, notes:

> The planning system has a fundamental role in delivering sustainable development in Wales ... In particular the planning system, through both development plans and the development control process, must provide for homes, infrastructure, investment and jobs in a way which is consistent with sustainability principles. (Welsh Assembly Government 2010a, para. 4.1.6)

A key sustainable development measure is the Ecological Footprint, and here it is pointed out that the Assembly Government has an ambition for Wales to use only its fair share of the Earth's resources, and this means that,

> within a generation, our ecological footprint is reduced to the global average availability of resources – 1.88 global hectares per person. The current footprint shows that, if everyone on the Earth lived as we

[Welsh citizens] do, we would use 2.7 planets worth of resources. Reducing Wales' ecological footprint will require a large reduction in the total resources used to sustain our lifestyles. The policy and guidance set out here in P[lanning] P[olicy] W[ales] will make an important contribution to reducing our footprint, whilst delivering sustainable development. (Welsh Assembly Government 2010a, para. 4.2.11)

Policy guidance has been supplemented with time series data on the Ecological Footprint at the local authority level (Dawkins et al. 2010).

Promoting the Ecological Footprint in Land Use Plan Development

The Assembly Government's guidance on the use of the Ecological Footprint in planning is too recent to assess its practical impact which will take some years to feed through, especially given the dramatic decline in development during the recession of 2008–2009. However, even before the publication of *Planning Policy Wales* (Welsh Assembly Government 2010b), the Footprint was being used to guide strategic land use policy making. A typical example is that of Swansea Council. Whilst at draft stage all land use plans (Local Development Plans – LDPs) must be assessed by a sustainability appraisal (SA) or SEA to identify and reduce negative environmental impacts and enhance positive features. In the Swansea SA/SEA the first objective is the promotion of sustainable development. The objective is to be assessed through answering key questions:

1. Will the LDP support the population of Swansea to live within environmental limits?
2. Will the LDP protect ecosystems?
3. Does the LDP encourage a resilient and sustainable economy?
4. Does the LDP promote safe, sustainable and attractive communities in which people have access to services and enjoy good health? (Swansea Council, n.d.)

These questions immediately point to two important issues. First, the recognition of environmental limits, and so providing a ready link to the Ecological Footprint; and second, the role of communities, a theme that we pursue further below. Data to answer the questions above is to be provided by monitoring a series of indicators:

1. Swansea's ecological footprint.
2. Percentage of LBAP [Local Biodiversity Action Plan] habitats and species recorded as stable or increasing.
3. Gross Value Added (GVA) and GVA per head.
4. Percentage of the population in low-income households.
5. Increase annually the number of people participating in sport and physical activity service and activities. (Swansea Council, n.d.)

Thus, what we are witnessing is the use of the Ecological Footprint in the assessment of the environmental sustainability of land use plans and in the monitoring of the plan over time. The role of the Ecological Footprint in steering more sustainable outcomes is an under-researched area (Welsh Assembly Government 2010b) (see below).

Using the Ecological Footprint to Monitor Land Use Plan Practice

Although the Welsh Government and individual councils have been innovative in their adoption of the Ecological Footprint as a headline environmental indicator and sought to adopt it in practice to land use planning, the effectiveness of the indicator in changing land use practices is more difficult to assess (Welsh Assembly Government 2010b). It remains a moot point as to whether the Ecological Footprint will be able to help promote an alternative development model.

CONCLUSIONS

For a number of Ecological Footprint practitioners, the methodological rigour of the technique and the numbers that emerge should be persuasive enough to encourage policy makers to reconsider their traditional perspectives. However, at a national level in Wales the use of numbers has not led to the Ecological Footprint having a significant influence on the policy process. Moreover, the Ecological Footprint has had only limited impact as a sustainability indicator. In large part this is because the practice of assessment techniques is somewhat different from the technical–rational model that many Ecological Footprint practitioners work with (see Owens et al. 2004; Hertin et al. 2009; Adelle et al. 2012). As Rayner (2003, p. 167) argues:

> Policy makers mostly treat technical analyses as background information. Where numbers are explicitly used, the existence of competing assessments allows decision makers to select the analysis that most closely conforms to their pre-existing preference. So, while the triumph of technique promises objectivity and transparency, it seems just as likely to be a means to buffer decisions from public scrutiny.

To this list we could also add scrutiny from other professionals and decision makers.

Meanwhile, as we have seen at a more local level, Cardiff Council's moves towards a more deliberative style of policy development have been important at both a prescriptive and an analytical level. The Ecological Footprint's power as a communication tool and as a single measure of ecological impact may make it well suited to a more advocacy style of decision making as it can be readily understood by diverse groups of professionals. The persuasive, advocacy or argumentative perspective draws upon the insights into the decision making process provided by Fischer and Forester (1993), who recognise that decisions are made by groups of actors who engage in debate. Actors hold values and aspirations that will differ from their peers and so decision making is a complex and collective process. The ability of individual actors to influence decision making will vary, and so those concerned with the promotion of sustainability or environmental concerns are often likely to find themselves needing to win arguments against well-entrenched developmental interests. As seen in Cardiff Council, there is a need to develop arguments that can gain the support of other interests. It is not simply about presenting a case based upon facts, but about persuading other actors of the merits of the case. So, as we have briefly discussed here and will do at further length in Chapter 3, there were efforts to create spaces for deliberation, for example a Task and Finish Group, in which officers could discuss data, methods and the assigning of environmental values to resource use, and evidence needs for policy development.

However, those using the Ecological Footprint and the study's results to persuade other actors to adopt a more sensitive environmental position must also recognise that some actors will be committed to their positions, and will deploy counter-arguments and prefer their own assessment tools. So although the Ecological Footprint raises challenging questions about the level of resource consumption, the balance of interests at both an official and a political level may mean that these are kept to the margins of an organisation. As Flyvbjerg (1998) has highlighted, a tool like the Ecological Footprint may simply rationalise decisions that are made by powerful actors, rather than providing an alternative development model.

NOTE

1. In the text we refer to the Welsh Government, National Assembly for Wales and Welsh Assembly Government. These different terms reflect the ongoing process of devolution in Wales. We have sought to use the term that was applicable to government at the time.

3. Consumption and the city: the Ecological Footprint of Cardiff

INTRODUCTION

This chapter begins by describing the process developed to undertake Cardiff's first Ecological Footprint study. Following this it then discusses the city's Ecological Footprint results, those factors that have influenced the size of its Footprint, and how Cardiff Council has since used the results. The chapter then compares Cardiff's Footprint results with those of other British, European and international cities. Finally, the chapter discusses how the 'model' process developed as part of the Cardiff Ecological Footprint project has been used to inform the approach of governments elsewhere.

CARDIFF'S ECOLOGICAL FOOTPRINT

Cardiff is the capital city of Wales, and is ranked as the tenth-largest city in the UK (UK Cities 2011). In 2001, the year that Cardiff's Ecological Footprint was first calculated, the city had a population of 307 300 residents, which accounted for approximately 10 per cent of the total population of Wales (2.9 million) (ONS 2001). Being the capital city of Wales, Cardiff is the centre for economic growth not only in South East Wales, but also for the country as a whole. In the last 10–15 years, Cardiff has witnessed a period of significant growth, including the development of retail, housing, leisure activities, and also the redevelopment of its Bay, which was a former docklands area. The city also boasts a thriving retail sector, and in 2008 was ranked ninth in a list of the top 20 UK retail towns and cities (Retail Week 2008), following closely behind other major UK cities such as Edinburgh, Leeds and

Manchester. The public, service and finance sectors dominate Cardiff's economy, and in 2001 total employment increased from 143 000 to 173 200 (Cardiff Council 2002a). In the same year, the city attracted over 10.6 million tourists, and since then major events including the FA Cup Final, Worthington Cup Final, Wales Rally Great Britain and the Ashes have all contributed to raising the profile of the city nationally as well as internationally.

Cardiff is one of a relatively small number of cities in the UK that have commissioned their own Ecological Footprint study. Other cities that have measured their Footprint include London, York, Liverpool and five cities in Scotland (Aberdeen, Dundee, Edinburgh, Glasgow and Inverness). In 2000, their respective Ecological Footprints per capita in global hectares (gha) were: York (6.98 gha), London (6.96 gha), Aberdeen (5.87 gha), Edinburgh (5.6 gha), Dundee (5.51 gha), Glasgow (5.37 gha), Inverness (5.47 gha) and Liverpool (4.15 gha) (see BFF 2002b, 2002c; Barrett and Scott 2001; Barrett et al. 2002). Although slightly different methodologies were used to calculate the Footprint of each city, the results highlight that there are variations amongst cities in terms of their consumption and resource use patterns, and subsequently their global ecological impact.

Background to Cardiff's Ecological Footprint Project

Between January 2003 and January 2005, an Ecological Footprint study was undertaken of Wales (see Barrett et al. 2005c). The 'Reducing Wales' Ecological Footprint' project was funded by a £300 000 Biffa Award,[1] and additional funding from the Welsh Assembly Government and two local councils in Wales, Cardiff and Gwynedd. This project represented the second time that Wales's Ecological Footprint was calculated. The first study was commissioned by the World Wide Fund for Nature (WWF) Cymru in 2001, and undertaken by UK Footprint consultants Best Foot Forward (BFF) as part of the 'All Wales Footprint as Global Indicator' project (see BFF 2002a). In the case of Wales's second Footprint study, the aims were, firstly, to measure the Ecological Footprint of Wales and two geographically contrasting areas: Cardiff, the capital city, which is located in industrial South Wales, and Gwynedd, which is located in a predominantly rural area in north Wales; and secondly, 'mainstreaming of sustainability within the City' (Collins et al. 2005, p. 5). In selecting these two local council areas, WWF Cymru wanted to compare and contrast the Ecological Footprints of an urban and a rural area, and identify those factors that were influencing the scale and composition of their individual Footprints. At the time of the project, Cardiff was the only local council in Wales to have considered and adopted a commitment to the Ecological Footprint in its Local Sustainability Strategy (see Cardiff Council 2000).

The 'Reducing Cardiff's Ecological Footprint' project involved a partnership of seven key organisations: WWF Cymru; the Stockholm Environment Institute – York (SEI–York), a research institute based at the University of York; the Economic and Social Research Council (ESRC) Centre for Business Relationships, Accountability, Sustainability and Society (BRASS) at Cardiff University; Cardiff Council,[2] Welsh Assembly Government, Welsh Development Agency, and the Environment Agency Wales. WWF Cymru had responsibility for managing the overall project. Ecological Footprint experts at SEI–York provided the methodological framework that was used to calculate the Ecological Footprint of Cardiff (and also Wales and Gwynedd). SEI–York also provided national-level data for the Ecological Footprint calculations when local data specific to Cardiff was not available. The research team at Cardiff University played a key role in collecting Cardiff-specific data on consumption and resource use from various departments across the Council, and provided officers with answers to specific questions they had about the Ecological Footprint and how data provided by their department was being used in the calculations. Cardiff University also developed a number of sustainable policy scenarios with the assistance of Council policy officers. During the first year of the project (2003–2004), Cardiff Council seconded its Sustainability Co-ordinator to Cardiff University to work specifically on the project. This was invaluable not only in enabling researchers at Cardiff University to gain access to Council officers and data for the Footprint calculations, but also in terms of reinforcing the legitimacy of the project to local stakeholders.

In 2003, Cardiff's Ecological Footprint project was one of the city's most high-profile environmental projects, and had widespread corporate commitment within the organisation. The Council initially considered the Ecological Footprint concept in 1999 whilst drafting its Local Sustainability Strategy (Cardiff Council 2000).

The decision to embrace the Ecological Footprint in 2000 was a reflection of the Sustainable Development Unit's (SDU) aim to 'reinforce pre-existing environmental integration institutions' (Collins et al. 2009, p. 1713). From the outset, relatively little effort was needed to persuade local politicians to commit to measuring the city's Ecological Footprint and including it in the Local Sustainability Strategy (Cardiff Council 2000). The Local Sustainability Strategy committed the Council to integrating sustainable development into its decision making process, raise awareness of sustainability issues, and use the Ecological Footprint to assess the city's ecological impact.

Cardiff Council's decision to measure the city's Ecological Footprint was fourfold. First, the Council's Local Sustainability Strategy (Cardiff Council 2000) and Community Strategy (Cardiff Council 2004) endorsed the Ecological Footprint, and the Council wanted to mainstream the project and its outcomes into existing policy. From the viewpoint of Cardiff Council's Sustainable Development Co-ordinator, the inclusion of the Ecological Footprint in these strategies meant there was the potential that Cardiff Council would be able to go beyond its rhetorical commitment to sustainable development and demonstrate that it was taking positive action. Second, measuring the city's Footprint would enable the Council to develop links between the local and global elements of sustainable development, a difficult issue being faced by a number of other councils across the UK. Policy officers within the Council wanted to understand the scale of the environmental challenge that the city faced in order to become more sustainable. The Ecological Footprint study would provide an initial benchmark for the city and be used to track the Council's performance and assess progress. Third, the Footprint would provide the Council with a resonant tool and metaphor from which to promote awareness of sustainable consumption and lifestyles. Fourth and finally, data relating to residents' resource use and its Ecological Footprint would provide policy officers with additional evidence from which to inform debate and policy development within the Council. More specifically, policy officers anticipated that the Footprint study would be able to provide answers to the following six questions:

1.   What is Cardiff's Ecological Footprint?
2.   What is the Footprint made up of?

3. What are residents' most significant areas of resource use?
4. Is the Council prioritising the right policy areas to reduce the city's Footprint?
5. Are the Council's current policies sufficient to enable Cardiff to become a more environmentally sustainable city?
6. How can data from the Footprint study be used to inform policy, manage resources more sustainably, and raise awareness of sustainable lifestyles?

Cardiff's Ecological Footprint: Process and Methodology

During the initial stages of Cardiff's Ecological Footprint project, the research team at Cardiff University undertook a review of previous Ecological Footprint studies undertaken at a UK local government level between 1999 and 2003 (see Collins and Flynn 2007). The purpose of the review was to consider how Footprint studies had been constructed and used elsewhere, and involved semi-structured interviews with local authority officers, researchers, Footprint consultants and non-governmental organisations that had either been directly involved with or were associated with projects. From the review a number of key themes emerged. First, the majority of studies had been developed through a narrow base in their organisation, often driven by an individual single officer who held a relatively junior position. This individual officer coordinated data collection across their organisation, which was subsequently given to a consultant to use alongside other data in the final Ecological Footprint calculations. Second, local government officers had minimal involvement in validating data and assumptions used by consultants in the final Footprint calculations, and subsequently had concerns about the credibility and accuracy of the Ecological Footprint results. Third and finally, none of the officers responsible for the studies reviewed had taken steps to obtain corporate support for their Ecological Footprint project or subsequent use of the results to inform policy development within their organisation. For many the production of the final report marked the end of Footprinting within their organisation. In instances where the Ecological Footprint had been used, this was primarily for education and awareness-raising activities with local communities rather than for policy development purposes.

To overcome the concerns surrounding previous Ecological Foot-print studies and provide credible answers to policy officers' questions, two types of methodological innovation were developed to enhance policy officer engagement in the Cardiff project. First, at the outset of the project policy officers received a formal introduc-tion to the Ecological Footprint, including an explanation of how it considers resource use and measures environmental impact. Second, to ensure policy officers would regard the Ecological Footprint results as reliable and sensitive to local circumstances, the data collection and analysis process was made as transparent as possible. At key stages in the project, policy officers were invited to check the quality of data and validity of assumptions used within the Footprint calculations. This process of engaging officers in the project – which resulted in the creation of spaces for deliberation – was significantly different to how previous Ecological Footprint studies had been undertaken for local and regional government elsewhere in the UK.

Putting the Ecological Footprint on the Agenda

In Cardiff Council, the SDU had responsibility for promoting sustainable development across the organisation, and took a lead role in promoting and developing the project. This involved a two-stage process of 'selling' the Ecological Footprint concept, firstly to senior management and politicians, and secondly to policy and technical officers across 22 departments in the Council. Obtain-ing initial support from the Council to measure the city's Ecological Footprint involved the preparation of a Cabinet Report for politi-cians in mid-2002 (prior to the start of the project) which outlined the case for the Council's participation in the study, and the request for financial contribution and other resource requirements including officer time to provide data and develop ideas for sustainable policy scenarios. Politicians involved in the Council's Environmental Scru-tiny Committee[3] were also informed about the project. The approach used to 'sell' the Ecological Footprint project to politi-cians focused on four key uses. First, measuring the city's Eco-logical Footprint would be a high-profile corporate project and enable the Council for the first time to measure the city's global environmental impact. Second, researchers at Cardiff University would support the Council by scrutinising the methodology and ensure the best-quality available data was used by SEI–York in the Footprint calculations. Third, the Ecological Footprint would identify those areas of residents' resource use that had the greatest environmental impact. Finally, measuring the city's Ecological Footprint would also provide the Council with evidence to demonstrate that the city was facing different resource use issues from the rest of Wales.

Politicians on the Environmental Scrutiny Committee received the request for corporate support enthusiastically and with minimal opposition, as they wanted the Council to be seen as taking a lead on sustainability issues within Wales. Obtaining political approval for the project represented an opportunity for the Ecological Footprint results to be considered alongside economic and social considerations when developing future local policies.

The SDU also took steps to 'sell' the Ecological Footprint project to the Council's Sustainability Advocates, who represented middle management from 22 different departments across the organisation who worked corporately on sustainable development issues. The ability of the SDU to present the study as a high-profile environmental project with corporate support enabled it to engage officers across different departments and gain access to a wider set of officers. Prior to the start of the project (early 2002), an initial briefing session was organised for the Council's Sustainability Advocates. This was used as an opportunity to explain the aim of the project, what the Ecological Footprint was and how it would be measured, and the various departments that would be required to provide data for the calculations. A second briefing session was held six months after the start of the project (June 2003). This involved SEI–York and the research team at Cardiff University providing more detailed information on the structure and organisation of the project, and specific data requirements. The approach used to 'sell' the Ecological Footprint project to advocates focused on how the results would be likely to reinforce a number of existing policies within the Council. Furthermore, officers were informed that the project's data collection and analysis process would be made as transparent as possible. Officers would be asked to provide locally specific data (where it existed), and also invited to check the quality of data and appropriateness of assumptions made within the Ecological Footprint calculations. The data collection and scrutiny role of the research team at Cardiff University was also highlighted and explained.

The Ecological Footprint

Throughout the Cardiff project a series of regular progress reports and meetings were prepared for the Council's Sustainability Advocates, highlighting how data provided by their department had been used within the Ecological Footprint calculation and the strategy for collecting any additional data. The process of regular reporting was specifically used to develop organisational ownership of the project and generate credibility for the project. It also signified that all departments had a role in the project and avoided the assumption that it was merely an environmental project. Adopting an open and corporate approach to selling the Ecological Footprint across the organisation was important for two main reasons. First, it would engender support for the data collection process as officers would develop confidence and 'raise the legitimacy of the Footprint within the organisation' (Collins and Flynn 2005, p. 282) as they would understand how their data was being used in the final Footprint calculation. Second, officers then would understand the Ecological Footprint results as they had opportunities throughout the project to raise queries about the methodology and how results could be used to inform policy decisions.

Project Task and Finish Group

A corporate Task and Finish Group – another opportunity for deliberation – was also established for the duration of the project, and included policy officers whose work related to the areas of resource use considered by the Footprint (transport, waste, economic development, housing, energy, sustainable development, tourism and research). The role of the Task and Finish Group was to provide the research team at Cardiff University with locally specific data for the Ecological Footprint calculations, and validate data and assumptions. The group also made suggestions on additional data sources, and how to address certain data gaps. In some instances they also acted as a gatekeeper to companies and organisations that held data the project would not otherwise have had access to for reasons of commercial confidentiality. For example, a local bus company provided the project with passenger numbers and distances travelled by its vehicle fleet within the city. This meant the Cardiff project was able to place less reliance on the use of proxy data, and enable the Ecological Footprint calculation to be as accurate and locally sensitive as possible.

Table 3.1 Ecological Footprint (EF) for Cardiff, Wales and the UK in 2001, by COICOP category for household consumption

COICOP	Consumption category	EF of Cardiff	EF of Wales	EF of United Kingdom
	HOUSEHOLD CONSUMPTION			
	Food and Drink	**gha/cap**	**gha/cap**	**gha/cap**
01.1	Food	0.759	0.748	0.771
01.2	Non-alcoholic beverages	0.050	0.048	0.050
02.1	Alcoholic beverages	0.090	0.083	0.078
11.1	Catering services	0.431	0.411	0.439
	Subtotal Food and Drink	**1.33**	**1.29**	**1.34**
	Energy			
	Domestic fuel consumption	0.57	0.512	0.546
04.5	Electricity and gas distribution	0.42	0.405	0.358
	Subtotal Energy	**0.99**	**0.92**	**0.90**
	Travel			
	Private transport (car fuel)	0.285	0.276	0.287
07.1	Purchase of vehicles	0.125	0.109	0.116
07.2	Operation of personal transport equipment	0.150	0.130	0.103
07.3	Transport services	0.091	0.066	0.092
	Aviation	0.336	0.198	0.124
	Subtotal Travel	**0.99**	**0.78**	**0.72**
	Infrastructure (Housing)			
04.1	Actual rentals for housing	0.032	0.034	0.033
04.2	Imputed rentals for housing	0.072	0.076	0.075
04.3	Maintenance and repair of the dwelling	0.054	0.057	0.067
	Subtotal Infrastructure	**0.16**	**0.17**	**0.18**
	Consumables and Durables			
	Consumables			
02.2	Tobacco	0.024	0.024	0.024
09.5	Newspapers, books and stationery	0.027	0.026	0.029

COICOP	Consumption category	EF of Cardiff	EF of Wales	EF of United Kingdom
12.1	Personal care	0.024	0.023	0.028
	Durables			
03.1	Clothing	0.023	0.022	0.029
03.2	Footwear	0.011	0.010	0.012
05.1	Furniture, furnishings, carpets and other floor coverings	0.049	0.049	0.057
05.2	Household textiles	0.012	0.013	0.013
05.3	Household appliances	0.091	0.095	0.115
05.4	Glassware, tableware and household utensils	0.007	0.007	0.011
05.5	Tools and equipment for house and garden	0.019	0.019	0.017
05.6	Goods and services for routine household maintenance	0.008	0.008	0.009
06.1	Medical products, appliances and equipment	0.008	0.008	0.010
08.2	Telephone and telefax equipment	0.0002	0.0002	0.0005
09.1	Audio-visual, photo and inf. processing equipment	0.076	0.072	0.069
09.2	Other major durables for recreation and culture	0.010	0.012	0.020
09.3	Other recreational items and equipment	0.200	0.200	0.187
12.3	Personal effects n.e.c.	0.083	0.080	0.123
	Subtotal Consumables and Durables	**0.67**	**0.67**	**0.75**
	Services			
04.4	Water supply and miscellaneous dwelling services	0.024	0.021	0.018
06.2	Out-patient services	0.003	0.002	0.006
06.3	Hospital services	0.004	0.004	0.004
08.1	Postal services	0.001	0.001	0.002
08.3	Telephone and telefax services	0.019	0.018	0.023
09.4	Recreational and cultural services	0.042	0.042	0.043
10.0	Education	0.017	0.013	0.026
11.2	Accommodation services	0.055	0.053	0.071

COICOP	Consumption category	EF of Cardiff	EF of Wales	EF of United Kingdom
12.4	Social protection	0.017	0.017	0.025
12.5	Insurance	0.038	0.037	0.046
12.6	Financial services n.e.c.	0.019	0.018	0.033
12.7	Other services n.e.c.	0.017	0.017	0.022
	Subtotal Services	**0.26**	**0.24**	**0.32**
	Holiday Activities			
	Resident holidays abroad	0.103	0.101	0.122
	OTHER CONSUMPTION			
	Capital Investment[1]			
	Gross fixed capital formation	0.744	0.744	0.744
	Government[2]			
	Central government	0.241	0.241	0.241
	Local government	0.167	0.167	0.167
	Subtotal Government	**0.41**	**0.41**	**0.41**
	Credits for recycling	-0.030	-0.027	-0.108
	Other[3]	-0.031	-0.031	-0.031
	TOTAL Ecological Footprint (gha/cap)	**5.59**	**5.25**	**5.35**

Notes:
n.e.c. = not elsewhere classified.
1. Capital investment or gross fixed capital formation (GFCF) relates principally to investment in tangible fixed assets such as plant and machinery, transport equipment, dwellings and other buildings and structures.
2. The Footprint calculations have assumed shared responsibility; therefore the Footprint per capita is the same for the UK, Wales and Cardiff.
3. 'Other' includes non-profit institutions serving households, valuables, changes in inventories and overseas tourists in the UK. Overseas tourists results in an overall negative Footprint in the Cardiff, Wales and UK results as this figure is included in the Footprint for visitors' country of origin.

Source: Collins et al. (2005).

Data Collection Process

Data collection for the project commenced in June 2003 (six months following the start of the project) and involved the research team at Cardiff University collating data on physical consumption for each of the component areas listed in Table 3.1 (food and drink; domestic energy use; travel; housing infrastructure; consumables and durables; services; holiday activities; capital investment; government). Data on waste and recycling, and tourism was also collected. Each component of the Footprint was considered in turn and involved the research team at Cardiff University contacting the relevant member of the Task and Finish Group to establish whether locally relevant data was available. This data was subsequently given to SEI–York for use in the Footprint calculation. The process involved a continuous dialogue between the research team at Cardiff University, Council officers and SEI–York in checking the quality of data and validity of assumptions used within the calculations. Where locally specific data was not available, proxy data from national data sources was incorporated into the Ecological Footprint calculation. Throughout the project, policy officers were kept informed about the data collection process. They were also provided with opportunities to submit queries to Cardiff University about data used, the robustness and accuracy of the methodological framework being used to calculate Cardiff's Footprint, and how the results related to their specific policy area.

Policy Scenario Development

During the final stages of the project, the research team at Cardiff University worked together with policy officers to develop a number of sustainable policy scenarios to assess whether the city's Ecological Footprint would increase, decrease or remain relatively unchanged. Examples of scenarios that were assessed included: increasing residents' consumption of organic, fresh and locally grown food and drink; increasing recycling rates and the range of items which are recycled and composted; switching domestic energy use from electric to renewable fuels; replacing car travel with other transport modes including public transport; and increasing the number of visitors (day and overnight) to Cardiff. The results of the individual policy scenarios are not discussed here; however a detailed description of each policy scenario and the results are available in Collins et al. (2005).

Novel Ecological Footprint Applications

During and following the Cardiff Ecological Footprint project, the research team at Cardiff University also developed several novel Footprint applications specific to Cardiff. These included Footprint studies of the 2004 FA Cup Final at Cardiff's Millennium Stadium (see Collins et al. 2007; Collins and Flynn 2008), a proposed large-scale development for an international sports village in Cardiff Bay (see Collins and Flynn 2005), sustainable food consumption (see Collins and Fairchild 2007) and school meals (see Fairchild and Collins 2011). These applications assisted in demonstrating the flexibility of the Ecological Footprint as a tool to predict the environmental impact of future developments within the city and the type of policies needed to mitigate negative ecological impacts. They also helped both to raise the profile of the Ecological Footprint across and beyond the Council, and to demonstrate its relevance to other development agendas outside the environment arena (Collins et al. 2009).

Presentation of Ecological Footprint Results and Policy Scenarios

The Ecological Footprint results for the various policy scenarios were presented and discussed with policy officers at a series of workshops during the last six months of the project. These workshops were important for four main reasons. First, they enabled policy officers to check the quality of data and appropriateness of assumptions made within the Ecological Footprint calculations. Second, they highlighted the interrelationship between different policy areas, for example food, waste and tourism. The third reason was that they considered whether current policies were efficient in addressing the most significant resource use demands of the city's residents. Fourth and finally, policy officers were encouraged to think differently about how they might address sustainability issues in their specific policy area. A deliberate attempt was made to present the results to officers and politicians in a non-threatening manner, and emphasis was placed on the environmental management value of the Ecological Footprint, as opposed to implications for particular policy goals (Collins et al. 2009). These workshops helped to generate further awareness of the Ecological Footprint project across the organisation as members of the Task and Finish group subsequently reported the Footprint results and policy implications to their respective management teams within the Council. Results were also presented to politicians at a Council scrutiny meeting.

CARDIFF'S ECOLOGICAL FOOTPRINT RESULTS (2001)

Cardiff's first Ecological Footprint was calculated for the year 2001 using the methodology developed by Footprint experts at SEI–York. In summary, this methodology uses National Footprint Accounts (NFAs) developed by the Global Footpring Network (GFN), and combined this with an input–output framework for various economics sectors within the UK. A detailed description of the methodology developed and used by SEI–York to calculate Cardiff's Ecological Footprint is available in Weidmann et al. (2006).

In 2001, Cardiff's Ecological Footprint was 1.72 million gha for its 307 300 residents. On a per capita basis the Footprint of the average Cardiff resident was 5.59 gha. To sustain Cardiff's resource demands on nature required significant imports of goods such as food, timber, and other materials and services into the local economy from beyond the city's geographical boundaries. Residents' ecological demands were equivalent to 17 200 km^2, and almost four times larger than the area of land that they physically occupied (4392 km^2).

The size of Cardiff's Ecological Footprint highlighted that residents' current level of resource consumption was not equitable or sustainable as they were using resources more than three times the available global biocapacity per capita of 1.8 gha. To achieve a more sustainable and equitable Footprint of 1.8 gha, Cardiff's residents would need to reduce their ecological demand by 68 per cent. This Ecological Footprint result raises significant challenges about residents' level of resource use and their preferred lifestyles. Compared to other studies that have used the same Footprint methodology, Cardiff's Footprint per capita was greater than that for the average UK and Welsh resident (5.35 gha/capita and 5.25 gha/capita, respectively) (see Barrett et al. 2005c). The size of its Ecological Footprint is considered to be attributable to the city's level of prosperity combined with the rapid increase in executive and single-occupied dwellings, whose occupants have greater levels of disposable income and consequently consume more resources (Collins and Flynn 2007). As the city's affluence continues to grow it is likely that Cardiff's Ecological Footprint will continue to increase.

A breakdown of Cardiff's Ecological Footprint results by the six different land and sea areas (carbon, grazing, forest, fishing, crop and built-up land) is shown in Table 3.2. The table also provides the sum total of all these areas, which is the total Ecological Footprint for Cardiff. Cardiff's relatively large Ecological Footprint is due to carbon land, which accounts for 63.0 per cent of the city's overall Footprint. Combined with crop land and fishing, these three land areas accounted for 76.5 per cent of the total Footprint. The size of the Carbon Footprint highlights the importance of reducing greenhouse gas (GHG) emissions. The results also highlight the significant ecological impact of residents' consumption of food and drink, and fish and seafood products.

Cardiff's Ecological Footprint results can also be classified by COICOP (Classification of Individual Consumption According to Purpose) final demand categories. For comparative purposes, Table 3.1 also shows the Footprint results for Wales and the UK. Cardiff's Ecological Footprint highlights that residents' food and drink was the single largest component and accounted for almost 25 per cent of the city's overall Footprint. When combined with three other components – travel, energy, and consumables and durables – they contribute to 70 per cent of the total Footprint. The dominance of these four components is indicative of how residents' lifestyles and associated consumption patterns have significant resource use implications. This also raises significant challenges regarding the long-term sustainability of the average Cardiff lifestyle. Significant lifestyle changes are required if the Cardiff Footprint is to be reduced to a sustainable level. In the following sections, we discuss the key findings from the study; however a more detailed account of Cardiff's Ecological Footprint results are available in Collins et al. (2005).

Table 3.2   Cardiff's Ecological Footprint results by land area (2001)

Footprint land categories	Cardiff's Ecological Footprint (gha/capita)	% total
Carbon land[1]	3.53	63.0
Grazing land[2]	0.34	6.1
Forest land[3]	0.32	5.7
Fishing land[4]	0.48	8.6
Crop land[5]	0.70	12.6
Built-up land[6]	0.23	4.0
Total	5.59	100.0

Notes:
1. Carbon land: the amount of forest land needed to absorb carbon dioxide (CO_2) emissions from the burning of fossil fuels, changes in land-use and chemical processes.
2. Grazing land: the area needed to raise livestock for meat and dairy products, hide and wool products.
3. Forest land: the amount of lumber, pulp, timber products and fuel wood consumed per annum.
4. Fishing land: the estimated primary production needed to support fish and seafood caught for human consumption (includes marine and freshwater species).
5. Crop land: the area used to produce food and fibre for human consumption, fed for livestock, oil crops and rubber.
6. Built-up land: the area of land covered by infrastructure (includes transportation, housing, industry and reservoirs for hydropower).

Source: Collins et al. (2005).

Food and Drink

The results show that food and drink was the largest single category, with a Footprint of 1.33 gha/capita, and was responsible for almost a quarter of Cardiff's total Ecological Footprint. Table 3.1 also highlights that Cardiff's Footprint per capita for food and drink was similar to that for the UK, but larger than that for Wales.

Cardiff has a significantly large Footprint for food and drink due to the scale, type and patterns of residents' consumption. In 2001, Cardiff residents consumed an estimated 0.2 million tonnes of food and drink, which is equivalent to 675 kilograms per resident per year. This is almost 6 per cent more than the average resident in

Wales (see Barrett et al. 2005c). Organic food and drink items accounted for only 1 per cent of the total amount purchased, compared to 99 per cent for items that had been produced using conventional methods. As conventional food production methods are more energy- and resource-intensive than organic methods, this was a further factor that contributed to the size of the city's Footprint.

A further reason for the size of the food and drink Footprint was that almost 10 per cent of the total amount of food and drink was prepared and consumed outside the home, for example in restaurants, fast food outlets and canteens. This was almost double that for the average resident in Wales (see Barrett et al. 2005c). Catering services (that is, eating out) accounted for almost one-third of Cardiff's Footprint for food and drink, compared to 0.900 gha/capita for what was consumed at home. The Footprint for eating out is disproportionately high as the production, preparation and service of food in eating-out establishments is considered more energy-intensive compared to that at home, and these indirect effects resulted in a large Footprint figure. Although almost one-third of food and drink consumed by residents was imported (215 kg/capita), its transportation to the UK and Cardiff was found not to contribute significantly to the food and drink Footprint.

In addition to the amount of food and drink purchased by residents, Cardiff's Footprint study also considered whether residents had consumed it or not. The study revealed that an estimated 30 605 tonnes of food and drink was disposed of as waste, which was equivalent to 16.4 per cent of the total food and drink consumed by residents at home that year.

Passenger Travel

Passenger travel had a Footprint of 0.99 gha/ capita, and was responsible for almost 18 per cent of the Cardiff Footprint. This Footprint figure for transport was larger than that for Wales (0.78 gha/capita) and the UK (0.72 gha/capita), and was primarily due to residents placing a heavy reliance on private modes of travel. As shown in Table 3.1, private transport accounted for 57 per cent of the travel Footprint and includes the ecological demand generated by the purchase of vehicles, associated fuel use and the operation of personal transport equipment. Fuel use alone was responsible for 30 per cent of the transport Footprint. This compares quite significantly with residents' use of public transport services, which was responsible for less than 10 per cent of the overall transport Footprint. A further factor that contributed to the size of Cardiff's Footprint for transport was residents' air travel (0.34 gha/capita), which accounted for 34 per cent of the travel Footprint. Cardiff has within close proximity two international airports (Cardiff and Bristol) from which a number of budget airlines operate (for example, BMIBaby, EasyJet and Ryanair), which residents use frequently to travel within the UK or overseas. The increase in vacations is also reflected in the size of the Footprint for residents' holidays abroad (0.103 gha/capita) (see Table 3.1). However, this figure excludes the impact of residents' travel to the final holiday destination, and so it is likely that the overall ecological demand was significantly more.

Domestic Energy Use

Similar to passenger travel, Cardiff's domestic energy use also had an Ecological Footprint of 0.99 gha/capita, of which 58 per cent was attributable to domestic fuel consumption (0.57 gha/capita) and 42 per cent to electricity and gas distribution (0.42 gha/capita). As shown in Table 3.1, both of these Footprint figures are higher than the respective numbers for Wales and the UK. In recent years, Cardiff has witnessed an increase in young and affluent professionals, which combined with a rise in the development of single-occupancy and executive type dwellings may provide an explanation for such a large Footprint for domestic fuel consumption. Residents living in this type of accommodation tend to have high levels of disposable income and are more likely to heat their homes throughout the year, and use more household electrical items.

Consumables and Durables

As shown in Table 3.1, residents' consumption of consumables and durables had an Ecological Footprint of 0.64 gha/capita, which was equivalent to 11.4 per cent of the city's total Footprint. This Footprint result is similar to that for Wales, but lower than that for the UK. Recreational items and equipment (which includes items and equipment for sports, outdoor recreation, gardening and veterinary services) was the single largest subcategory and responsible for 31 per cent of the Footprint for consumables and durables. Thirty-nine per cent of the consumables and durables Footprint was attributable to audio-visual equipment, household appliances and personal effects (which includes jewellery, handbags and wallets). The results within this category highlight that with an increasing number of the city's residents having high levels of disposable incomes, they are purchasing more high-cost items and replacing them on a more frequent basis. However, as the results also show, affluent lifestyles do have significant resource demands and can contribute to a larger Ecological Footprint.

Other Consumption Categories

Of the other consumption categories listed in Table 3.1, gross fixed capital formation (capital investment), which includes fixed assets such as transport equipment, houses and other buildings, had the largest Footprint (0.74 gha/capita). This figure is the same for Wales and the UK as the Footprint methodology assumed that all UK residents have equal responsibility for capital investment. On grounds of equity it may be sensible to apportion such investments; however if we consider consumption practices it could be considered anomalous as Cardiff is a capital city. Although by European standards, Cardiff is considered a relatively small city but it does contain the infrastructure associated with a capital such as government administrative buildings, museums, arenas and major sporting stadiums. The presence of these will influence the consumption activities of residents living in the city and also their Footprint.

Waste

The methodology used by SEI–York to calculate Cardiff's Ecological Footprint only considered the impact of consumables (that is, an input) and did not include the environmental impact of waste (that is, an output). To avoid issues relating to double counting, waste was treated as a satellite account. The reason for this is that the impacts of household consumption can only be counted once, either as an 'input' when products are bought or consumed, or as an 'output' when products are disposed of (see Barrett et al. 2005c,

p. 117). In 2001, Cardiff's residents generated 164 989 tonnes of waste, of which 94.5 per cent went to landfill and 5.5 per cent was recycled (see Collins et al. 2005). This resulted in a Footprint of 0.81gha/capita, 17 per cent larger than that for Wales and the UK. Due to the relatively small proportion of waste that was recycled and composted, this only resulted in a small number of credits for recycling (–0.03gha/capita) (see Table 3.1). This Footprint result for waste provides only a partial account of its impact as the figure only refers to household waste and excludes other types of waste such as construction, demolition and commercial wastes which would also have been related to residents' consumption and resource use.

Tourism

Within SEI–York's Footprint methodology, tourism is also treated as a satellite account. Using a top-down approach to calculating tourists' Footprint that was based on modelling tourist expenditure in five key areas (catering and accommodation services, clothing, other products, UK transport services, and other services), the Ecological Footprint of Cardiff's tourists was estimated to be 280 000 gha, or 8.5 gha/tourist. As the top-down approach to calculating tourists' Footprint was unable to account for their travel to the UK, data from a Cardiff visitors' survey was used to calculate the Footprint of overseas travel to the UK (Cardiff Council 2002b). From this, Cardiff visitors' air travel to the UK was found to have generated an additional Ecological Footprint of 5 536 gha, or 0.17 gha/visitor. Combined with the top-down Footprint figure, the total Footprint for Cardiff's tourists was 286 000 gha (8.67 gha/tourist), and equivalent to 17 per cent of Cardiff's total Ecological Footprint for the same year (1.72 million gha). Although the promotion of Cardiff as a visitor and events destination is an important part of the city's development strategy, these Ecological Footprint results high-light the resource demands and ecological impact that can result from Cardiff promoting itself as a tourist destination.

Responses and Reactions to Cardiff's Ecological Footprint Results

The Cardiff Ecological Footprint project provided policy officers with quantifiable evidence of residents' physical consumption, its global ecological impact and the extent to which it compared to the Footprint of the average UK and Welsh resident. It also provided support for officers in terms of thinking about policy in a more integrated way, and showed how the activities of one department was generating additional costs for another; costs which did not appear to have been taken into account in event planning or tourism promotion. For example, promoting tourism and large-scale events in the city can generate significant amounts of additional visitor waste. This could also support and enable officers to consider whether current policies were effective in addressing the most significant issues and reducing the city's Footprint.

In some policy areas where there were long-established models for assessing impact and policy effectiveness, and commitments to particular policy solutions, policy officers reacted cautiously to the Ecological Footprint findings and in some instances raised counter-arguments on the Footprint model and data. However, in other policy areas where their role within the organisation was under threat, officers reacted more enthusiastically towards the results and in one instance used them to reinforce the importance of their area of work. Whilst at a day-to-day level transport policy staff could resist the Ecological Footprint model (see Chapter 2) at a strategic level, the Ecological Footprint appealed to the Head of Transport, who considered the results as additional evidence to justify greener transport policy (Collins et al. 2009). The Waste Department also considered the Footprint as an attractive approach from which to communicate alternative waste management options to managers, politicians and the general public. Some officers suggested further policy applications for the Footprint, for example community planning, food procurement and schools.

The Cardiff Ecological Footprint study also resulted in two key outputs. The first was a joint report by Cardiff University and Cardiff Council that provided a summary of the key results and the policy changes needed to slow the growth of the city's Footprint (see Collins et al. 2005). A key message deriving from this report was that in the future, Cardiff would encounter the challenge of slowing the growth of its Footprint before it could begin to think about how it could reduce it. Policies suggested in the report included consuming more organic and seasonal food and drink; using energy from renewable sources such as solar, wind and tidal; reducing the amount of paper and cardboard entering the waste stream; reducing travel by car and air; considering the resource use implications of a development over its lifetime and not just its infrastructure; and considering the resource use implications of tourism and major events. A second output from the project was the adoption of the Ecological Footprint as a headline indicator in the Council's Community Strategy in 2004, a key document which deals with council planning structure, as it would enable the Council to be 'well-positioned to respond to urgent global problems like climate change, and to balance growth and development against environmental imperatives' (Cardiff Council 2004, p. 16). The Council's Sustainable Development Action Programme also contained commitments to recalculate the city's Footprint and use it 'to inform policy formulation within the Council' (Cardiff Council 2009, p. 8) – for example spatial development options within the Local Development Plan and waste management options – and incorporate it as an element of the Eco-Schools Programme. Although the Ecological Footprint and study received corporate commitment and policy officers recognised its value and had few concerns regarding the methodology, to date the Footprint has still to be shown to influence specific policy decisions. As we shall see in the section below, Cardiff has one of the larger Ecological Footprints per capita. From an environmental management perspective this makes the lack of policy action rather worrying.

COMPARISON OF CARDIFF'S ECOLOGICAL FOOTPRINT RESULTS WITH OTHER CITIES

In 2008, more than half of the world's population (3.3 billion) were living in urban towns and cities (UNFPA 2007). This figure is expected to increase to 4.9 billion by 2030, some 80 per cent of the world's population, and the majority of this growth will take place in developing countries. As cities continue to grow they become increasingly dependent on the ecological resources beyond their geographical boundaries in order to provide for their needs and sustain themselves, such as importing goods and services from elsewhere. As a consequence, this will increase the Ecological Footprints of our cities and those who live in them.

Cardiff is a major European city, and as already discussed in this chapter, the city's first Ecological Footprint study demonstrated that the resource use of its residents has large ecological demands and Footprints. A key question might be whether or not Cardiff is typical of other British and European cities. As Cardiff continues to develop and its Council aspires the city to be an international destination (Cardiff Council 2007), how does the city's Footprint compare to other cities internationally?

Ecological Footprint results for a selection of British, European and international cities, and their corresponding countries, are shown in Table 3.3. Although these Footprint results have been drawn from a number of reports, using different methodologies and baseline years, they still provide a useful starting point from which to compare and contrast the resource use impacts of different cities. However, as the level of data reported within published reports is variable, comparisons between cities is limited to the overall Ecological Footprint results rather than individual components.

The same methodological framework used to calculate Cardiff's Ecological Footprint for 2001 has more recently been used to recalculate the Footprint for a number of cities across the UK including Cardiff (see Calcott and Bull 2007). Similar to many other indicators, methodologies are subject to constant development in terms of modelling techniques and the data sources that are used. In Table 3.3 we present the 2007 Ecological Footprint results for Cardiff, as they are the most recent results available for the city. They are also more directly comparable with the Footprint results of other British cities as they have been calculated for the same year.

Although the Ecological Footprints for 2001 and 2007 were calculated using the same methodological framework, the figure per capita in 2007 (5.2 gha/capita) is lower than that for 2001 (5.59 gha/capita). The difference between the Footprint results is due to methodological developments and changes to the way in which the Footprint estimates were calculated. It is unlikely that Cardiff's Footprint would have reduced during that period as the city has seen a number of significant developments and the level of affluence has continued to increase.

Table 3.3   Ecological Footprints of cities: UK, European and international

	Year of Ecological Footprint results	Ecological Footprint per capita (gha/capita)
United Kingdom[1] (ranking of city)	2007	4.9
Newport[3] (= 1)	2007	5.01
Plymouth[3] (= 1)	2007	5.01
Cardiff [3] (= 15)	2007	5.20
Glasgow (= 15)	2007	5.21
Bradford[3] (= 17)	2007	5.21
Bristol[3] (= 17)	2007	5.22
Birmingham[3] (= 17)	2007	5.22
Liverpool[3] (= 21)	2007	5.25
Nottingham[3] (= 21)	2007	5.26
Manchester[3] (= 37)	2007	5.36
London[3] (44)	2007	5.48
Edinburgh[3] (50)	2007	5.76
Winchester[3] (60)	2007	6.52
Norway[1]	2007	5.55
Oslo[13]	2000	7.76
Austria[1]	2007	5.31
Vienna[9]	2009	3.9
Italy[2]	2007 (2001)	4.98 (3.8)
Piacenza[15]	2002	3.79
China[1]	2007	2.21
Beijing[4]	2008	3.9
Shanghai[4]	2008	3.8
Tianjin[4]	2008	2.7
Chongqing[4]	2008	2.2
Hong Kong[5]	2007	4.0
Australia[1]	2007	5.31
Adelaide[6]	2001	6.53
Sydney[7]	2001	5.92

	Year of Ecological Footprint results	Ecological Footprint per capita (gha/capita)
Canada[1]	2007	7.0
Edmonton[11]	2008	8.56
Calgary[8]	2007	9.5–9.9
Toronto[10]	1996	7.6
Brazil[1]	2007	2.9
Curitiba[12]	2009	2.6
South Africa[1]	2007	2.3
Cape Town[14]	2007	4.28

Notes:
1. Estimates for the United Kingdom, Austria, Brazil, China, Australia, South Africa, Canada, Norway have been taken from the *Living Planet Report 2010* (WWF 2010).
2. Estimates for Italy (2001) have been taken from *Living Planet Report 2004* (WWF 2004). The results are included here as the year base is closer to that of the Piacenza study.
3. Estimates for UK cities have been taken from a report by Calcott and Bull (2007).
4. Estimates for Beijing, Shanghai, Tianjin and Chonqing have been taken from WWF China (2010). Estimates are based on per capita Ecological Footprint for the urban population.
5. Estimates for Hong Kong have been taken from the *Hong Kong Ecological Footprint Report* (WWF Hong Kong 2010).
6. Estimates for Adelaide have been taken from Agrawal et al. (2008).
7. Estimates for Sydney have been taken from Lenzen (2008).
8. Estimates for Calgary have been taken from City of Calgary (2007).
9. Estimates for Vienna have been taken from Vienna City Administration (2009).
10. Estimates for Toronto have been taken from Onisto et al. (1998).
11. Estimates for Edmonton have been taken from Anielski (2010).
12. Estimates for Curitiba have been taken from GFN (2010a).
13. Estimates for Oslo have been taken from Aall and Norland (2005).
14. Estimates for Cape Town have been taken from City of Cape Town (2007).
15. Estimates for Piacenza have been taken from Scotti et al. (2009).

In 2007, Cardiff's Ecological Footprint per capita was 5.2 gha/capita (see Table 3.3). Like most Western cities, Cardiff's Ecological Footprint greatly exceeds its geographical boundaries and fair share of the available global capacity. This Footprint is 48.1 per cent greater than the global average biocapacity (1.8 gha/capita) and 65.4 per cent more than the global average Footprint (2.7 gha/capita). The size of Cardiff's Ecological Footprint highlights that the city's residents have a highly consumptive and material lifestyle. If everyone living on the planet had similar lifestyles and consumption patterns as Cardiff residents, almost three planets worth of resources would be needed to support that level of resource consumption.

A report published by the World Wide Fund for Nature UK (WWF UK) in 2007 ranked 60 British cities according to the size of their average Ecological Footprint (see Calcott and Bull 2007). Overall, Cardiff is ranked joint fifteenth, with the city of Newport (Wales) being ranked first with the smallest Ecological Footprint (5.01 gha/capita), and Winchester being ranked sixtieth with the largest (6.52 gha/capita). Compared with other British cities, Cardiff has an Ecological Footprint comparable to other cities such as Coventry, Nottingham and Leicester which have similar-sized populations (300 000–330 000) (see Table 3.3). Cardiff's Footprint per capita is similar to some of Britain's larger cities, such as Glasgow, Bradford, Birmingham and Liverpool. However, its per capita Ecological Footprint is smaller than other British capital cities, London and Edinburgh, but larger than other key cities in Wales (Newport, 5.01 gha/capita and Swansea, 5.12 gha/capita). These comparisons highlight that although Cardiff is considered a relatively small city in terms of its population size, the consumption and resource use patterns of its residents are on a par with much larger British cities. This may be attributable to its increasing affluence and that, being a capital city, residents have access to a wider range of services and facilities which may facilitate greater consumption, such as leisure facilities, retail developments and airports. However, the city's geographical location and having few public transport links to the rest of Britain may also be factors that are contributing to the size of its Ecological Footprint.

In the case of European cities, Table 3.3 shows that with the exception of Vienna (Austria), the Ecological Footprints of cities per capita exceed that of their respective country: Oslo by 28.3 per cent and Piacenza by 23.9 per cent. In Canada, the Footprints of its cities are more closely aligned with that of their country's average Ecological Footprint (7.6–9.9 per cent greater). With the exception of Curitiba (Brazil), the Footprints of cities in other countries were much greater: Australia (10.3–18.7 per cent), China (0.5–43.3 per cent) and South Africa (46.3 per cent), which may be a signal of the increasing affluence and materialistic lifestyles of residents living in those cities.

Compared to those European cities listed in Table 3.3, Cardiff's Ecological Footprint is 33 per cent smaller than that for Oslo, but 27 per cent and 33 per cent larger, respectively, than that for Piacenza and Vienna. However, Cardiff's Ecological Footprint per capita is significantly lower than those of cities in the developed countries of Australia and Canada. The Canadian cities of Vancouver, Calgary and Toronto are useful benchmarks against which to compare Cardiff's Ecological Footprint as they have similar climatic conditions. However, as shown in Table 3.3, their Footprints are between 32 and 47 per cent greater. Whilst the per capita Ecological Footprint of cities in Australia is lower than those in Canada, they are still 1.1–1.3 per cent greater than that for Cardiff. Compared with cities in the developing countries of China and Brazil, Cardiff's Footprint is between 1.3 and 2.4 times greater. However within the rapidly developing economies of China and Brazil, it is likely that with increasing levels of disposable incomes the Ecological Footprint of residents living in these cities will grow significantly in the future, as their lifestyles converge towards that of Western and developed cities.

The Ecological Footprint of cities, their future growth and policies needed to address sustainability are important issues for city planners. Key questions include: How can the economic development of a city be considered alongside environmental sustainability? Do cities place unsustainable pressures on their countries and regions? What types of policies are required to reduce the Ecological Footprints of cities now and in the future?

The Cardiff Model: Informing the Approach of other Ecological Footprint Studies

During the course of Cardiff's Ecological Footprint project, WWF UK was also closely involved in a number of other Footprint-related activities in the UK, including Scotland's Ecological Footprint project (see Aberdeen City Council 2006; North Lanarkshire Council 2006). A key part of WWF UK's strategy for promoting the Ecological Footprint in the UK was through its published guide on the Ecological Footprint for local councils called *Taking the First Step* (see Bond and Matthews 2006). This guide explained the Ecological Footprint concept, the methodologies, and how it could be used by local government to promote sustainable development, be integrated into policy and used in education. The guide also presented the case studies of three local councils in the UK that were considered to have undertaken 'effective Footprint work', and also the outcomes that resulted from those individual projects. A key message communicated within the guide was that an effective Footprint required 'a series of clear and distinct stages or "steps", each of which would help ensure that the Footprinting work is properly integrated within the wider work of the council' (Bond and Matthews 2006, p. 11). One of the case studies included within this publication was Cardiff, and the guide outlined the process developed to address concerns relating to previous Ecological Footprint studies. The guide concluded that in adopting this approach, the Cardiff project 'helped to move the Footprint out of the academic and into the policy arena' (Bond and Matthews 2006, p. 21). A number of local councils throughout the UK have since used the WWF UK guidance to assist them in developing their own Ecological Footprint studies.

More recently the Cardiff approach has also been used to inform the development of Ecological Footprint studies in countries outside the UK, including the United Arab Emirates (UAE). In the 2006 *Living Planet Report*, the UAE was ranked as the country with the largest Ecological Footprint per capita (11.68 gha) (see WWF 2006). In response to concerns about the size of their country's reported Ecological Footprint, the UAE held discussions with WWF and GFN to understand the methodology behind the analysis and factors influencing the size of its estimated Ecological Footprint. From these discussions there was recognition that not all land types included within the Footprint methodology were appropriate, or that they had been overestimated (for example, built-up land and existing biodiversity), and that some areas of consumption were significantly underestimated (for example, fishing). It was agreed amongst all parties that a more robust analysis was required in order to provide a more accurate account of the country's Footprint. The UAE is the third country in the world to have embarked on in-depth research to understand its Ecological Footprint, after Switzerland and Japan.

UAE Ecological Footprint Initiative: Al Basma Al Beeiyah Initiative

Following on from these initial discussions and wanting to seize the opportunity to develop more sustainably, the UAE launched its own Ecological Footprint Initiative, the Al Basma Al Beeiyah Initiative, in October 2007. This involved a partnership of four key organisations: the Ministry of Environment and Water, the Environment Agency-Abu Dhabi's AGEDI (Abu Dhabi Global Environmental Data Initiative) programme, the Emirates Wildlife Society in association with WWF (EWS-WWF), and GFN. A key aim of the Ecological Footprint Initiative was to 'better understand the Ecological Footprint of the UAE, and monitor consumption patterns in the country' (EWS-WWF 2010, p. 3). Specific objectives included: sourcing data integrity, conducting nation-specific research, contributing to methodological improvements, fostering capacity-building, recommending and assisting in the development of policies, and raising awareness amongst all sectors. Partners involved in the Initiative anticipated that it would provide answers to the following questions: What is the Ecological Footprint? What does it measure? What factors are driving the UAE's Footprint? What strategies are needed to manage and reduce the Ecological Footprint? The process used by the UAE to construct a more accurate Ecological Footprint was informed by the approach and experiences of Cardiff, and involved a number of key stages.

First, from the outset it was imperative that the Initiative had 'buy-in' and EWS-WWF (the Initiative's coordinators), embarked on high-level strategic engagement. A number of key federal organisations were engaged as partners of the initiative and contributed to the research. Second, to enhance the credibility of the Initiative a project steering committee was established whose membership included the Ministry of Economy and senior-level government representation from the different Emirate countries. Third, to raise awareness of the Initiative and establish the credibility of the Ecological Footprint in the wider community, a series of workshops were organised for various government institutions and ministries to explain the Ecological Footprint concept and the methodology behind its calculation. GFN played a key role in this process as well as undertaking the final Ecological Footprint calculations. Third, UAE partners worked alongside GFN to develop and improve the accuracy of the methodology. To ensure that the method was robust and scientific, and the final Footprint results were as accurate as possible, policy and technical officers from organisations represented on the steering committee were involved in providing and verifying data used by GFN in constructing the UAE's Ecological Footprint. This was particularly important given the UAE's very distinctive geography. As the UAE is a relatively young country, at a very early stage the Initiative revealed that not all data was streamlined in all of the Emirate countries and a number of data gaps existed. A key outcome from the Initiative was the development of a National Bureau of Statistics that would coordinate and standardise data collection across all of the Emirate countries.

The UAE's recalculation of its Ecological Footprint for the year 2007 identified that 57 per cent was attributable to household consumption (see EWS-WWF 2010). From this EWS-WWF and the Environment Agency Abu Dhabi launched a sustainable lifestyle campaign entitled 'Heroes of the UAE', to engage the government, public, private and education sectors on the importance of conserving resources such as energy and water. The UAE Government has been interested in the Ecological Footprint not only as a useful awareness raising tool and indicator of global environmental impact, but also as a tool that can be used to inform policy decisions, and this may well result from a more sympathetic approach to technocratic perspectives that is found in the West (see Chapter 1). The Government has also invested heavily in the development of a 'first of a kind' science-based tool to assist policy makers and make the Ecological Footprint policy relevant. This model was developed by Masdar Institute, the UAE's scientific institute of technology (with input from GFN) and used to assess the effectiveness of existing policy (for example, energy and water) and included the Ecological Footprint and carbon dioxide as indicators. Data contained within the model was provided by key stakeholders, thereby helping to generate ownership of the model and ensure the results would be considered credible and could be interpreted by policy makers, policy and technical advisors within key organisations. Policies considered in the first instance have focused on electricity and the water sector, although at the time of writing this book (2014), the Initiative was not yet at a stage of making policy recommendations to its government.

CONCLUSIONS

For those conducting earlier Ecological Footprint studies, a great deal of emphasis was placed on standardising and increasing the robustness and accuracy of the Ecological Footprint methodology. From the viewpoint of leading UK Ecological Footprint organisations, the standardisation of the Ecological Footprint methodology is key to the Footprint being used by decision making organisations such as local government (see Chapter 6). Standardisation is also important if organisations such as Cardiff Council want to make comparisons with others. However, building the capacity of organisations to use the Ecological Footprint was not a focus for studies undertaken prior to Cardiff, as funding packages tended to support the communication and awareness-raising aspects of the Footprint, and focused less on engaging decision makers with the tool. There has been relatively limited investment by funding regimes for capacity building, which can be very resource-intensive. Building the capacity of partners involved in the Cardiff Ecological Footprint study was a key element, and from the outset Council officers were engaged in the process of constructing a Footprint for the city.

The process used to conduct the Cardiff Ecological Footprint study was significantly different to that used previously for other UK local and regional government studies, as it involved a unique consortium of researchers at Cardiff University and Cardiff Council policy officers in checking the quality of data used in the calculations and the validating of any assumptions that were made. This process has required researchers at Cardiff University to liaise closely with officers when interpreting local data and considering their appropriateness and use in the Ecological Footprint calculation. Although this aspect of the Cardiff study was extremely resource-intensive and required a great deal of investment by the three partners, it helped to ensure that the Ecological Footprint calculation was as accurate as possible and raised the credibility of the whole process and project within Cardiff Council.

The value of the Ecological Footprint as a communication tool that can provide a resonant chord with diverse policy interests, and the efforts to create a deliberative process to promote engagement with the Ecological Footprint across Cardiff Council, together produced a more participative process. This has been key to ensuring that Cardiff's commitment to the Ecological Footprint has been more widely dispersed amongst policy officers than was the case for other UK Councils. Compared with the concept of Environmental Space (Opschoor and Reijinders 1991; Carley and Spapens 1998), the Ecological Footprint and its calculations can be communicated in a relatively straightforward manner. Building upon existing administrative structures, policy officers were able to create spaces for deliberation on the Ecological Footprint, and discuss issues of data, method and assigning ecological value to resource use, and to shape the process to produce data that they felt would be helpful to them in policy analysis. Consequently, awareness of the Ecological Footprint spread throughout much of the organisation, rather than being contained within environment departments which appears to have happened in many previous local government experiences. It is important, though, to provide a note of caution on the experiences of a more persuasive style of engagement. Our evidence indicates that deliberation and argumentation were taking place across the organisation and engaging middle management. There is little to suggest that senior management or politicians engaged in a more advocacy style of decision making. Instead, high-level commitment to the Ecological Footprint and its results was secured through texts, via key corporate documents that were adopted by Cardiff Council.

The Ecological Footprint results for Cardiff and other cities discussed in this chapter has shown that the Footprint is a useful tool by which organisations can consider whether their residents' resource use is sustainable and equitable – to which the answer is clearly no. Cardiff's first detailed Ecological Footprint study allows the identification of areas of priority for policy and can help officers and local politicians to contribute to more informed debates about a vision of a sustainable Cardiff. Even so, interest in the Ecological Footprint results is variable, in part depending upon calculations of whether particular interests will be furthered or stifled by promoting the Footprint. For example, in novel policy areas for Cardiff Council such as food, or climate change, some officers have been keen to utilise the Ecological Footprint results and champion it as a tool as a way of bolstering their position and credibility within the organisation. Meanwhile, other officers have felt that the Ecological Footprint results may challenge long-held policy objectives or favoured policy evaluation tools, and have sought to dismiss or discredit the findings. The debates that the process has provoked have subjected the methodology to considerable scrutiny.

As officers within Cardiff Council have become more confident in the robustness of the Ecological Footprint as a tool and the legitimacy of its data, they (similarly to the UAE) have been keen to engage in evaluations of different policy options. Here the Ecological Footprint provides an innovative perspective on environmental pressures and is able to communicate them to officers in a readily understandable form. On its own, though, it is unlikely that the Ecological Footprint will change decisions within the Council (or any other organisation). Economic factors will continue to dominate, and the interpretation of the Ecological Footprint results or the development of alternative developmental perspectives based on the Footprint will probably remain within the shadow of a pro-growth agenda. The next chapter will consider the extent to which organisations in the UK have engaged with the Ecological Footprint, drawing comparisons with what has happened in Australia.

NOTES

1. Biffa Waste Services (the Biffa Group Ltd, a leading integrated waste management business operator in the UK) generated the Biffa Award through the introduction of a landfill tax credit scheme in the UK in 1996.
2. In the case of the Gwynedd project, the partnership organisations included Gwynedd Council, Bangor University, WWF Cymru and SEI–York.
3. Cardiff Council has five Scrutiny Committees whose role includes reviewing, proposing and monitoring Council policies, practices and strategies.

4. Ecological Footprinting in the United Kingdom

INTRODUCTION

Organisations in the UK were amongst the first to engage with the Ecological Footprint as a measure of ecological impact. The pace of uptake has been quite remarkable and quite different compared to what has happened elsewhere. A number of key factors – namely funding opportunities, and the role of Ecological Footprint consultancies and environmental non-governmental organisations (NGOs) – have influenced the speed of uptake and direction of its development. This chapter describes how the Ecological Footprint has developed in the UK since the late 1990s. It begins by considering the UK's Ecological Footprint results from 1996 through to 2008, the most recent year for which they have been published by the World Wide Fund for Nature (WWF). We then consider the level of interest that the Ecological Footprint has generated in the UK. The chapter then discusses those key factors that have influenced the uptake and development of the Ecological Footprint in the UK. Throughout this chapter comparisons are made with what has happened in Australia, where although organisations started to engage with the Ecological Footprint at a similar time, its uptake and development has differed.

THE UNITED KINGDOM'S NATIONAL ECOLOGICAL FOOTPRINT, 1996–2008

Since 2000, WWF – a world-leading conservation organisation – has published through its *Living Planet Report* (LPR), a biennial publication on the 'state of the planet'. In its first LPR, the average person living on the Earth in 1996 was estimated to have an

Ecological Footprint of 2.85 global hectares (gha) (WWF 2000). The available biocapacity for the same year was estimated to be 2.0 gha/capita. Compared to this available biocapacity, the average person living on the Earth had an Ecological Footprint that exceeded this by as much as 30 per cent (2.85 gha/capita – 2.0 gha/capita). The 2012 edition of the LRP reported that the Earth's available biocapacity was 1.8 gha/capita in 2008. Its Ecological Footprint was 2.7 global hectares per capita, and so exceeded the available biocapacity by 33.3 per cent (WWF 2012). So the Earth's population have been living in a situation of 'ecological overshoot' since 1970; in other words, human annual demand for natural resources has been exceeding what the Earth can renew for almost 75 years.

Table 4.1 shows the LPR's Ecological Footprint results for the UK from 1996 through to 2008, the corresponding Footprint for different land types (carbon, grazing, forest, fishing, crop and built-up land), and the country's world ranking. In 1996, the UK was ranked as having the 18th-largest Ecological Footprint per capita, with the average resident having an estimated Footprint of 6.29 gha. Countries with larger Footprints in the same year included the UAE (15.99 gha/capita, 1st), the USA (12.22 gha/capita, 3rd), Australia (8.49 gha/capita, 7th), Ireland (7.27 gha/capita, 9th) and the Czech Republic (6.3 gha/capita, 17th). On a per capita basis the Ecological Footprint of the average person living in the UK was similar to that for an average Western European. However, it was 46 per cent larger than the global Footprint average (2.87 gha/capita) (WWF 2000), and is indicative of the level of resource consumption by residents living in the UK. In the same year, the land types with the largest Ecological Footprints were carbon, crop and grazing land, and these combined accounted for 88 per cent of the country's Footprint, highlighting the significant ecological impact of UK energy use, as well as its production and consumption of food products. Between 1996 and 2008, the UK's Ecological Footprint results for the different land types was fairly constant, with the greatest decrease being its Carbon Footprint (from 3.80 gha/capita to 2.64 gha/capita, a reduction of 30 per cent), and the greatest increase being its Forest Footprint (0.36 gha/capita to 0.52 gha/capita, an increase of 44 per cent).

*Table 4.1   The United Kingdom's Ecological Footprint (EF)
            (1996–2008)*

Year	1996	1999	2001	2003	2005	2007	2008
Population (millions)	58.4	59.5	59.1	59.5	59.9	61.1	61.5
Total EF (per capita)	6.29	5.35	5.4	5.6	5.3	4.9	4.71
Crop land	1.03	0.68	0.69	0.68	0.87	0.87	0.88
Grazing land	0.69	0.33	0.27	0.30	0.21	0.27	0.45
Forest land	0.36	0.32	0.44	0.46	0.46	0.61	0.53
Fishing land	0.05	0.47	0.25	0.25	0.08	0.13	0.06
Carbon land	3.80	3.3	3.4	3.52	3.51	2.87	2.65
Built-up land	0.37	0.21	0.34	0.38	0.20	0.15	0.15
World ranking	18th	9th	15th	14th	15th	31st	27th
Average Europe EF (per capita)	6.28[1]	4.97[1]	5.1[1]	4.8[2]	4.7[2]	4.7[3]	4.72[2]
World average EF (per capita)	2.85	2.3	2.2	2.2	2.7	2.7	2.7
World's biocapacity (per capita)	2.0	1.9	1.8	1.8	2.1	1.8	1.8

Notes:
1. Results refer to Western European countries (incl. EU countries plus Norway and Switzerland).
2. Results refer to European Union (EU) countries.
3. Result refers to countries in Europe.

Sources: Compiled from WWF (2000, 2002, 2004, 2006, 2008, 2010, 2012).

Between 1996 and 1999, the UK's world ranking for its Ecological Footprint per capita climbed from 18th to 9th position (see Table 4.1). However by 2008, the UK was reported as having an estimated Ecological Footprint of 4.67 gha/capita, some 26 per cent lower than what it was in 1996. This result might suggest that the UK is consuming fewer resources, but is more likely to be due to methodological advances in how GFN calculates national Ecological Footprints, as Barrett and Scott (2001, p. 14) have highlighted that, 'each year the ecological footprint has become more refined, portraying a more and more accurate figure of the land appropriated by humans'. The UK's drop in world ranking to 27th position in 2008 also highlights that resource use levels and the corresponding Ecological Footprints of an increasing number of countries are becoming ever more unsustainable and inequitable, and depleting the Earth's natural resources at an ever faster rate.

UPTAKE OF THE ECOLOGICAL FOOTPRINT IN THE UNITED KINGDOM

Following the initial creation of the Ecological Footprint concept, and within a relatively short period of time, a number of organisations in the UK started to engage with it as a measure of ecological impact. To date, there is no complete catalogue of which organisations have been engaging with the Ecological Footprint, or how. To help provide an insight as to which organisations in the UK and Australia have been engaging with the Ecological Footprint, in 2011, the search engine Google was used to undertake a search of the term 'ecological footprint' on both UK and Australian websites. Although this type of search does not provide a complete account of the uptake of the Ecological Footprint in both countries, it can provide a useful snapshot as to what type of organisations are engaging with the Footprint and how, thereby enabling some broad comparisons to be made between both countries.

Our initial search of the term 'ecological footprint' resulted in 1.11 million hits on UK websites and 0.54 million hits on Australian websites, and so initially suggests that interest in the Ecological Footprint has been greater in the UK compared to Australia. For each country, the first 45 hits for the following categories of organisations were identified as they were considered to be engaging the most with the Ecological Footprint: academics, research institutes, corporations, consultancies, governments and their agencies, and social benefit, NGOs and not-for-profit organisations. Our search excluded those organisations whose website only made brief reference to the Ecological Footprint or contained a link to a Footprint calculator hosted by another organisation. The website of each organisation was then examined in turn for information relating to how it was engaging with the Ecological Footprint as well as its geographical location (by UK region, Australian state or country-wide).

The geographical location of organisations that are engaging with the Ecological Footprint can provide us with a useful indication as to the spread of interest and uptake in both countries. In the UK, the Ecological Footprint has been picked up by organisations across all four countries (see Figure 4.1). The largest proportion of organisations was located in England (37.8 per cent), while 35.6 per cent were UK-wide based. The remaining organisations were located in Wales (15.6 per cent), Scotland (6.7 per cent) and Northern Ireland (4.4 per cent). In Australia, however, of those organisations that were engaging with the Ecological Footprint, almost 69 per cent were located in the three specific states: New South Wales, Victoria and South Australia. This result is not surprising given that some of the key organisations that have led on work relating to the Ecological Footprint are located in these three states, namely the Environment Protection Authority (EPA) Victoria, the Australian Conservation Foundation (ACF), and the Centre for Integrated Sustainability Analysis (ISA) at the University of Sydney.

The results from our web search also show that a wide range of organisations in both countries have been engaging with the Ecological Footprint. Although the category of organisations does not show the extent of organisational interest or engagement, it does provide us with a useful indication as to how the Ecological Footprint is being used in each country. As shown in Table 4.2, in both countries the organisation category that was found to be engaging the most in terms of hits was social benefit, NGO and not-for-profit organisations, followed by consultancies and research institutes, and academic. When combined, these three categories of organisations accounted for 64.4 per cent and 60.0 per cent of our sample for websites in the UK and Australia, respectively. However, on closer inspection our sample also reveals some distinct similarities and differences between the two countries. First, in the UK, a larger proportion of social benefit, NGO and not-for-profit organisations, and government and government agency organisations, were found to be engaging with the Ecological Footprint. In the latter category, there was a notable difference in engagement by both local and national government. Second, in Australia a larger proportion of organisations were academic and corporations compared to the UK. Finally, in both countries a similar proportion of consultancies and research institutes were found to have been engaging with the Ecological Footprint. It could be argued that it is these differences and similarities which have influenced the direction and development of the Ecological Footprint in each country.

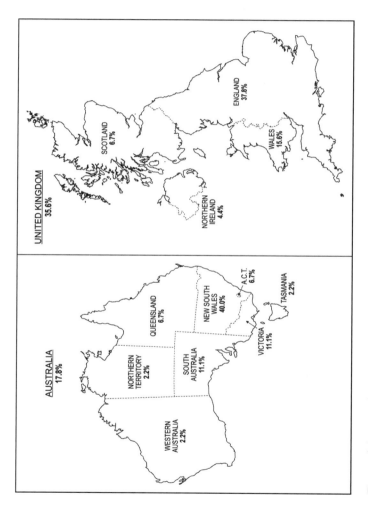

Figure 4.1 Uptake of the Ecological Footprint in the United Kingdom and Australia (2010)

Table 4.2   Category of organisations engaging with the Ecological
             Footprint in the UK and Australia (2010)

Category of organisation		United Kingdom (%) (n = 45)	Australia (%) (n = 45)
Academic		11.1	17.8
Consultancies and research institutes		13.1	11.1
Corporations		0.0	11.1
Government and government agencies	Government agencies	2.2	4.4
	Local government	15.6	11.1
	Regional/state government	11.1	11.1
	National government	6.7	2.2
Social benefit/NGO/not-for-profit		40.0	31.1
Total		100.0	100.0

FACTORS INFLUENCING THE DEVELOPMENT OF THE ECOLOGICAL FOOTPRINT IN THE UK

The uptake of the Ecological Footprint in the UK since the late 1990s has been quite spectacular, and compares quite differently to what has happened elsewhere. There are several key factors that have been instrumental to its uptake and development. The first of these relates to the role of funding organisations, in particular Biffa Waste Services Limited, which provided the necessary financial support through its Biffa Award scheme, for studies and research on the Ecological Footprint in the UK. The second factor relates to the role of Ecological Footprint consultancies, namely Best Foot Forward (BFF) and the Stockhold Environment Institute – York (SEI–York), which conducted the vast majority of Ecological Footprint studies in the UK and played a key role in creating markets for its further development. The third factor relates to the role of environmental NGOs, in particular WWF UK, the efforts of which focused on promoting the Ecological Footprint as an educational and awareness-raising tool, and identifying opportunities through which it could inform government policy. The influence and contribution made by each of these factors are discussed in turn below.

The Role of Funders

In the UK, funding opportunities for facilitating the uptake and development of the Ecological Footprint have been unique. Between 1996 and 2006, revenues generated through landfill tax credits funded a significant amount of work on the Ecological Footprint. In 1996, following the introduction of a landfill tax credit scheme in the UK, Biffa Waste Services Limited under the fund name 'Biffa Award' (and managed by the Royal Society of Wildlife Trusts), committed some £10 million funding for 60 projects which examined material resource flows in the United Kingdom as part of its Mass Balance Programme. Biffa's primary reason for investing landfill tax credits on work relating to the Ecological Footprint was twofold: first, to develop a better understanding of different waste flows and their geographical boundaries; and second, to inform corporate decisions on which new waste processing technologies they should invest in the future (Biffa Award 2010). The first of these funded projects was one of the world's first mass balance flow analysis for a distinct geographical region, the Isle of Wight, which was undertaken by BFF (see BFF and Imperial College 2000). Projects were also undertaken for UK regions and devolved countries, as well as for specific materials and industry sectors, and other so-called 'complementary studies' (Biffa Award 2006). As shown in Table 4.3, Biffa Award provided funding for almost 50 per cent of published Ecological Footprint studies at different government levels (local, regional and national).

One of the most comprehensive projects to be undertaken was Ecological Budget UK, a £520 000 project that produced detailed material flows, Ecological Footprint analysis and carbon dioxide emissions data for the United Kingdom by industrial sector and

Table 4.3 Summary of published UK Ecological Footprint studies (1999–2008)

Study number	Study title	Year of publication	Funder	Scope of study: EF = Ecological Footprint MF = material flow analysis SC = policy scenarios	Level of government	Organisation(s) conducting study	Reference
1	Oxfordshire's Ecological Footprint	1999	Oxfordshire County Council	EF	Local	BFF	BFF and Oxfordshire County Council (1999)
2	Island State: An Ecological Footprint Analysis of the Isle of Wight	2000	Biffa Award	EF, MF	Local	BFF and Imperial College	BFF and Imperial College (2000)
3	An Ecological Footprint of Liverpool: Developing Sustainable Scenarios	2001	Liverpool City Council, Environment Agency, Northwest Development Agency, Government Office for the Northwest, Northwest Water Ltd	EF, SC	Local	SEI-York and Sustainable Steps Consultants	Barrett and Scott (2001)
4	Herefordshire's Ecological Footprint	2001	Herefordshire County Council	EF	Local	BFF	BFF (2001)
5	A Material Flow Analysis and Ecological Footprint of York	2002	Norwich Union	EF, MF, SC	Local	SEI-York	Barrett et al. (2002)

	Title	Year	Commissioned by				Reference
6	City Limits – A Resource Flow and Ecological Footprint Analysis of Greater London	2002	Biffa Award	EF, MF, SC	Local	BFF	BFF (2002b)
7	Ol-troed Cymru / The Footprint of Wales	2002	WWF Cymru (Wales)	EF, MF, SC	Regional	BFF	BFF (2002a)
8	Five Cities Footprint: Estimating the Ecological Footprint of Aberdeen, Dundee, Edinburgh, Glasgow and Inverness	2002	Scottish Executive	EF	Local	BFF	BFF (2002c)
9	An Ecological Footprint of the United Kingdom: Providing a Tool to Measure the Sustainability of Local Authorities	2003	United Kingdom Government, Department for Transport (New Horizons Programme)	EF	National	SEI-York and BFF	Barrett and Simmons (2003)
10	An Ecological Footprint of Angus, Scotland	2003	Angus Council	EF	Local	BFF	Vergoulas et al. (2003)
11	Taking Stock: A Material Flow Analysis and Ecological Footprint of the South East	2004	Biffa Award	EF, MF, SC	Regional	SEI-York	Barrett et al. (2006)

Study number	Study title	Year of publication	Funder	Scope of study: EF = Ecological Footprint MF = material flow analysis SC = policy scenarios	Level of government	Organisation(s) conducting study	Reference
12	*Northern Limits: A Resource Flow Analysis and Ecological Footprint for Northern Ireland*	2004	Biffa Award	EF, MF, SC	Regional	EnviroCentre, BFF, Queen's University Belfast	Curry et al. (2004)
13	*Ecological Footprint of Inverness*	2004	Sustainable Development Research Centre (Inverness, Scotland)	EF, SC	Local	SEI-York and BFF	Birch et al. (2004a)
14	*Ecological Footprint of North Lincolnshire and North East Lincolnshire*	2004	North East Lincolnshire Council North Lincolnshire Council, North East Lincolnshire Primary Care Trust and North Lincolnshire Primary Care Trust	EF	Local	SEI-York	Birch et al. (2004c)
15	*Footprint North West – A Preliminary Ecological Footprint of the North West Region*	2004	North West Regional Assembly		Regional	SEI-York	Birch et al. (2004b)

No.	Title	Year	Commissioned by	Components	Scale	Method	Reference
16	*Scotland's Footprint – A Resource Flow and Ecological Footprint Analysis of Scotland*	2004	Biffa Award, Scottish Executive and The Institution of Civil Engineers	EF, MF	Regional	BFF	Chambers et al. (2004)
17	*An Ecological Footprint Analysis of Essex – East of England*	2004	Essex County Council	EF, MF, SC	Local	BFF	Vergoulas and Simmons (2004)
18	*An Ecological Footprint Analysis of Buckinghamshire – South East England*	2004	Buckinghamshire County Council	EF	Local	BFF	Vergoulas (2004)
19	*Stepping Forward: A Resource Flow and Ecological Footprint Analysis of the South West of England*	2005	Biffa Award, South West Regional Development Agency	EF	Regional	BFF	Chambers et al. (2005)
20	*The Ecological Footprint of Greater Nottingham and Nottinghamshire*	2005	Nottinghamshire County and Greater Nottinghamshire District Councils	EF, MF, SC	Local	SEI-York	Birch et al. (2005)
21	*Reducing Wales' Ecological Footprint: A Resource Accounting Tool for Sustainable Consumption*	2005	Biffa Award, Cardiff Council, Environment Agency Wales, Gwynedd Council	EF, MF, SC	Regional	SEI-York	Barrett et al. (2005c)

Study number	Study title	Year of publication	Funder	Scope of study: EF = Ecological Footprint MF = material flow analysis SC = policy scenarios	Level of government	Organisation(s) conducting study	Reference
22	*Reducing Cardiff's Ecological Footprint: A Resource Accounting Tool for Sustainable Consumption*	2005	Biffa Award, Cardiff Council, Environment Agency Wales, Gwynedd Council	EF, MF, SC	Local	SEI-York and Cardiff University	Collins et al. (2005)
23	*Reducing Gwynedd's Ecological Footprint: A Resource Accounting Tool for Sustainable Consumption*	2005	Biffa Award, Cardiff Council, Environment Agency Wales, Gwynedd Council	EF, MF, SC	Local	SEI-York and Bangor University	Farrer and Nason (2005)
24	*The Ecological Footprint of Kingston upon Thames*	2006	Kingston Council	EF	Local	SEI-York	Birch et al. (2006)
25	*North East Scotland Global Footprint Reduction Report*	2006	Scottish Executive, WWF Scotland, Aberdeen City Council, Aberdeenshire Council, Scottish Heritage, Scottish Environmental Protection Agency, Scottish Power	EF, SC	Local	SEI-York	Aberdeen City Council (2006)

No.	Title	Year	Commissioner	Components	Scale	Method	Reference
26	*North Lanarkshire Global Footprint Project*	2006	Scottish Executive, WWF Scotland, Aberdeen City Council, Aberdeenshire County Council, Scottish Heritage, Scottish Environmental Protection Agency, Scottish Power	EF, SC	Local	SEI-York	North Lanarkshire Council (2006)
27	*Ecological Budget North East*	2006	Biffa Award	EF, MF, SC	Regional	SEI-York and CURE	Paul et al. (2006)
28	*Ecological Budget West Midlands*	2006	Biffa Award	EF, MF, SC	Regional	SEI-York and CURE	Ravetz et al. (2006)
29	*The Ecological Footprint of Hertfordshire: Results and Scenarios*	2006	Hertfordshire Environment Forum	EF, MF, SC	Local	SEI-York and GFN	Barrett et al. (2003)
30	*Ecological Budget United Kingdom Counting Consumption*	2006	Biffa Award	EF, MF, SC	National	SEI-York and CURE	WWF UK (2006)
31	*Wales' Ecological Footprint: Scenarios to 2020*	2008	Welsh Assembly Government	EF, SC	Regional	SEI-York	Dawkins et al. (2008)

geographical area (by English region and devolved country) (WWF UK 2006):

> Ecological Budget United Kingdom provides a much needed evidence base to better understand the important issues of Sustainable Consumption and Production (SCP). It provides a statistical and scientific basis for SCP strategies in the United Kingdom at national and regional levels. It shows the total global impact of United Kingdom consumption, not only by accounting for direct resource flows and emissions within the United Kingdom, but also by including the manufacture of imported products and materials. Ecological Budget United Kingdom's three headline indicators – CO_2 emissions, material flow analysis, and the Ecological Footprint can be used together or side-by-side for different purposes ... [It] has taken the first step in understanding how the decisions we take every day affect the environment around us. It is an essential step in creating a platform to enable us to move from the current United Kingdom 'three planet economy' to a 'One Planet Economy'. (WWF UK 2006, p. 3)

The Ecological Budget UK project was undertaken by a second Ecological Footprint research consultancy, SEI–York, in collaboration with the Centre for Urban and Regional Ecology (CURE) at Manchester University, and Cambridge Econometrics, and produced a number of key research outputs including the *Ecological Budget United Kingdom Report* (WWF UK 2006), several regional project reports (see Paul et al. 2006; Ravetz et al. 2006), and a software tool called REAP (Resources and Energy Analysis Programme). This tool was designed with the specific intention that it could be used by governments to inform decisions and the development of more sustainable policies on resource consumption (www.resource accounting.org.uk) (Dawkins et al. 2010). The development and design of the REAP tool is discussed further in Chapter 5. A sustainable production and consumption network and website (SCPnet) was also established as part of the Ecological Budget UK project with the support of UK English regions, WWF UK and the UK's Environment Agency.

In Australia, however, similar funding opportunities did not exist. The availability of funding for work on the Ecological Footprint has been much more limited, and the majority of this has come from two key organisations: EPA Victoria and the Commonwealth Scientific and Industrial Research Organisation (CSIRO).

EPA Victoria is the second-oldest Environmental Protection Authority in the world and a statutory body with responsibility for protecting the Victorian environment. EPA Victoria was one of the founding members of GFN, and its Chairman at the time was a member of its Science and Policy Advisory Council. During the late 1990s, EPA Victoria was considering ways in which it could measure the environmental impacts of natural resource consumption. EPA Victoria's decision to engage with the Ecological Footprint was threefold. First, being a scientific organisation, according to one senior figure EPA Victoria considered the Ecological Footprint as 'the best available tool [which also] seemed to have some credibility in the expert field'. As the Ecological Footprint calculations incorporated quality data, it was considered rigorous enough to inform policy decisions. Second was the value of the Ecological Footprint as an education and awareness-raising tool, and its ability to influence behaviour changes on resource use. Third and finally was its potential to inform policy decisions relating to resource use.

EPA Victoria initially funded a pilot programme, involving 12 organisations (including businesses, local government, schools and individuals), which studied how they might use the Ecological Footprint to assess their environmental impacts. EPA Victoria was keen 'to take the Ecological Footprint out of just the academic arena in Australia and into the wider community' (Interview with senior official), and this led it to fund the development of five innovative online Ecological Footprint calculators that were designed to engage specific user groups: individuals, schools, retail tenants, retail centres and events.[1] To promote further interest in the Ecological Footprint, EPA Victoria also funded the first Ecological Footprint study of an Australian state – Victoria – as part of an attempt to synthesise the different Footprint methodologies advocated by the Global Footprint Network (GFN) and ISA at the University of Sydney (see EPA Victoria 2005). A second study, *An Ecological Footprint of Consumption in Victoria*, was also funded in 2008 as part of EPA Victoria's reporting in its first State of the Environment Report (see EPA Victoria 2008a). The funding of these novel online Ecological Footprint calculators and state-focused studies generated a significant amount of interest and assisted EPA Victoria in raising awareness of the Ecological Footprint not only across the Victorian state, but also across other states in Australia.

The second organisation in Australia to fund work on the Ecological Footprint was CSIRO, the national government body for scientific research in Australia. In 2000, CSIRO commissioned academics at ISA at the University of Sydney to undertake the first ever triple bottom line analysis of the Australian economy. The reason for this study was to encourage Australian industry, government and institutions 'to make decision on a broader basis than just the financial bottom line' (CSIRO 2005, p. 1). The study resulted in a key publication, *Balancing Act*, a four-volume report that quantified the impact and contributions of 135 sectors of the Australian economy across ten social, environmental and financial indicators, and covered some key components of an Ecological Footprint analysis (see CSIRO 2005, Vol. 1). Alongside this, CSIRO also funded the development of a triple bottom line (TBL) software tool (later marketed as 'BottomLine'[3]), as part of an attempt to overcome issues of trying to develop an aggregate indicator that was scientifically robust (Interview with senior academic). This was also undertaken by ISA at the University of Sydney and was designed with the specific intention that it could be used by businesses to select and measure progress on indicators most applicable to them, and to consider other trade-offs. Both the 'Balancing Act' report and BottomLine[3] software tool received a 'considerable amount of interest not only across government, but also by manufacturers and various industry sectors' (Interview with senior academic), and assisted in raising awareness and interest in the Ecological Footprint.

The Role of Ecological Footprint Consultants

In the UK, there have been two consultancy organisations that have been important advocates of the Ecological Footprint and have undertaken an extensive range of studies which have assisted in its development: BFF, a sustainability consultancy based in Oxford (UK); and SEI–York, a research consultancy based at the University of York. There is currently no complete catalogue of ecological studies undertaken in the UK; however, based on information available on BFF and SEI–York's websites and interviews with key individuals from both organisations, it is estimated that between 1999 and 2013 some 234 Ecological Footprint studies were undertaken (see Table 4.3). Those studies which have been undertaken and the associated software tools are discussed further in Chapter 5. In this chapter we describe the role played by both organisations in promoting and creating further markets for the development of the Ecological Footprint in the UK.

Best Foot Forward Limited

BFF Limited is a sustainability consultancy based in Oxford, UK, which specialises in Ecological and Carbon Footprint analysis. The company was co-founded in 1997 by Nicky Chambers and Craig Simmons, and was amongst one of the first environmental consultancies in the UK and Europe to use the Ecological Footprint.

At a relatively early stage, BFF's co-founders identified opportunities and recognised the benefits and flexibility of applying the Ecological Footprint to convey impacts at different scales:

> there was a great potential for the Ecological Footprint to measure and we moved that to the first Footprint study in the United Kingdom and we looked beyond what it had been used for up to that time, which was just to look at international issues, but to look at more regional and local issues, whether it's lifestyle, products or services, and so we decided to set up Best Foot Forward, and we did that in '97 to start taking forward some of these ideas. (Interview with BFF co-founders)

It was this potential of applying the Ecological Footprint to a range of applications which gave BFF its edge in the market. Whereas much of the earlier research undertaken by Mathis Wackernagel and William Rees had focused on the Ecological Footprint's application at a macro level, BFF took the Footprint beyond this initial application and applied it at different micro levels: individuals, cities, regions, corporations and products. In doing so they achieved a number of 'firsts' in the field of Ecological Footprinting.

In 1996, BFF first promoted the Ecological Footprint through the development of EcoCal™, which was one of the first computer-based calculators to be developed that measured personal and household Ecological Footprints (Simmons and Chambers 1998; Chambers et al. 2000). EcoCal™ was developed as part of the UK Government's Going for Green Campaign, and was aimed at raising public awareness of environmental issues and influencing behaviour change. Putting EcoCal™ through rigorous market testing provided BFF with an opportunity to collect data on household activities and their Ecological Footprints, and identify those with the greatest impact (Chambers et al. 2000).

BFF was particularly interested in developing a method that could be used to calculate the Footprint of household consumption activities such as travel, energy use, food and drink, and the production of waste. However, in the late 1990s there was limited information and guidance available on how to undertake Ecological Footprint calculations for specific consumption activities. So BFF set about working with CAG Consultants to develop algorithms for converting consumption activity data into Footprint equivalents, and using official government data on household travel and energy use (Simmons et al. 2000). This calculation method was later named the 'component-based' Footprint method, and was considered to be complementary to the original 'compound-based' method, but also 'more sensitive to underlying data variations' (Simmons et al. 2000, p. 377). Furthermore, it sought to build on the Ecological Footprint's strength as a metaphor that resonates with the public with its pedagogical structure enabling individuals, organisations and decision makers to understand the impact of their consumption activities (Simmons et al. 2000, p. 378), something which was more difficult with the original compound-based method. The validity of the component-based method was assessed through collaboration with John Barrett, a doctoral student at Liverpool John Moores University (who later worked on Ecological Footprint studies at SEI–York), whose thesis involved calculating an Ecological Footprint analysis of Guernsey in the Channel Islands. Barrett's PhD thesis represented the first attempt to compare both methods for calculating the Ecological Footprint of a region, and concluded that the component-based approach was able to provide similar results to the compound-based approach (Barrett 1998).

Following the assessment of the compound-based approach and the successful market testing of EcoCal™, BFF developed one of the first regional Ecological Footprint calculators, Regional Stepwise. As discussed earlier in this chapter, with the support of Biffa Award funding, BFF was able to apply Regional Stepwise and undertake the first large-scale study at a local government level in the UK, the Isle of Wight (see BFF and Imperial College 2000). Although this study took over a year to complete, mostly due to the extensive amount of primary data collection required, it acted as a test of whether or not the Ecological Footprint could be applied at a local government level:

> we used that [Isle of Wight] as sort of a test study, if you like, to see whether it's possible to do a detailed analysis down to the regional level and our conclusion was very much that it was and it's found to be a useful study and because of that other people have said, we'd like studies done of our areas. (Interview with BFF co-founders)

Following this, BFF then undertook further local and regional studies, the majority of which were also supported by Biffa Award funding (see Table 4.3). In undertaking these studies, BFF was able to invest its resources and develop different methodological innovations around the Ecological Footprint calculations, including the incorporation of official datasets such as Prodcom (a European database for almost 4800 products). The investment of Biffa Award funding was important for two main reasons. First, it enabled BFF to calculate more accurate Ecological Footprint calculations and provide a more reliable measure of resource use and environmental impact. Second, it also enabled BFF to create further markets for the Ecological Footprint by developing a range of novel applications and calculators, a theme which is discussed further in Chapter 5. In an interview with BFF, its co-founders considered that they were responsible for 'creating a market for the footprint in the United Kingdom ... and Europe' (Interview with BFF co-founders), and as a result of their various applications and methodological innovations and developments, their organisation has continued to grow steadily.

Stockholm Environment Institute – York
The second consultancy to play a key role in the development of the Ecological Footprint in the UK was SEI–York, based at the University of York. SEI is a not-for-profit, independent international research institute, which was formally established in 1989 by the Swedish Government. In 2012, SEI was ranked in the Global Go To Think Tank Index as the sixth most influential environmental think tank in the world, and the most influential outside the USA (McGann 2013). A key objective of SEI is to bring change for sustainable development by bridging the gap between science and policy through integrated analysis that supports decision makers

(SEI 2010). Although SEI's headquarters are in Stockholm (Sweden), it has an international network of centres in Boston (USA), Tallinn (Estonia), York and Oxford (UK), Bangkok (Thailand) and Dar Es Salaam (Tanzania). In York, SEI is a self-funded multidisciplinary research unit based in the Environment Department at the University of York. A key area of its work has been on consumption and behaviour and its environmental impacts, and this has included work on the Ecological Footprint. A key individual behind SEI's work on the Ecological Footprint and development of the REAP software tool was John Barrett, who joined SEI–York as a research associate in 2000. As previously discussed, Barrett had prior experience in calculating Ecological Footprints as part of his PhD thesis, and had also briefly worked with BFF on its Footprint study of the Isle of Wight. On joining SEI–York, Barrett initially worked on Ecological Footprint projects with Liverpool City Council, Mersey Travel (the integrated transport authority for Merseyside) and York City Council (see Barrett and Scott 2001; Barrett et al. 2002). This was followed by a number of single and cluster studies, which were either partly or fully funded by Biffa Award (see Table 4.3), and enabled the development of a new input–output methodology for calculating Ecological Footprints (see Wiedmann et al. 2006).

SEI–York continued to undertake further Ecological Footprint studies including several cluster studies: the Reducing Wales Ecological Footprint project which included a Footprint study of Cardiff and Gwynedd; Nottingham and Nottinghamshire; Scotland; Yorkshire and the Humber; and the UK's North West Region (see Barrett et al. 2005c; Collins et al. 2005; Farrer and Nason 2005; Birch et al. 2004b; Birch et al. 2005; Aberdeen City Council 2006; North Lanarkshire Council 2006). Its work on UK regions went beyond the Ecological Footprint and it considered a number of other indicators, including carbon dioxide and material flow analysis, to understand the consequences of resource consumption.

Although SEI–York had been approached to develop Ecological Footprint models for businesses, an interview with senior researchers at SEI–York highlighted that they made a conscious decision in 2002 to invest their resources on studies that would ultimately enable them to develop the methodological framework needed to create their novel REAP software program:

We've had a vision I suppose for a while on what we want to do. We wanted to do an environmental modelling scenario tool ... We [SEI–York] wouldn't do a project if it didn't build on the last one. We have very strict criteria now ... on what projects we take and what projects we don't. If a local authority doesn't want REAP then we don't do a project with them ... that's all we want to develop and we've got to be focused on a particular approach at one time. (Interview with senior researchers)

REAP is an interactive modelling software tool, based on an input–output methodology (Wiedmann and Barrett 2005), which was developed to help legitimise the Ecological Footprint in the UK and enable policy makers to understand and measure the environmental impacts associated with human consumption and production (SEI–York 2007; Paul et al. 2010). It also supported SEI's organisational objective of bridging the gap between science and policy. However, it was only when SEI–York embarked on the Biffa Award's Ecological Budget UK Project that it had the necessary resources to develop a more sophisticated REAP decision support tool. REAP was first launched by SEI–York in 2006 as part of the Ecological Budget UK project, with a further update being produced in 2007 (see Dawkins et al. 2010). To help promote the tool and encourage take-up amongst local and regional governments in the UK, SEI–York also provided training and support for end users as a means of increasing capacity within organisations. Further discussion relating to the design of the REAP software is provided in Chapter 5.

SEI–York considers that the development of REAP development has played an important role in evidence on the impacts associated with consumption to government policy makers in the UK (Paul et al. 2010). Since its initial launch in 2006 the tool has been used in more than 100 projects to assess regional strategies and specific policies in relation to food, transport and housing (Paul et al. 2010).

In Australia, organisations similar to BFF and SEI–York did not emerge. This has mainly been due to the different funding situation that has existed. Although there have been consultancies that have engaged with the Ecological Footprint and undertaken various studies, most of the methodological developments on the Footprint have been undertaken by academics such as Manfred Lenzen and his colleagues at the University of Sydney.

Role of Environmental NGOs

As discussed earlier in this chapter, the organisation category that was found to be engaging the most with the Ecological Footprint in terms of Google hits was social benefits, NGOs and not-for-profit organisations. In the UK, the environmental NGO WWF UK has played a prominent and leading role and has actively promoted the Ecological Footprint as part of its One Planet Living™ campaign, a global initiative based on ten principles of sustainability developed with Bioregional Group (another environmental NGO). WWF UK has actively promoted the Ecological Footprint in the UK in two main ways: first, through education and awareness raising; and second, by providing advice and demonstrating through various projects how it can be used to inform government policy.

At an individual level, WWF UK collaborated with SEI–York to develop an online Ecological Footprint calculator designed to enable individuals to measure their own Footprint, as well as providing tips on how to reduce it (for further information see Chapter 5). WWF UK has also been active in promoting the Ecological Footprint as a tool for developing more sustainable strategies and encouraging its uptake at different levels of government. At a UK level, WWF UK was a key partner in the Biffa Award Ecological Budget UK project. As already discussed, a key outcome from the EcoBudget project was the REAP software, from which data would contribute to the evidence base needed for developing a One Planet Economy in the UK. WWF UK published with SEI–York several Footprint reports for several English regions (the North East, West Midlands and South East) based on consumption and production data contained within REAP (Barrett et al. 2006; Ravetz et al. 2006; Paul et al. 2006).

In Wales, WWF Cymru has promoted the Ecological Footprint since 2000, and in 2001 commissioned BFF to undertake the first Footprint study of Wales (see BFF 2002a). WWF Cymru was also instrumental in the Ecological Footprint being adopted by the National Assembly for Wales in 2001 as one of its headline indicators for sustainable development (see Chapter 2). One year later, WWF Cymru was successful in securing funding through Biffa Award to measure the Ecological Footprint of Wales and two of its sub-regions (Cardiff and Gwynedd) (see Barrett et al. 2005c). Through this project WWF Cymru established a Wales Footprint

Network with other project partners to share experiences and provide advice to other local authorities and organisations considering using the Ecological Footprint, and was also a leading steering group member for the recalculation of Wales's Ecological Footprint in 2008 (see Dawkins et al. 2010).

In Scotland, WWF Scotland secured funding via the Scottish Executive's Sustainable Action Fund to undertake a Global Footprint Project (2003–2006) involving North Lanarkshire, Aberdeen City and Aberdeenshire Councils to measure the Ecological Footprint of their respective area and identify policies that could reduce their local and global environmental impact (see Aberdeen City Council 2006; North Lanarkshire Council 2006). Further funding was secured to develop an Ecological Footprint tool for schools to measure their own Footprint as part of the Scotland Global Ecological Footprint project. WWF Scotland also played a key role in the Ecological Footprint being adopted as a national indicator by the Scottish Executive.

Experiences and lessons learnt from these and other Ecological Footprint studies in the UK were published by WWF UK in a series of reports aimed at helping local and regional governments implementing Footprint reduction strategies for their areas. The first publication was *A Guide for Local Authorities*, which explained what the Ecological Footprint is and how it is calculated, and its value as a policy and education and environmental awareness tool (see Bond 2002). The second publication was also a guide for local councils, *Ecological Footprints: Taking the First Step* (see Bond and Matthews 2006), and provided local government with guidance on how to gain organisation buy-in and undertake an Ecological Footprint study.

Ecological Footprints: The Journey so Far was the third report in the series and was specifically targeted at policy officers responsible for developing Ecological Footprint strategies (Ross 2006). It drew upon the experiences of officers who were involved in eight UK projects across Wales, Scotland and England (and at different stages of completion), and provided a useful summary of the main lessons learnt from those projects. A further publication commissioned by WWF UK involved a study of British city residents, which explored those factors that were contributing to cities' Footprints, particularly income levels (see Calcott and Bull 2007). The study's report ranked the Ecological Footprints of 60 cities in

Britain (by gha per capita), and provided some key recommendations on how residents could reduce their Footprint in the future. A breakdown of Ecological Footprint results for each city was also provided, thereby enabling some useful comparisons to be made. In Australia, WWF has not had the same degree of influence and has played a less active role in promoting the Footprint, focusing mostly on awareness raising through its online Ecological Footprint calculator. WWF Australia has not sought to promote the Ecological Footprint as a policy tool, or support its development in the same way to the UK, but instead has focused its efforts on engaging corporations in thinking about climate change and reducing CO_2 emissions associated with their business activities and supply chains. This has involved encouraging business leaders to use triple bottom line tools to assess the sustainability performance of their supply chains, and promoting 'Sustainability Supply Chain Leaders'.

However, the environmental NGO Australian Conservation Foundation (ACF) has played a more prominent role in promoting the development of the Ecological Footprint. ACF is the largest environmental organisation in Australia and has a long history of advocating for Australia's natural environment. In 2000, ACF published its *Natural Advantage: A Blueprint for a Sustainable Australia* (Krockenberger et al. 2000) which outlined 32 environmental reforms that were needed for a sustainable environment, and the importance of reducing Australia's Ecological Footprint. Following on from that, ACF secured funding from the New South Wales Government's Environment Fund in 2003 to undertake a collaborative project with academics at ISA, the University of Sydney to develop an innovative interactive 'Consumption Atlas', which was designed to show household greenhouse gas (GHG) emissions for different geographical areas across Australia (see http://www.acfonline.org.au/sites/default/files/resource/index67.swf). This Consumption Atlas was part of a bigger push by ACF to engage the Australian public and communities in adopting sustainable lifestyle changes, and to make the environmental impacts of lifestyles and household consumption (transport, goods, services and energy use) more meaningful to them. The Consumption Atlas was launched in 2007, and its findings generated a considerable amount of interest amongst national media as well as local government (see ACF 2007), and provided ACF with opportunities to initiate further discussions on lifestyles and environmental impacts. The baseline data with the Atlas has since provided ACF with the necessary information from which to develop its Greenhouse Outreach Programme:

> Greenhouse Outreach Programme and Atlas was really an attempt to model the environmental impact of household consumption activities and it was very deliberately pitched at that sort of household level ... it was something to bridge the gap between global and national indicators and then right down to the individual, to be able to say this is the local consumption. (Interview with ACF Strategies Director)

THE ROLE OF GLOBAL FOOTPRINT NETWORK

In the UK, GFN has played a less prominent and direct role in the promotion and development of the Ecological Footprint compared to Australia. There are two possible reasons for this. First, in the UK there were in existence several organisations promoting the Ecological Footprint which also had the necessary expertise (namely, BFF, SEI–York and WWF UK) to explain the science behind the Footprint calculations and provide credibility to the tool. A second reason for GFN's less prominent role may have been related to competing methodologies on calculating Ecological Footprints.

In Australia, however, GFN has had greater involvement in promoting the Ecological Footprint. Between 2002 and 2007, EPA Victoria funded three separate visits by Mathis Wackernagel, co-creator and Executive Director of GFN. Together EPA Victoria and GFN facilitated training workshop events and meetings in Melbourne and Sydney to explain the science behind the Ecological Footprint calculation, and to provide credibility and demonstrate the 'scientific prominence, integrity and robustness of the methodology' (Interview with senior official). To promote the Ecological Footprint even further and encourage further uptake by organisations, in 2008 GFN and EPA Victoria signed a Sustainability Covenant, a voluntary statutory agreement between organisations under the Environmental Protection Act 1970. This Covenant contained six key commitments including sharing knowledge on the Ecological Footprint, and building the technical and communicative capacities of the Ecological Footprint in Australia (EPA Victoria

2008b). Later in 2008, EPA Victoria and GFN launched Australia's first personal Ecological Footprint calculator.

CONCLUSIONS

The analysis in this chapter suggests that the UK has had a more positive experience with the Ecological Footprint than other countries. It has had a significant number of organisations involved in Ecological Footprint studies, and there has been a wide variety of applications developed, including for new developments, tourism, major sporting events and products. The availability of Biffa Award funding has played a major part in the activities that have taken place. Funding has also enabled consultants and academics to make methodological innovations which have, in turn, helped to develop new markets. For example, BFF pioneered the application of the Ecological Footprint to products. The nature of the funding process has also encouraged collaborative working, for example between local government, consultants, academics and WWF UK. WWF UK's involvement in projects has also enabled it to promote its lobbying role with government because it can demonstrate its expertise in relation to the Ecological Footprint, thus adding to its credibility. Involvement with the Ecological Footprint has also enabled WWF UK to develop its work on education and communication.

In Australia, the experience of the Ecological Footprint has been different. A key promoter of the Ecological Footprint has been EPA Victoria (in collaboration with GFN), ACF and academics at the University of Sydney. In contrast to the UK, the Australian take-up of the Ecological Footprint has been much more reliant on the efforts of a small number of individuals and organisations. In the UK, there has been wider involvement of people and organisations, though even here the Ecological Footprint community is small. The devolved nature of UK government also means that Ecological Footprint initiatives have taken place in England, Northern Ireland, Scotland and Wales. Although activity may have been more apparent, there are very few indications that the Ecological Footprint has become mainstreamed in organisational thinking or practice. Even though the Welsh Government, Scottish Executive and Northern Irish Executive have made public declarations in support of the

Ecological Footprint, changing practice has proved to be much more difficult. Nevertheless, governments in the UK have generally been much more sympathetic to environmental issues than in Australia. As a result, WWF Australia has worked with businesses as a way of promoting the Ecological Footprint.

Funding of Ecological Footprint projects has undoubtedly enabled the Footprint to enter public and political arenas in a more rapid and pervasive way than would otherwise have been the case. Aside from numerous projects and communication of Ecological Footprint results to communities, what has the funding achieved? What might be the longer-term legacy of investment in the Ecological Footprint? First, the results from Ecological Footprint studies have generated debates about the link between consumption and the environment. For example, there is now a much greater awareness of the environmental significance of food production and consumption, and as a result some questioning of traditional environmental priorities. Second, there have been efforts by local governments and environmental NGOs to personalise an environmental message. Through the Ecological Footprint, citizens now have a much greater understanding of the links between their local consumption and the global environment. Third, work on the Ecological Footprint has brought the measurement of environmental impacts into areas where it had not previously been considered in a systematic way, such as major events. It is to the development and application of novel uses of the Ecological Footprint that we turn to in the following chapter.

NOTE

1. http://www.epa.vic.gov.au/ecologicalfootprint/calculators.

5. Novel applications, Ecological Footprint calculators and communication

INTRODUCTION

Since the initial creation of the Ecological Footprint in the early 1990s, a number of innovations and novelties have surrounded the concept. This has been facilitated by a great deal of interaction between academic debates on the Footprint and its application in practice. The Ecological Footprint is not unique in this respect since there have also been some interesting crossovers between academic application and practice with other environmental assessment tools, such as life cycle analysis (LCA), for example interlinkages between the physical sciences and engineering disciplines, and the business application of LCA (see Horne et al. 2009). The innovations and novelties that have surrounded the Ecological Footprint have involved a number of key players: academics, environmental consultants, environmental NGOs and funders. Although their involvement has been interconnected, for reasons of clarity their contributions are discussed separately in this chapter.

This chapter begins by considering the extent of interest and debates that have surrounded the Ecological Footprint within the global academic community. It then moves on to consider how the concept has been marketed through the development of a range of novel applications by Ecological Footprint consultancies, focusing particularly on the activities of Best Foot Forward (BFF) and the Stockholm Environment Institute – York (SEI–York) in the UK. The following section considers the growing popularity of Ecological Footprint calculators, and compares and contrasts the most popular online personal calculators, and what implications their results have for constructing a sustainable future. The chapter then discusses how the Ecological Footprint has been used by environmental non-governmental organisations (NGOs) to interact with different audiences and communicate information on resource use, and the scale of change required to live within the Earth's ecological limits. Here the focus is specifically on the Global Footprint Network (GFN)'s high-profile Earth Overshoot Day Campaign. The final section draws conclusions.

NOVELTY THROUGH ACADEMIC STUDIES

Since the late 1990s, interest in the Ecological Footprint within the global academic community has grown steadily. There have been two main reasons for this. First, its contribution as a method for measuring biocapacity and assessing the environmental impacts of natural resource use; and second, its potential value as a policy tool and its link to practice. To help us appreciate the extent of interest and debates that have surrounded the Ecological Footprint within the global academic community, the Google Scholar search engine was used to undertake a broad search of online published scholarly literature on the Ecological Footprint. Google Scholar was used as it has the ability to identify a wide range of scholarly literature in all languages across different academic disciplines, including peer-reviewed online journals of Europe and the USA's largest scholarly publishers, as well as a range of 'grey literature' including theses, books, preprints of scientific papers, conference abstracts and papers, and technical and government reports. Google Scholar ranks published articles on a range of criteria including the weight of the article text, words included in the article title, the author(s), the publication in which an article appears, and how frequently it is cited in other scholarly literature. As Google Scholar places high weighting on citation counts and words included in an article title, the first results of a search are often the mostly frequently cited articles on a given subject.

Our initial search of the term 'ecological footprint' (in English) using Google Scholar produced some 28 900 search results (see Table 5.1). The term 'ecological footprint' was also translated into 18 other languages using Google Translator, based on those countries where Footprint studies have been conducted or where applications have related to them. Searches of the term 'ecological footprint' in these languages also generated a significant number of results (see Table 5.1), and clearly demonstrate that scholarly publications on the Ecological Footprint have not been restricted to publications whose print language is English.

Table 5.1   Google Scholar search results for the term 'ecological footprint' in 19 languages

Language	Translation of term 'ecological footprint' using Google Translator	Number of Google Scholar search results
English	ecological footprint	28 900
Spanish	huella ecológica	21 300
French	empreinte écologique	17 500
Russian	Экологический след	14 900
Chinese (Simplified)	生态足迹	12 400
Portuguese	pegada ecológica	11 800
Italian	impronta ecologica	11 200
Chinese (Traditional)	生態足跡	2 320
German	ökologische Fußabdruck	1 500
Danish	økologiske fodaftryk	600
Swedish	ekologiska fotavtryck	431
Dutch	ecologische voetafdruk	422
Finnish	ekologinen jalanjälki	393
Norwegian	økologisk fotavtrykk	280
Japanese	エコロジカル・フットプリント	143
Arabic	البصمة البيئية	113
Welsh	ôl-troed ecolegol	3
Hebrew	טביעת רגל אקולוגית	1
Irish	lorg éiceolaíoch	1

Of the scholarly publications listed on the first ten web pages of the English search of the term 'ecological footprint' (that is, 67 results), 94 per cent (63) had been published in academic peer-reviewed journals and 6 per cent (4) in technical reports. These publications were examined in further detail and provide a number of fascinating insights into the rate and pattern of publications, the range of academic disciplines that have shown an interest in the Ecological Footprint, and also the range of applications it has received.

The first observation relates to the rate and pattern of scholarly publications on the Ecological Footprint. From our search, publications on the Ecological Footprint started to emerge in 1998 (see Figure 5.1), soon after the publication of *Our Ecological Footprint: Reducing Human Impact on the Earth* by Mathis Wackernagel and William Rees in 1996 (Wackernagel and Rees 1996), which had helped to popularise the concept and make it more mainstream as a sustainability metric. As shown in Figure 5.1, academic interest in the Ecological Footprint continued with a rapid explosion in the number of scholarly publications following 2000, with the number peaking in 2007 (15 per cent of our overall sample). However, since 2008 the number of publications has dropped quite dramatically with only 4 per cent of our sample being published between 2010 and 2012. There are several factors which may have contributed to this drop in scholarly publications. First, the shortfall in funding provided by governments and other organisations worldwide to undertake original academic research not only on the Ecological Footprint, but research more generally. Second, the Ecological Footprint has become trapped in recent environmental debates on climate change, and increased policy interest around resource limit issues, including peak oil and peak food. As the Carbon Footprint relates more directly to policy debates on climate change, this has resulted in the Ecological Footprint being sidelined by academics as well as policy makers, a theme which was discussed in Chapter 1.

The second observation that can be made from the peer-reviewed journal articles in our sample (62) is that studies relating to the Ecological Footprint have spread across a number of key academic disciplines, such as the natural sciences and environmental economics, as well as to the margins of others. Table 5.2 shows the broad categories of peer-reviewed journals that featured articles on the Ecological Footprint between 1998 and 2012, and provides an indication of the contribution made by different academic disciplinary interests. The majority of earlier articles were published in journals relating to environmental planning and management, the natural and social sciences, and policy. However, the Ecological Footprint has also spilled over into other disciplines with some academics working at the margins of their area of expertise. In

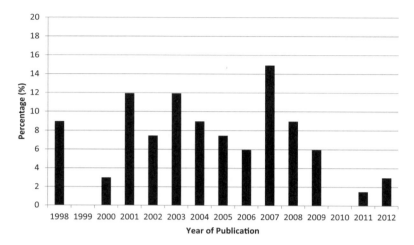

*Figure 5.1   Percentage of scholarly articles published on the
            Ecological Footprint (1998–2012)*

2001, contributions to debates started to emerge in sustainability
and resource use related journals.

Overall, academic studies on Ecological Footprint applications
have been both interdisciplinary as well as at the fringe of certain
academic disciplines. From our Google Scholar search results, the
academic discipline with the greatest contributions to debates on
the Ecological Footprint in terms of the number of published
articles has been the social sciences, accounting for 30.6 per cent of
our sample. A large number of articles have also been published in
journals whose academic discipline relates to environmental planning and management (14.5 per cent), and also planning and
development (17.7 per cent).

A third observation from our search is that the geographical
focus of studies has changed rapidly over time. Although the
Ecological Footprint concept was initially developed in Canada in
the early 1990s, as a source of information on environmental
impacts it has travelled relatively quickly, and within the space of
20 years, studies have related to five continents. The rapid transfer
of environmental ideas on resource use impacts and growth in the
application of the Ecological Footprint has followed a similar
pattern to how ideas on environmental impact assessment (EIA)

Table 5.2 Categories of academic journals featuring articles on the Ecological Footprint (1998–2012)

Year of publication	Ecology and natural sciences	Ecology and social sciences	Environmental planning and management	Planning and development	Policy	Sustainability and resource use	Total number of articles (n = 62)
1998	1	1	2	–	1	–	5 (8.1%)
1999	–	–	–	–	–	–	0 (0.0%)
2000	–	2	–	–	–	–	2 (3.2%)
2001	-	3	2	–	–	3	8 (12.9%)
2002	1	1	–	2	–	–	4 (6.5%)
2003	–	1	–	2	2	1	6 (9.7%)
2004	–	1	1	2	2	1	6 (9.7%)
2005	1	2	–	–	1	–	5 (8.1%)
2006	1	2	–	1	–	–	4 (6.5%)
2007	–	3	–	3	2	1	9 (14.5%)
2008	2	1	3	–	–	–	6 (9.7%)
2009	1	1	1	1	–	–	4 (6.5%)
2010	–	–	–	–	–	–	0 (0.0%)
2011	–	–	–	–	1	–	1 (1.6%)
2012	1	1	–	–	–	–	2 (3.2%)
Total	8	19	9	11	9	6	62
(%)	(12.9)	(30.6)	(14.5)	(17.7)	(14.5)	(9.7)	(100.0%)

spread from the USA in 1969, then to other developed countries including Canada, the UK and other EU member states during the 1970s and 1980s, and then to developing countries including those in Africa and South America as early as the 1990s (Glasson et al. 2012).

Between 1998 and 2001, Ecological Footprint studies focused predominately on Europe, Australia and New Zealand, and North America (see Table 5.3). However, from 2002 onwards there has been an increase in the number of studies relating to Asia and South America, as well as a number of comparative studies of European and North American countries with those in Asia and South America. In 2007, when the number of country-related studies was at its highest level (16.1 per cent of our sample), the number that related to Europe and Asia were almost equal. Overall, the continent with the largest number of Ecological Footprint-related studies has been Europe (51.6 per cent), followed by Asia (16.1 per cent) and then Australia (12.9 per cent). At a country level, the largest number of studies have related to the UK (24.2 per cent), followed by China (9.7 per cent) and Italy (8.1 per cent).

Differences in the level of interest in the Ecological Footprint within specific countries are closely related to its intended use, again highlighting the interactions between key user groups. In some countries, studies have focused primarily on the Ecological Footprint as a research tool, and so the focus has primarily been on identifying applications. However in other countries, particularly the UK, the focus has also included how the Ecological Footprint can be used to introduce environmental knowledge into policy making circles. In the UK, local and regional government have shown a great deal of interest in the Ecological Footprint (Collins and Flynn 2007). As previously discussed in Chapter 2, the National Assembly for Wales formally adopted the Ecological Footprint as one of six headline indicators for measuring progress towards sustainable development.

A fourth observation that can be made from our sample of scholarly articles is that the Ecological Footprint has received a wide range of interesting and novel applications. Although the majority of initial studies published between 1998 and 2000 involved the application of the Ecological Footprint to countries, cities, households, and products and services (see Table 5.4), this has quickly spread to a range of other areas of interest. In 2001,

Table 5.3 Ecological Footprint studies that have related to specific continents (1998–2012)

Year of publication	Europe	North America	Australia	South America	Asia	Comparative studies	Total continent-related studies (n = 62)
1998	2	1	1	1	–	–	5 (8.1%)
1999	–	–	–	–	–	–	0 (0.0%)
2000	–	–	–	–	–	2	2 (3.2%)
2001	3	1	4	–	–	–	8 (12.9%)
2002	1	–	–	–	2	1	4 (6.5%)
2003	5	–	2	–	–	1	8 (12.9%)
2004	4	–	1	–	–	1	6 (9.7%)
2005	3	–	–	1	1	–	5 (8.1%)
2006	1	–	–	–	1	1	3 (4.8%)
2007	5	–	–	–	4	1	10 (16.1%)
2008	4	–	–	–	1	–	5 (4.8%)
2009	3	–	–	–	–	–	3 (4.8%)
2010	–	–	–	–	–	–	0 (0.0%)
2011	1	–	–	–	–	–	1 (1.6%)
2012	–	–	–	–	1	1	2 (3.2%)
Total	32	2	8	2	10	8	62
(%)	(51.6)	(3.2)	(12.9)	(3.2)	(16.1)	(12.9)	(100.0%)

Table 5.4 Categories of Ecological Footprint applications by year (1998–2012)

Year	Countries, regions and cities			Products, production and services			Institutions		Tourism	Households	International trade	Transport and travel	Mapping	Debt	Total (n = 67) (%)
	Countries	Regions	Cities	Energy and fuel	Food and agriculture	Products and services	Businesses and corporations	Education institutions							
1998	2	–	2	–	1	–	–	–	–	1	–	–	–	–	6 (9.0)
1999	–	–	–	–	–	–	–	–	–	–	–	–	–	–	0 (0.0)
2000	1	–	–	–	–	–	–	–	1	–	–	–	–	–	2 (3.0)
2001	2	–	1	–	1	–	–	2	3	1	–	–	–	–	8 (11.9)
2002	–	–	1	1	1	–	–	1	–	–	–	–	1	–	5 (7.5)
2003	–	–	–	–	–	–	2	1	1	2	1	1	–	1	8 (11.9)
2004	3	–	1	–	–	–	–	1	–	1	–	1	–	–	6 (9.0)
2005	–	1	–	1	1	–	–	–	1	–	–	1	–	–	5 (7.5)
2006	2	–	1	–	–	1	–	–	–	–	–	–	–	–	4 (6.0)
2007	2	3	2	–	2	2	–	–	–	–	1	–	–	–	12 (17.9)
2008	–	–	–	–	1	–	–	1	2	–	–	–	–	–	4 (6.0)
2009	–	1	1	1	1	–	–	–	–	–	–	–	–	–	4 (6.0)
2010	–	–	–	–	–	–	–	–	–	–	–	–	–	–	0 (0.0)
2011	–	–	–	–	1	–	–	–	–	–	–	–	–	–	1 (1.5)
2012	1	–	–	–	–	–	–	–	1	–	–	–	1	–	2 (3.0)
Total	13	5	7	3	8	3	2	6	9	5	2	2	1	1	67
(%)	(19.4)	(7.5)	(10.4)	(4.5)	(11.9)	(4.5)	(3.0)	(9.0)	(13.4)	(7.5)	(3.0)	(3.0)	(1.5)	(1.5)	(100.0)

applications were developed for regions, tourism, transport and travel, and then in 2003 for educational institutions and international trade. By 2005, application of the Ecological Footprint had extended to energy and fuel, as well as food and agriculture, and then to businesses in 2006.

Overall, the core of Ecological Footprint applications (37.3 per cent) have related to countries, regions and cities. Footprints have been calculated for cities including Santiago de Chile (Chile), Toronto (Canada), York, Bath and Swindon (UK), a group of 60 British cities, and Piacenza (Italy); regions, including Guernsey (UK), provinces of Gansu and Shaanxi (China), Val di Merse and Siena (Italy); and countries, including Australia, New Zealand, China, Austria, Benin, Bhutan, Costa Rica, the Netherlands, the Philippines and South Korea (see Table 5.5). The majority of these studies were undertaken for a single year, but for some, Ecological Footprints have been calculated over longer time periods (see Haberl et al. 2001; Erb 2004; Wackernagel et al. 2004a; Yue et al. 2006; Chen and Chen 2007).

However, Ecological Footprint studies have also been extended to other novel areas of research interest. The second-largest category of applications have related to products, production and services (20.9 per cent), which include energy and fuel, food and agriculture, and other products and services (see Table 5.4). There has also been a great deal of academic interest in the Footprint's application to tourism (13.4 per cent), food and agriculture (11.9 per cent) and institutions (11.9 per cent). Households have also been the focus of Ecological Footprint analysis (7.5 per cent), with applications on individual households, the comparison of different housing types (that is, eco versus conventional) and different urban forms.

The various academic applications of the Ecological Footprint have helped to enrich debates on the environmental impact of resource use, and provide data which is more accessible and can be used to communicate environmental information to a range of audiences including professionals and communities. These applications have also assisted in providing alternative perspectives and a more comprehensive assessment of the impacts of resource use. For example, earlier debates on the environmental impact of food consumption focused primarily on 'food miles'; the application of the Ecological Footprint to food has highlighted the ever more significant environmental impacts associated with different stages of the supply chain and production processes, that is, conventional versus organic. An application of the Ecological Footprint to wine production by Niccolucci et al. (2008, p. 162) concluded that a 'viable means of reducing the Ecological Footprint of wine production could include organic procedures, a decrease in the consumption of fuel and chemicals, and an increase in the use of recycled materials in the packaging phase'.

Table 5.5   Academic journal articles published on the Ecological Footprint (1998–2012)

Application category	Application subcategory	References
Cities, regions and countries	Cities	York (UK) (Barrett et al. 2002) 60 UK cities (Calcott and Bull 2007) Bath (UK) (Doughty and Hammond 2004) Swindon (UK) (Eaton et al. 2007) Toronto (Canada) (Onisto et al. 1998) Municipality of Piacenza (Italy) (Scotti et al. 2009) Santiago de Chile (Chile) (Wackernagel 1998)
	Regions	Siena (Italy) (Bagliani et al. 2008) Guernsey (Channel Islands) (Barrett 1998) Shaanxi Province (China) (Huang et al. 2007) Gansu Province (China) (Yue et al. 2006) Val di Merse (Italy) (Patterson et al. 2007)
	Countries	22 countries (Wackernagel et al. 2006) 200 nations (Sutton et al. 2012) New Zealand (Fricker 1998; Bicknell et al. 1998; McDonald and Patterson 2004) Benin, Bhutan, Costa Rica and Netherlands (van Vuuren and Smeets 2000) Australia (Lenzen and Murray 2001) Austria (Haberl et al. 2001; Erb 2004) Austria, Philippines and South Korea (Wackernagel et al. 2004a) Slovenia (Medved 2006) China (Chen et al. 2007; Chen and Chen 2007)
Institutions	Businesses and corporations	Businesses (Holland 2003) Water supply corporation (Lenzen et al. 2003)
	Education establishments	Tertiary college (Dawe et al., 2004) High school (Gottlieb et al. 2012) Universities (Flint 2001; Venetoulis 2001; Wood and Lenzen 2003; Li et al. 2008)

Application category	Application subcategory	References
Products, production and services	Energy and fuels	Ethanol (Dias de Oliveria et al. 2005) Alternative fuels (Holden and Hoyer 2005) Biofuels (Stoeglhner and Narodoslawsky 2009)
	Food and agriculture	Aquaculture (Roth et al. 2000; Bunting 2001) Diet (White 2000; Collins and Fairchild 2007) School meals (Fairchild and Collins 2011) Paddy fields (Ferng 2005) Seafood (Folke et al. 1998) Wine (Niccolucci et al. 2008) Apple production (Mamouri Limnos et al. 2009)
	Other products and services	Mobile phones (Frey et al. 2006) Textiles (Herva et al. 2008) Products and services (Huijbregts et al. 2008)
Households		General (Simmons and Chambers 1998) Eco versus conventional living (Haraldsson et al. 2001) Urban planning and household consumption (Holden 2004; Hoyer and Holden 2003) Sustainability rating of homes (Wiedmann et al. 2003)
Transport and travel		Passenger transport (Barrett and Scott 2003) Commuting (Muniz and Galindo 2005)
International trade		Export production (Hubacek and Giljun 2003) Embodied energy and international trade (Hong et al. 2007)
Tourism		Accommodation sector (Becken et al. 2001) Tourism developments and infrastructure (Cole and Sinclair 2002; Collins and Flynn 2005) Seasonal tourism (Patterson et al. 2008) Major events (Collins et al. 2007; Collins et al. 2009) Island tourism (Gössling et al. 2002) Sustainable tourism (Hunter 2002; Hunter and Shaw 2007)
Mapping		Sanderson et al. (2002)
Debt		Torras (2003)

A further example is Collins and Flynn (2005, p. 299), whose application of the Ecological Footprint to Cardiff's International Sports Village highlighted the relationship between increased urban tourism and its environmental impact:

> From a marketing perspective, increasing the number of visitors who stay overnight is positive since it increases spending in the local economy. The philosophy of the International Sports Village developed, though, is to increase visitor days by encouraging repeat visits to the

facilities. As visitors are more likely to use private transport to travel to the International Sports Village, especially to travel by car and travel further by car, this would have negative consequences for the ecological footprint.

The final observation that can be made from our Google Scholar search results is that most scholarly articles related to one-off studies, and limited comparisons made to other related applications due to different methodologies being used to calculate the Ecological Footprints (see, for example, Flint 2001; Lenzen and Murray 2001; Lenzen et al. 2003; Dawe et al. 2004; McDonald and Patterson 2004). Several studies have involved modifications of the original Ecological Footprint methodology developed by Mathis Wackernagel and William Rees in the early and mid-1990s, due to perceived limitations of its value as a planning policy tool (see Lenzen and Murray 2001; Wood and Lenzen 2003). For example, methodologies involving the use of input–output tables for various national economies have been developed and applied by several academics to calculate Ecological Footprints (see Bicknell et al. 1998; Wood and Lenzen 2003; McDonald and Patterson 2004; Barrett et al. 2002; Wiedmann et al. 2003). The Ecological Footprint has also been considered alongside other measures of environmental impacts, for example the LCA of products (see Frey et al. 2006; Huijbregts et al. 2008) as well as other assessment measures, including nutritional analysis (see Collins and Fairchild 2007; Fairchild and Collins 2011) and monetary analysis (see Sutton et al. 2012).

NOVELTY THROUGH FOOTPRINT APPLICATIONS IN THE UK

This part of the chapter considers the novel applications and calculators that have developed around the Ecological Footprint, and how this has helped to create distinctive markets for it. The focus here is on the UK: as previously discussed, this is the country with the largest number of Ecological Footprint-related studies. The activities of two leading Ecological Footprint organisations in the UK, BFF and SEI–York, are discussed as they were the first organisations in the UK to promote and develop markets around the Ecological Footprint. Similar types of organisations have not emerged in other countries, and there are two key reasons for this. First, a large number of Ecological Footprint and material flow analysis studies in the UK were supported by Biffa Award funding (Collins and Flynn 2007). Biffa Award was generated by Biffa Waste Services Ltd (the Biffa Group, a leading integrated waste management business operator in the UK), through the introduction of a landfill tax credit scheme in the UK in 1996. The availability of these landfill tax credit monies meant that BFF and SEI–York were able to utilise the funding in their research and development of Ecological Footprint methodologies, and ensure their robustness and reliability as well as compatibility with national and international data sets. The second reason is that GFN set up partnerships with local organisations and academics in several other countries, and this may have had the effect of suppressing the emergence of alternative and competing organisations developing the Ecological Footprint. In the UK, though, BFF and SEI–York had sufficient capacity to work independently of GFN on the Ecological Footprint. This capacity was of two types: first, to conduct their own Ecological Footprint studies; and second, to innovate and develop novel Footprint applications. Below we discuss the background to each organisation, and show how through their innovations and novel applications they sought to create distinctive markets for the Ecological Footprint in the UK.

Best Foot Forward

As previously discussed in Chapter 4, BFF's co-founders identified at an early stage a range of potential applications for the Ecological Footprint, and this gave BFF its edge in the market. Although the Ecological Footprint was still evolving as a methodology in the mid-1990s, BFF considered it sufficient to form the basis of a household Ecological Footprint calculator (Simmons and Chambers 1998). BFF subsequently created EcoCal™, which was one of the first computer-based calculators to be developed that measured personal and household Ecological Footprints (Simmons and Chambers 1998; Chambers et al. 2000).

Following the successful market testing of EcoCal™, BFF then developed a second Ecological Footprint calculator, Regional Step-wise, which was one of the first local and regional calculators of its time. As previously discussed in Chapter 4, with the support of

Biffa Award funding, BFF was able to apply Regional Stepwise and undertake the first large-scale study at a local government level in the UK, of the Isle of Wight (see BFF and Imperial College 2000). BFF then undertook further local and regional Ecological Footprint studies, the majority of which were also supported by Biffa Award funding. Examples of other studies included *City Limits*, the first Ecological Footprint study of a major city, Greater London (BFF 2002b); Wales (BFF 2002a); five cities in Scotland (Simmons 2002); the UK (Barrett and Simmons 2003); Angus (Scotland) (Vergoulas et al. 2003) and Scotland (Chambers et al. 2004); and the South West region of England (Chambers et al. 2005).

Running alongside these novel applications, BFF simultaneously developed a range of Ecological Footprint tools and calculators aimed at specific target groups and end users. Examples include Lifestyle Stepwise, one of the first online calculators aimed at individuals; CampusCal, a university campus calculator created for People and Planet (a British student network which campaigns on environmental protection issues); and Footprinter, a calculator developed for small and medium-sized companies. In response to the increased attention being given to carbon emissions and carbon reduction, BFF also extended its portfolio to include Carbon Footprint studies and calculators including a Footprint Reporter for small and medium-sized businesses. Customised versions of this tool have also been developed for the aviation sector, dairy farmers and producers, general practitioners, and producers. A Product Portfolio Footprinter tool for businesses with complex supply chains was also launched in 2011, and products were piloted with the supermarket chain Tesco, Pepsico, Crown Paints and WRAP (a not-for-profit company funded by the UK Government which supports organisations in reducing waste and recycling). More recently BFF has extended its portfolio to include Water Footprinting.

Through its novel applications and methodological innovations around Footprinting more generally, BFF has worked with a wide range of clients including: retail and fast-moving consumer goods; entertainment and hospitality; transport; health and pharmaceuticals; construction and buildings; public sector; not-for-profit organisations; business services; sustainability and research; energy; technology and communications; and agriculture and forestry. In recognition of its innovation and achievements, BFF has received several awards, including the Green Apple Award for Best Environmental Practice

(2003), an Association of Chartered Certified Accountants (ACCA) Accounting Award (2003), a Queen's Award for Enterprise in Sustainable Development for its Ecological Footprint work with businesses (2005), and more recently the Environment Product/Service Award (2012) for its Product Portfolio Footprinter tool, designed to help multinational corporations tackle their supply chain footprint.

Data and publications available on the websites of BFF and SEI–York at the start of 2013 was collated to provide some understanding of the range and number of Ecological Footprint projects undertaken by both organisations to date, as well as identifying the different markets that have been developed around the Ecological Footprint (see Table 5.6). Although at the outset both organisations' efforts focused on local and regional Ecological Footprint projects, mainly due to the availability of Biffa Award funding, their different expertise, interests and innovations have since led them to create separate but complementary markets for the Ecological Footprint. In the case of BFF, the main focus of their work has been organisations, products, and tool development. In contrast however, SEI–York has mostly focused on three key areas: policy and strategy, local and regional applications, and methodological development.

Table 5.6   *Range and number of Ecological Footprint projects undertaken by BFF and SEI–York*

Project category	BFF (%)	SEI–York (%)
Events and tourism	11 (7.7)	1 (1.1)
Local and regional	13 (9.1)	29 (31.5)
Methodological development	0 (0.0)	22 (23.9)
Organisations	39 (27.3)	5 (5.4)
Policy and strategy	13 (9.1)	25 (27.2)
Products	32 (22.4)	2 (2.2)
Tool development	16 (11.2)	5 (5.4)
Training and communications	11 (7.7)	1 (1.1)
Transport	8 (5.6)	2 (2.2)
Total (%)	143 (100.0)	92 (100.0)

Note: Projects that related to two project categories, for example 'Local and regional' and 'Policy and strategy' have been counted twice.

Stockholm Environment Institute – York

SEI–York has undertaken an extensive number of local and regional Ecological Footprint studies across all parts of the UK, and its work has developed to include other indicators alongside the Ecological Footprint, such as carbon emissions and material flow analysis. SEI–York's work on the Ecological Footprint has also involved the development of the Resources and Energy Analysis Programme (REAP), which can assess the environmental impacts of various policy scenarios (Wiedmann and Barrett 2005; SEI 2007). REAP is an interactive modelling software tool which is based on an input–output methodology (Wiedmann and Barrett 2005). It was developed to help legitimise the Ecological Footprint in the UK and enable policy makers to understand and measure the environmental impacts associated with human consumption and production (SEI 2007; Paul et al. 2010). It also supported SEI's objective of bridging the gap between science and policy. However, it was only when SEI–York embarked on the Ecological Budget UK project in 2006, and through that received funding from Biffa Award (see WWF UK 2006), that it had the necessary resources to develop the REAP tool.

The REAP software was designed in such a way that it related to specific policy areas, including transport, housing and energy. It contained consumption and production data for the UK at local, regional and national levels, and its indicators included the Ecological Footprint, carbon dioxide (CO_2), greenhouse gas (GHG) emissions and material flows. SEI–York wanted users (that is, policy makers) to identify with and have ownership of the tool, and this was achieved in two ways. The first was by including a scenario editor function, which could be used to explore the environmental impacts associated with various policy scenarios on consumption and production, as well as changes in population size. Second, users could update their own Ecological Footprint annually by inputting more recent data for their area, rather than relying on SEI–York's assistance. In developing REAP, SEI–York developed several methodological innovations, including the use of Classification of Individual Consumption According to Purpose (COICOP) categories, and socio-economic profile data (using A Classification Of Residential Neighbourhoods, ACORN, groupings for subnational areas). To enable sustained used of REAP, SEI–York also offered transparency in the methodology used within the software by publishing it widely in academic journal articles as well as reports.

REAP was first launched by SEI–York in 2006 as part of the Ecological Budget UK project, and an update was produced in 2007 (see Dawkins et al. 2010). Alongside the main REAP tool, SEI–York also developed a family of REAP tools, which focused on specific sectors of the economy in more detail: education, the National Health Service and tourism (Paul et al. 2010; Whittlesea and Owen 2009, 2012). The efficiency factors generated by the input–output tables behind REAP (that is, emissions per pound spent on a range of consumer items) has also been used to develop an Ecological Footprint calculator for the WWF UK (referred to in Chapter 4), which according to Paul et al. (2010) was accessed by the public 250 000 times between 2007 and 2010.

Between September 2009 and November 2011, a version of REAP (known as EUREAPA) was developed through the One Planet Economy Network (OPEN), a two-year European Union (EU)-funded project (under the EU 7th Framework Programme for Research and Technological Development). The project involved eight international partners (including SEI–York, WWF UK and GFN), and focused on developing a 'Footprint Family' of indicators: Ecological, Carbon and Water Footprints, which would enable decision makers 'to track and measure the impact of consumption on the Earth's natural resources and ecological assets' (OPEN 2013).

THE ECOLOGICAL FOOTPRINT: COMPARING HUMAN DEPENDENCY ON NATURE THROUGH CALCULATORS

The growing popularity of the role of the individual in making a difference and addressing sustainable consumption has meant that the Ecological Footprint has gained increasing popularity as an indicator of environmental sustainability. The Ecological Footprint is now accessible worldwide, and this has been facilitated through the development of several novel online Footprint calculators. As previously discussed, one of the first Ecological Footprint calculators to be produced was EcoCal™, by BFF in the mid-1990s. Since then a significant number of organisations including several environmental NGOs (for example, Bioregional Group, Conservation International, Earth Day Network, GFN and WWF), governments and their agencies (for example, Education Scotland; Powerhouse Museum and the Environment Protection Authority, EPA, in Victoria, Australia) and consultants (for example, BFF, the Centre for Sustainable Economy, and SEI–York) now offer a range of Ecological Footprint calculators on their websites that enable individuals, households, schools and businesses to assess their impact on the environment, and provide feedback in the form of an Ecological Footprint, and in some cases the associated Carbon Footprint.

Some of these have been developed as stand-alone calculators, whereas others have been developed to support further work by organisations on the Ecological Footprint. For example, as discussed in Chapter 4, EPA Victoria in Australia has supported the development of a number of calculators (personal, schools, retail and events) as part of its effort to promote the Ecological Footprint and encourage sustainable consumption amongst those living and working in the state of Victoria (EPA Victoria 2013; Verghese and Hes 2007). In the UK, environmental NGOs such as WWF UK and Bioregional Group have also made personal Ecological Footprint calculators available on their websites, as part of their wider One Planet Future campaign aimed at promoting sustainability and equity in production, trade and consumption. An increasing number of organisations also now include links to Ecological Footprint (and Carbon Footprint) calculators on their websites. For example, the New Zealand Ministry for the Environment website page on 'Calculating your Ecological Footprint' contains links to calculators provided by EPA Victoria, GFN and Redefining Progress, as well as a Carbon Footprint calculator on the New Zealand Government's Landcare Research Institute's website.[1]

Table 5.7 lists the four most popular online Ecological Footprint calculators based on the highest rate of return by the search engine Google, using the term 'ecological footprint calculator'. Although these calculators aim to provide an assessment of the environmental impact associated with different lifestyles, they do contain a number of differences as well as similarities.

All four calculators are branded, and those organisations have authority and influence, which helps to add to the credibility and

confidence in the science behind the calculators and their Ecological Footprint results. With the exception of GFN, the other
Ecological Footprint calculators do not provide information on their
methodology, baseline year or assumptions behind the calculations.
In the case of GFN, a web link is provided to a separate webpage
that provides answers to 13 'Footprint calculator frequently asked
questions'. For example, 'How does the Personal Footprint calculator work?' and 'How is this calculator different from other Footprint
calculators, and which one should I use?'. Bioregional's calculator
does however include links to separate windows that explain why
certain data is required for particular questions. For example, a
low-fat vegetarian diet versus a high-fat diet with lots of meat.
WWF UK's calculator includes 'Did you know?' facts for particular
consumption activities, for example, 'Air travel has the fastest-
growing carbon emissions of any business'.

All four calculators included questions that related to the following consumption activities: food, waste, energy use at home, travel,
and goods/stuff. With the exception of BFF, the other calculators
group their questions into distinct consumption categories, although
as shown in Table 5.7 (row 5), there are slight variations in the
actual category terms used included within each. For example,
Bioregional's calculator includes a separate category for waste,
while WWF UK and GFN include waste-related questions in their
goods/stuff category.

The comprehensiveness of the four personal Ecological Footprint
calculators was also found to vary. The number of questions
included for each consumption activity is shown in Table 5.7 (row
6). Based on the total number of questions, the most comprehensive
calculators were GFN and Bioregional. BFF included the least
number of questions in its calculator (11). The number of questions
included for each theme is also shown in Table 5.7 (row 6). Across
all calculators, questions on transport and home (including energy
use) were the most detailed.

The calculators reviewed here take 3–15 minutes to complete,
depending on the number of questions the user is required to
complete. Some calculators (BioRegional and WWF UK) ask for
specific data on some consumption activities, for example, expenditure on certain products, hours or distance travelled by different

Table 5.7 Comparison of online personal Ecological Footprint calculators

Personal EF calculators	WWF UK	BFF	Bioregional (detailed version)	GFN (detailed version)
Organisation type	Environmental NGO	Sustainability consultancy	Environmental NGO	Environmental NGO
Calculator name	Footprint Calculator	What's Your Ecological Footprint?	Take the One Planet Challenge	Footprint Calculator
Website address	http://footprint.wwf.org.uk/	http://www.ecologicalfootprint.com/	http://calculator.bioregional.com/	http://www.footprintnetwork.org/en/index.php/GFN/page/calculators/
Is the methodology explained to the user?	No	No, but contains links that open windows which provides 'Did you know?' facts	No, but contains links which explain why certain data is required	Yes, contains link to a separate webpage that contains answers to 13 'Footprint Calculator frequently asked questions'
Consumption categories included	4 components: food, travel, home, stuff	Calculator questions are not divided into specific consumption categories	5 components: carbon, waste, transport, local and sustainable materials, local and sustainable food	4 components: food, goods, home, mobility
Number of questions included in calculator	23 = Total 6 = home (incl. energy) 4 = food 7 = travel 6 = stuff (incl. waste)	11 = Total 5 = housing (incl. energy) 2 = food 2 = travel 2 = waste	36 = Total 10 = carbon (including energy) 6 = local and sustainable food 5 = sustainable transport 5 = waste 10 = local and sustainable materials	37 = Total 7 = home 6 = energy 9 = mobility 7 = food 8 = goods (incl. waste)

	Planets; Carbon Footprint	Planets; Ecological Footprint; Carbon Footprint	Planets; Ecological Footprint; Carbon Footprint	Planet Earths; Ecological Footprint; Carbon Footprint. Ecological Footprint and breakdown by land type and category Carbon dioxide emissions
How are results communicated?				
Ecological footprint results (based on most sustainable scenario)	1.45 planets 5.05 tonnes carbon dioxide	1.4 planets 2.3 gha 4.5 tonnes carbon dioxide	1.2 planets 2.2 gha 4.7 tonnes carbon dioxide	1.3 Planet Earths 2.4 gha 6.7 tonnes carbon
Are results broken down by component/ consumption activity?	Breakdown for planets by consumption activity 20% food 4% travel 28% home 48% stuff	Breakdown for Carbon Footprint by consumption activity 27% home and energy 17% transport 23% food 14% goods 7% government 4% capital assets 9% services	Breakdown by Ecological Footprint (gha) 11% home and energy 7% transport 21% food 8% goods 27% government 10% capital assets 16% services	Breakdown by Ecological Footprint 27% food 16% shelter 29% goods 28% services
Advice on how to reduce your Ecological Footprint	Yes, one generic tip for each consumption activity	None	Yes, one generic tip for each consumption activity	Option to explore up to five 'What if?' scenarios to reduce your Footprint Scenarios focus on: reducing consumption of animal products; reducing travel (car, motorbike and air); installing solar panels; using energy-efficient appliances

modes of transport, or the amount of energy used (in kilowatts) per year. However, the majority of questions include predefined responses and require the user to select the frequency of behaviours and consumption of particular products. For example, WWF UK asks, 'How often do you eat meat or fish?' with a scale response including 'more than once a week', 'once a day', 'few times a week', 'once a week' or 'less than once a week'. Similarly BioRegional's questions on household waste ask, 'Approximately how full is your general rubbish wheely bin by the end of one week?' with a scale response including 'less than ¼', '¼', '½' and 'full'. As Gottlieb at al. (2012) have highlighted, obtaining data on individual consumption in this way is not as precise as those questions that ask for specific amounts. They are however convenient, and do make the calculators more accessible and user-friendly to a wide range of potential users with different abilities and levels of understanding.

All of the calculators in communicating their results refer to the number of planets required to support a certain level of consumption, if the world's population had similar consumption patterns. With the exception of WWF UK, the other calculators also report on the Ecological Footprint results (that is, global hectares, gha). In addition, several calculators provide users with a percentage breakdown of their Ecological Footprint results by consumption activity, although BFF's is by carbon emissions. This enables the user to identify the resource use area with the greatest impact, and rank order the contribution to their overall Footprint.

Further differences between the four calculators can be shown by assessing and comparing the impact of a sustainable lifestyle. The scenario used here was based on a family of four, living in a four-bedroom semi-detached house in the UK, and selecting the most sustainable options for all questions. In the case of GFN's calculator, where the 'United Kingdom' did not exist as a country option, 'Switzerland' was selected instead, as geographically it was the country closest to the UK.

Overall, all four calculators produced results ranging from 1.2 planets through to 1.45 planets (Table 5.7, row 8). From this there is no conclusive evidence to suggest that there is a link between the level of comprehensiveness and difference in the Ecological Footprint results. Even when the most sustainable options were selected, the personal Footprint results for all four calculators still exceeded the current available biocapacity of 1.8 gha/capita (WWF 2012).

The process of achieving sustainability requires the involvement of individuals in altering their consumption behaviours and patterns. With the exception of BFF, all other calculators provide advice and tips, albeit generic, on how an individual can reduce their Footprint score (Table 5.7, row 11). The GFN calculator goes further and includes a scenario model that enables the user to assess the reduction in their Ecological Footprint by considering up to five individual behaviour changes.

In terms of achieving sustainable consumption in an increasingly resource-constrained world, these findings highlight two important points. First, there is a limit to how far individuals in developed countries can reduce their Ecological Footprint through lifestyle changes. Second, as shown by the percentage breakdown of results for all four calculators (see Table 5.7, row 9), the construction of a sustainable future and achieving something close to a One Planet Lifestyle (that is, 1.8 gha) requires national and local governments to play a significant role in that process, and consider the accumulative and long-term impacts of investment decisions, for example the planning and design of future housing provision, transport, other services and infrastructure.

INNOVATIONS IN COMMUNICATING FOOTPRINTS

The Ecological Footprint is frequently used by environmental NGOs to illustrate and inform different audiences about sustainable development. Further innovations surrounding the Ecological Footprint relate to how it has been used to communicate information about our increasingly resource-constrained world, and the scale of change required to live within the Earth's ecological limits. One of the most high-profile examples is Ecological Debt Day, also known as Earth Overshoot Day, an idea originally devised by the New Economics Foundation (NEF) an independent UK think tank, to help conceptualise how unsustainable our current resource use is in relation to the Earth's capacity to replenish its natural capital.

Earth Overshoot Day is based on the Ecological Footprint concept, and is used to symbolise the approximate date in the year that humanity's annual demand on nature exceeds what the Earth is able to renew in a year (GFN 2013a). The date is calculated by dividing the world's biocapacity (the amount of natural resources generated by the Earth in a given year) by the world's Ecological Footprint (human consumption of the Earth's natural resources for that particular year), and then multiplying it by the total number of days in a year. It is expressed as:

$$(Earth's \ Biocapacity/Earth's \ Ecological \ Footprint) \times 365$$
$$= Earth \ Overshoot \ Day$$

For the remainder of the year, the Earth's population goes into what is known as 'ecological overshoot' or deficit, as it depletes resource stocks from the land and oceans, and accumulates increasing amounts of carbon dioxide in the atmosphere and oceans. This not only places an increasing burden on our environment, but can also undermine national economies.

GFN recognised the value of having an annual yet changeable date, to help promote the Ecological Footprint even further world-wide, and in 2006 it launched its own Earth Overshoot Day Campaign. GFN has estimated that the first date on which human consumption exceeded the Earth's available biocapacity for a given year was 29 December 1970. Since then the date has on average arrived earlier each year (see Table 5.8). However, for some years (for example 1995 and 2011) the date has arrived later than in the previous year, which is due to data adjustments and revised calculations by GFN rather than ecological advancements made by humanity.

In 2013, Earth Overshoot Day arrived on 20 August, and so just 34 weeks into the year the Earth's human population had used up the resources and CO_2 sequestration the Earth could sustainably provide in a year, and were operating in deficit for the remainder of the year (GFN 2013a). GFN calculates the estimated date for Earth Overshoot Day annually and publicises it through a range of media as well as through its Global Network Partners. In preparation for the 2013 Earth Overshoot Day, GFN produced a press release as well as a detailed media pack for its network partners to use and support any locally planned media activities relating to the day.

Table 5.8 *World Ecological Overshoot Day (1986–2013)*

Year	Estimated Ecological Overshoot Day
1970	29 December
1986	31 December
1987	19 December
1990	7 December
1995	21 November
2000	1 November
2005	20 October
2006	9 October
2007	6 October
2008	23 September
2009	25 September
2010	21 August
2011	27 September
2012	22 August
2013	20 August

Sources: GFN, NEF and Bioregional.

The 2013 press release and media pack prepared by GFN contained five key messages which were directed towards individuals as well as organisations, governments and financial institutions. First, humanity is living in an increasing resource-constrained world. Second, we are currently using resources at a rate of 1.5 Earths, and on track to requiring two Earths before 2050. Third, there are global inequalities in resource use, and 'ecological debtor' countries (such as Japan, China, the USA and Qatar) are using more than their ecological systems can provide, and are getting them from elsewhere, while the ecological reserves of 'ecological creditor' countries (such as Brazil, Madagascar and Indonesia) is continuing to shrink. Fourth, ecological debtors have a role to reduce their resource dependency, and ecological creditors have an economic, political and strategic motive to preserve their ecological capital. Finally, organisations, governments and financial institutions globally should consider resources as wealth, rather than liquidating them, and align decisions with resource use in mind.

To help us appreciate the extent of interest and coverage of Earth Overshoot Day worldwide, the search engine Google was used to undertake a search of the term 'Earth Overshoot Day 2013' (in English). This search generated some 209 000 results. On closer inspection, articles surrounding 'Earth Overshoot Day' were found on the websites of a range of organisations including the media (general, environmental and business-focused), environmental organisations and universities, in the following countries: the UK, the USA, Ireland, Germany, the Netherlands, Russia, the Philippines, Japan, Switzerland, Cambodia, New Zealand, Vietnam, Pakistan, Greece, Kenya and Italy. Examples of news and article headings included: 'Humans consume more than planet can produce on Earth Overshoot Day' (Euronews), 'The day the Earth ran out' (Council on Foreign Affairs). 'We've exhausted Earth's natural resources for 2013 already, campaigners claim' (Metro), 'Never mind the economic deficit. What about the environmental one?' (*Guardian*), 'Two planets not enough to sustain mankind' (*Independent Online*, UK), 'China, USA, Qatar singled out on Earth Overshoot Day' (Capital News, Kenya; Breaking News, Vietnam).

Although Earth Overshoot Day represents an approximate rather than an exact date, as its calculation is generated using large aggregated country data sets, it still represents a valuable and innovative approach from which to communicate trends surrounding inequalities in resource use and living beyond our means, and to communicate key messages about the gap that exists between our human demands for ecological resources and how much it exceeds what the planet can provide.

CONCLUSIONS

This chapter set out to discuss the innovations and novelties that have surrounded the Ecological Footprint since the early 1990s. In doing so it has gone some way towards enhancing our understanding of how the Ecological Footprint has attracted so much global attention as a measure of environmental sustainability. The innovations and novelties that have developed around the Ecological Footprint have enabled it to mature relatively quickly within its 20 years or so years of existence. These innovations and novelties have been facilitated by the activities of several different actors, and without this degree of interaction the Ecological Footprint may not have experienced the same level of interest it has received to date.

In the academic community the Ecological Footprint has had significant global reach, with some 14 187 scholarly articles published in at least 19 languages, and across five continents. The level of academic interest is related to its dual interest: as an impact assessment method, and as a policy tool with links to practice. Due to the Ecological Footprint's widespread appeal, interest within the academic community has spread across many key academic disciplines, such as ecological economics, as well as at the margins of others. Through different disciplinary interests, academics have developed a wide range of novel Ecological Footprint applications, ranging from agriculture to cities, to tourism and transport, and this has enabled the Footprint to make some valuable contributions to debates on environmental impact. These novel applications have taken the Ecological Footprint on a particular journey, generating debates about the methodology and its value as a policy tool. This has gone some way to enhancing the Footprint's credibility and robustness as a measure of environmental impact.

The availability of funding for original research on the Ecological Footprint has in many ways been pivotal to the success it experienced. The novel applications and calculators that have been developed have clearly helped to create a set of distinctive markets, and this has been particularly evident in the UK. The Ecological Footprint has been picked up in different countries, for different reasons depending on its intended use. The capacity and funding of work by BFF and SEI–York to apply the Ecological Footprint at different scales and develop different methodological innovations has helped to legitimise the Footprint, and making it ever more popular.

The growing popularity of the Ecological Footprint worldwide has also been facilitated by the development of novel online Footprint calculators, and their value in educating the general public about the environmental impacts associated with their chosen lifestyles, and how they might make changes in order to reduce their footprint. The most popular calculators have been branded by high-profile NGOs, which has helped to add credibility to the science behind the calculators and the results. Whilst they can be a valuable education and communication tool, in the case of our UK scenario they do highlight that there are limits to what individuals can do to reduce their Ecological Footprint, and the need for government support and intervention.

NOTE

1. http://www.mfe.govt.nz/withyou/do/footprint/.

6. Building a network for the Ecological Footprint community

INTRODUCTION

Networks as forms of organisation and as analytical categories have become an increasingly important phenomenon. Although much effort has been devoted to classifying different networks (or categories of networks) (see Borgatti and Foster 2003) and understanding their effectiveness, much of the work has been undertaken in the field of organisational management. Much less attention has been given to the emergence of networks within the field of environmental management. In this chapter we begin to rectify the situation by exploring the work of the Global Footprint Network (GFN). GFN has quickly established itself as 'the' partner network for the global Ecological Footprint community. The network is relatively young (founded in 2002 and launched the following year), and it is timely to review the experiences of GFN and to identify some of the challenges that it may face in the future.

The chapter is organised as follows. In the section below we outline the key goals and values held by GFN, and those activities it has developed to promote and facilitate the uptake of the Ecological Footprint by lead institutions across the world. Here we also describe the structure of the network including its partnerships. In the following section we highlight why the standardisation of the Ecological Footprint has been so important for GFN and what it may mean for its partners, and what standardisation means for its use in policy circles. Following this, we describe the methodology used to investigate the relationship between GFN and its partners, the values partners attach to the network, and their reasons for using the Ecological Footprint. This research was conducted at a time of growth of interest in the Ecological Footprint (see Chapter 4) and increase in membership for GFN. It thus provides a valuable insight into the way in which an environmental network operates at a time of confidence in GFN and the Ecological Footprint. Our survey provides an insight into the motivations, perceptions and aspirations of Footprint practitioners. In the penultimate section we present some of the key findings from our research. In the concluding section we map out potential challenges for GFN in the future.

GLOBAL FOOTPRINT NETWORK: GOALS AND VALUES

GFN was formally established in 2003 with a specific mission to 'support the transition to a sustainable economy by advancing the Ecological Footprint' as a resource accounting tool (GFN 2004, p. 1). GFN performs multiple roles, which makes it distinctive as a network. For example, a key function of GFN is to provide the scientific data (including conversion factors) which is required to calculate Ecological Footprints. In this way GFN acts as a classic professional network seeking to raise standards and ensure consistency of practice amongst its members. GFN is also involved in other typical network activities, such as sharing expertise, for example through its regular partner newsletter and involvement in biennial conferences. Another example includes the provision of technical training workshops for its partners and other interested bodies, on the methodological and scientific basis of the Ecological Footprint. Since its establishment, GFN has also developed a number of programmes designed to influence a range of decision makers and facilitate the uptake of the Ecological Footprint by leading institutions across the world. Here GFN is operating in a similar way to an environmental non-governmental organisation (NGO). Specific programmes promoted by GFN since 2004 include its Ten in Ten campaign,[1] a Sustainable Human Development Initiative,[2] programmes for cities and businesses,[3] and the development of National Footprint Accounts (NFAs)[4] and Footprint Standards.[5] With such a diverse range of roles it is not surprising that GFN also attracts a varied membership. In seeking to analyse GFN we can ask a number of questions: Why do its partners value GFN? How does GFN engage with its partners? What messages and environmental information does GFN provide to its partners? Finally, what challenges does the global Ecological Footprint community face in terms of further developing a network-based model of communication and engagement?

STRUCTURE OF GLOBAL FOOTPRINT NETWORK

GFN consists of a number of key components. At its core is GFN headquarters which is based in California (USA). GFN has as its President Mathis Wackernagel, co-creator of the Ecological Footprint concept, and a team of 26 staff[6] whose work remit includes research on NFAs and Footprint Standards (GFN 2009b), production of technical publications, development of Footprint applications, project development, policy advice, fund raising, donor engagement, communications, marketing and partnerships. GFN also has 12 research affiliates who have collaborated on various Footprint-related projects. In addition to its head office in California, GFN also has a sub-office in Switzerland.

Alongside its core, GFN has an Advisory Council with 24 members who include leading environmental scientists, economists and policy leaders in environmental and sustainability issues. The role of the Advisory Council is to provide specific scientific and policy advice to GFN and the network's committees with respect to the development of NFA and Footprint Standards.

Partners

GFN also has a partner network that in its peak year of 2008 had more than 100 organisations, but by 2013 that had gradually declined to about 70 (see Table 1A.1). Partners include government (local, regional and national), government agencies, consultancies, NGOs, businesses and individuals who are leaders in ecological resource accounting and sustainability. Partnership of the network is open to those organisations whose mission aligns with that of GFN: living within the means of one planet. The network offers two types of partnerships: Participating Partners and the Corporate Leadership Circle. Participating Partners include those who want to be part of the global Footprint community, have access to Footprinting expertise within the network, and can receive scientific and communications support directly from GFN. The second form of partnership, the Corporate Leadership Circle, in addition to the services offered to Participating Partners can also receive annual customised collaboration activities with GFN. Examples include advisory work, research, reports and a licence to specific Ecological Footprint tools developed by GFN. Both types of partner were invited to participate in our survey (see below).

All partners of the network are required to comply with the most recent Ecological Footprint Standards adopted by GFN, accept partnership responsibilities as outlined in GFN's Partnership Agreement (GFN 2014), and pay an annual partnership contribution according to the type of organisation and annual turnover or project budget. Partners can also play a central role in guiding the research agenda of GFN and contribute to the development of the Ecological Footprint methodology and standards through its two committees.

Global Footprint Network Committees

In response to the increasing number of Ecological Footprint practitioners, and a growing concern that different approaches to calculating Footprints could result in increased fragmentation and divergence of the methodology, in 2005 GFN established two working committees: a National Accounts Committee and a Standards Committee. The role of both committees is to oversee the scientific review procedures and standards for Footprint calculations, thereby helping to maintain the credibility and accuracy of Footprint calculations. A Committees Charter was also produced by GFN, outlining the scope of each committee, detailing regulations regarding membership, procedures for operation, the role of the network's Advisory Council, meetings and communications, and the process for the approval of Footprint Standards (for further details see GFN 2006b).

The National Accounts Committee has responsibility for supporting the improvement of the scientific basis of the NFAs. The NFAs provide the conversion factors and calculations required to convert human resource consumption into a Footprint measure. The Standards Committee has responsibility for developing standards to ensure the Footprint is applied consistently in a variety of contexts, different spatial scales and over time. In addition, the Standards Committee is also responsible for developing standards and best practices for communicating Footprint results. The Standards Committee currently consists of 20 members[7] who are also network partners, and includes representatives from academia, government, consultancies, NGOs and GFN.

Standardising the Ecological Footprint

As a number of commentators have pointed out (Brunsson and Jacobsson 2000; Brunsson et al. 2012; Timmermans and Epstein 2010), standards are an often little-noticed but nevertheless remarkable feature of contemporary life. Creating a standard for the Ecological Footprint and the process by which it was created provides an important window through which the authority of the Footprint can be asserted in the wider public and policy realms. Greater authority for the GFN-inspired Footprint will also enhance the credibility of those who work with it. Producing and using a standard Footprint methodology will therefore also help to provide some of the glue to keep GFN working effectively as a network. After all, partners in the network may well perceive that they have a stake in the wider promotion of a standard Footprint as this will help to give them and their use of the Footprint credibility.

There are a number of interpretations of what constitutes a standard. According to Brunsson et al. (2012, p. 615) there are three characteristics of standards. First, a standard is a specific type of rule: 'Standards reflect explicitly formulated and explicitly decided rules and thus differ from more implicit social norms. The rule-based character of standards makes them important tools for regulating individual as well as collective behaviour and achieving social order'. Second, standards are voluntary for those who wish to use them. On joining GFN a partner agrees to accept that they will work with the network's standards. The decision to comply with a standard is one for those who wish to use the standard. This means that if a standard is to be effective it must be seen to be legitimate by those who use it, and further accentuate the legitimacy of an action. Third, standards are meant to be widely used. Those who formulate standards, the so-called standardisers, are looking to 'provide rules for the many... They offer standards – which could be described as pieces of general advice offered to a large number of potential adopters' (Brunsson and Jacobsson 2000, p. 2). Most standards are intended for use beyond the standardisation formulating body, for example those relating to quality management which are developed by the International Organization for Standardization

(ISO). In short, standards 'define normative rules. They prescribe what those who adopt these rules should do and hence enable and restrict behaviour' (Brunsson et al. 2012, p. 616). As GFN argues in relation to its standards, there 'are those elements that are required for Footprint studies to be certified. In other words, all (unless they are not applicable) must be met in order to quality for certification' (GFN 2006b, p. 1).

By developing rules that apply across space, the standards for calculating the Ecological Footprint can bring together those who are in a producer community (for example, consultants and researchers) and those in a user community (for example, local and national governments), as they enable the two to speak to one another with greater confidence in the robustness of the methodology. According to one Footprint practitioner who we interviewed, GFN's role in promoting a standardised Ecological Footprint is highly important in bringing assurance to the Ecological Footprint market. Poorly conducted studies could undermine:

> that trust [in the Ecological Footprint] which, you know … [has] taken years to build up and in many ways, what we've done is created a market for the Footprint … opened up markets for the Footprint within the UK and Europe. But the proliferation of the Footprint if it's badly done can undermine it. [O]ur concern is that [robust Footprint studies] might not have happened in all cases that all these studies have been done.

The interviewee added, 'that's one of our concerns about the future of the Footprint and why the GFN has to develop trust [in the Footprint]'.

By generating trust in the robustness and reliability of the Ecological Footprint, its advocates hope it will develop further the producer and user communities and the interactions between them. As GFN have argued in their report on standards, 'The purpose of Standards for Ecological Footprint applications is to encourage the generation of mutually comparable and high-quality results. Such standards serve to make analyses robust, transparent, and reliable, and therefore lead to results that are trusted and relevant for decision makers at all levels'. (GFN 2006b, p. 1)

The process of standardisation is thus intimately linked to the ability of the Ecological Footprint to speak with authority. In turn, the more authority generated by the Ecological Footprint then the greater the research and market opportunities.

Origins of the Ecological Footprint Standard

Standards are often related to more privatised forms of governance. Market and non-market actors 'rely increasingly on standards to manage reputations, make claims credible, and rationalize competition, especially when traditional forms of regulation (for example, governmental) have been politically delegitimized' (Timmermans and Epstein 2010, p. 77). Standards have come to the fore in food and agricultural policy (see Busch 2000; Henson and Humphrey 2009) where corporate interests have a key role in securing food safety (Marsden et al. 2010). By way of contrast, environmental policy has traditionally been dominated by governmental activities, and the private sector and NGOs have played a lesser role in delivering public policy. So, for an environmental NGO (such as GFN) to create an environmental standard is unusual (but see WWF's support for the Forest Stewardship Council). That the promotion of a standard should happen within a relatively short space of time is all the more remarkable (the first UK Ecological Footprint study was undertaken in 1999 and GFN was created in 2003).

During our research one interviewee recalled early work on standardisation with GFN:

[W]e were all really pushing for the idea of legal standardisation and because I come from a bit of a standards background I was interested in pushing it down and trying to work out which route it should go down. Then we tried to put our results into GFN and they said 'how'? They [GFN] should set the standard and then you [another organisation] would then be able to apply for certification; you know, 'this tool is certified to comply with a particular standard'. And that's how that works, but it never happened. All the reports or analysis are certifiable to a standard but that has never happened because it [GFN] was trying this quality control thing and I think that all those quality control things are part of the reason why things haven't moved on – haven't really been picked up because we couldn't get any, you know, buy-in. To a certain extent I think it needs to – they needed to do that if they are going to do any certification but again I don't really know where they decided to go.

The interviewee continued:

> [It was] just a question of prioritising really. I think GFN spent a long time going around in circles to work out what they actually wanted – what they were about and what they were supposed to do. I don't think there was necessarily resistance. I think that we all recognised that there was a need it was just where to put your priorities really and who paid for it.

In an interview with one leading Footprint expert in the mid-2000s, they noted:

> In fact, we're very much part of the new Global Footprint Network looking at supporting his [Wackernagel's] work on national accounts because that makes it easier to put our work, that is to say more micro level compared to his [Wackernagel's] work, in a very stable context. We see the work that we're doing as very complementary to his but we've developed, you know, we took the choice from a very early stage to make sure all our work was compatible with his. We use the same basic methodology although we apply it ... to very different levels [for example, company rather than national or international level] because we see the strength in both approaches [company to nation] as being consistent.

Amongst early advocates and practitioners of the Ecological Footprint, standardisation was believed to be essential if the method was to have credibility in policy and academic debates. For one interviewee the concern was expressed as follows:

> everyone has to really push behind the standardisation issue because if it [the Ecological Footprint] is going to be mainstreamed then it has to be standardised. [S]tandardisation I think is absolutely vital. [T]he biggest criticism that policy-makers [make] who, for whatever reason, don't want to take it on [use the Footprint] hide behind [is lack of standardisation]. [When] ... the numbers come out different; people don't like inexplicable changes in them.

For another interviewee, the importance of standardisation was illustrated through an example. The numbers emerging from Ecological Footprint calculations need to be compared:

> Well, when you are saying a number ... they ... [have to be] comparable numbers otherwise you might as well not put a number on

it. If you are just using it for diagnostics it doesn't matter. If you are being just internally consistent it doesn't matter whether you are standardised. It's just for your internal system. But, let us say for example, there were Footprints of two chains of hotels. I come up with one room night number and you come up with another room night number then there has to be – to make it kind of adoptable there has to be some understanding to what those numbers are comparable to and if they [the hotel chains] are going to use them for communication – they are going to communicate that number – so you have to have some kind of summarisation process, and because the Footprint is so complex, there are so many variables in it, that, depending on what you choose, the number that you choose can change dramatically... But you need to have that sort of standardisation if you are going to use those numbers to compare. So, obviously there is a need for that if it is going to be fully adopted.

In terms of governance, the formulation of an Ecological Footprint standard was not because of a demand from government for a more robust method and neither was it to help deliver on a government regulation. Rather, the need for standardisation was recognised within the practitioner community as a way of helping them to reach out to the user community.

Formulating the Ecological Footprint Standards

In 2004, GFN 'initiated a consensus, committee-based process' (GFN 2006a) to develop application and communication standards. The latter have never been published for consultation with GFN partners. In addition, there was another committee, the National Accounts Committee, that was to review the science behind the Footprint methodology. Both committees were established in spring 2005 and continue their work today, though with a much changed membership. Membership of the committees was drawn from the GFN partners and covered its producer and user communities. For example, Standards Committee members from the producer community included UK partners the Stockholm Environment Institute – York (SEI–York) and Best Foot Forward (BFF), and from the user community the Environment Protection Authority Victoria (EPA Victoria) from Australia (GFN 2006b). Committee membership is to be representative of the countries where there is Footprint activity and of those who produce and use Footprints (GFN 2006a, p. 2). Membership of committees appears to be a mix of partly nomination by GFN partner organisations and partly by invitation. GFN staff has one place reserved on each committee. Typically organisations that develop standards draw upon their membership (Brunsson et al. 2012). Those involved in the Standards Committee have a keen interest in adopting a standard, because they are either a user or producer of Ecological Footprints.

At the outset the Standards Committee had 18 members, though the number has since grown to 20.[8] The work of the committees and the way in which they worked was specified in a charter (GFN 2006a). Decision making where possible was to be by consensus within the committee. Each member of the committee has equal rights. Once agreement had been reached on a proposal it would be forwarded to GFN's Advisory Council – its highest-level public decision making body – for approval. A committee-based approach to developing standards development has a number of advantages. First, it helps to coordinate the views of key interests. Second, it provides legitimacy because standards are formulated by GFN partners rather than by GFN diktat. Brunsson et al. (2012, p. 619) point out that:

> Standardization organizations face the challenge of endowing the rules they develop with legitimacy, especially since they do not possess any legal authority. Without legitimacy would-be adopters are unlikely to follow a standard. One way to achieve legitimacy is to try to include different stakeholders and encourage consensus among them while developing a standard.

Third, the committee includes those who are most likely to adopt the standard in their work. The process by which the Ecological Footprint Standard was devised by GFN was typical of many committee-based standardisation bodies (see Brunsson et al. 2012).

The Ecological Footprint Standard and Legitimacy

GFN adopted its first Ecological Footprint Standard in 2006 (GFN 2006b). An update soon followed in 2009 (GFN 2009b). As we have argued above, the Ecological Footprint Standard can gain legitimacy because it was developed in an inclusive and consensual manner by those who are most likely to wish to adopt the standard. More than that, though, those who are likely to adopt the standard also bring with them expertise. The expertise of those who have been involved in the development of the Ecological Footprint, such as Wackernagel, BFF and SEI–York, 'lends legitimacy and authority to the content of a standard' (Brunsson et al. 2012, p. 619). When the representative of one Ecological Footprint organisation was asked how it distinguished itself from others, they pointed to its expertise and the importance of being part of a network that could promote a standard Ecological Footprint methodology:

> We are the ones who've been involved in the European standardization programme on the Ecological Footprint. We led that. We led the international team on that. We're one of the main people in the UK, and in Europe ... So I think we're very much, you know, we're interested in, not just ... our own commercial well-being but in the future of the Ecological Footprint and the standardisation which is key. That's what people want. They want to know that when they get results, it's not just any old results. They're [Ecological Footprint] is [not] going to change, that they're stable results, that any changes reflect actual changes in consumption.

The authority that is gained from standardisation in turn bolsters the expert knowledge of those who produce Footprints. In reflecting upon how the Ecological Footprint had been adopted as an environmental indicator by city and national governments one interviewee commented:

> I probably wouldn't have believed it, but they have, and they have done that for a reason, and that's because it's a very powerful tool and because we have been incredibly careful about maintaining its robustness, reputability, standardisation, the whole range of things that make a good indicator and that needs to not be underestimated ... [a]nd that's why we're backing the Global Footprint Network on the standardisation thing because it's absolutely essential if it's ever to be embedded as a real proper indicator, that it is robust and credible and whatever. We have really pushed the whole credibility thing and everything we possibly can to maintain that. [We want to] maintain the robustness and the standardisation so it is actually very attractive to users.

Whilst the adoption of an Ecological Footprint standard can bolster the legitimacy of the Footprint within its communities of practice and to external audiences, legitimation is an ongoing political and social process. Timmermans and Epstein (2010, p. 84) have pointed out that standardisation is:

a soft form of stratification, employed by myriad stakeholders to elevate some at the expense of others ... Standardization is an active process that aspires to stability and order. Any order is a hard-won achievement that requires the submission of diverse actors. Standardization consists of building a society around a standard with an implied script that brings people and things together in a world already full of competing conventions and standards.

So, what stratification might we observe in the construction of the Ecological Footprint Standard? First, the influence of expertise in the formulation of the standard is variable. For example, it was a small community of experts led by Wackernagel who recognised the need for a standard and were the driving force behind its content. Moreover, GFN committee members 'serve without compensation and ... will be responsible for any travel expenses required for Committee meetings' (GFN 2006a, p. 2). Boström and Tamm Hallström (2010) show how differences in the material resources of NGOs (for example, travel budgets) limit their participation in transnational processes of standard development and thus the content of the resulting standards. Second, the authority that has stemmed from the standardisation of the Ecological Footprint has had implications for other environmental tools, such as the Ecological Rucksack. Lacking the legitimacy and wider stakeholder support that the Ecological Footprint has been able to gather has meant that the Rucksack has only marginal appeal. Third, the Footprint as a metaphor has now become part of the currency of environmental debate. The Carbon Footprint and the Water Footprint, for example, have quickly become established methods for understanding resource use.

Finally, it is worth exploring why GFN partners and others may be interested in the use of a Footprint Standard. For some partners in the network their belief in the Footprint makes a standard worthwhile because it is the right thing to do. As one interviewee argued:

I think the danger at the moment with proliferation of Footprints is that because ... we've set up this standard that people don't apply it and I think that weakens the Footprint for everyone and we realise that, so we've tried to put a lot of our effort and a lot of our time into making standardisation issues [a priority] and securing that. That's why I became so closely involved in Global Footprint Network.

There are also economic reasons as to why standards are adopted (Brunsson et al. 2012). These can include benefits to users and wider interest in a product or service. Certainly from the point of view of one very active Footprint practitioner, standardisation was about opening up opportunities in the marketplace, not closing them down: 'we've chosen to focus on and to standardise [in this area] and to get out there, but it [the Ecological Footprint] can be applied at any level that you choose'. The key, though, for this interviewee was to ensure that innovations in application drew upon the standard Ecological Footprint method promoted by GFN.

In the following section, we explore the attitudes of GFN's partners to the network. Our data collection was undertaken at a time of considerable growth for GFN. It had more than 75 members in 2006, more than 80 in the following year and in its peak year of 2008 had more than 100 members. We were keen to analyse how GFN's strategy to promote the standardisation of the Ecological Footprint would be received by the Footprint community. We also wanted to know more about why organisations joined GFN and what Footprinting activities they were undertaking.

METHODOLOGY

The methodology chosen for this research involved developing an online survey for partners of GFN in June 2008. The survey was restricted to partners of GFN since they were likely to be the most knowledgeable about the network and Ecological Footprint community. The survey was developed in conjunction with staff at GFN headquarters, and contained questions relating to knowledge and practice within the network and partners' views on the network.

Piloting the Online Survey

Prior to launching the online survey, it was piloted with selected partners from the network. This was necessary for checking partners' experiences of completing the survey online, in particular the clarity of questions, if there were difficulties in understanding any of the questions, the appropriateness of response categories for questions with predefined answers, the length of time taken to complete the survey, and whether or not they experienced any technical difficulties in accessing or completing the online survey. The survey was developed using the Bristol Online Survey (BOS). The BOS service is hosted on the Bristol University website and is used by more than 200 UK organisations including universities, public bodies and companies. As well as providing an easy to use service for developing, monitoring and analysing surveys via the web, BOS also offers those taking part in a survey with a user-friendly interface, and a safe and secure method for completing surveys and storing survey results.

Partners invited to take part in the pilot survey were selected with the assistance of GFN staff. This was to ensure that we obtained feedback from a range of different organisations within the network and from different regions of the world. A total of five partners were invited to take part in the pilot study, of which three responded and provided valuable feedback on its content and their experience of completing the survey online. Based on these responses some minor changes were made to the survey, including: changing the order of some questions; rephrasing of some questions to improve their clarity; improving the clarity of instructions for completing questions where partners were asked to prioritise their responses; and providing further response categories for some questions with predefined answers.

Final Online Survey

The final online survey was launched on 2 June 2008 and initially made available to all partners (including Participating Partners and those from the Corporate Leadership Circle) of GFN for a period of four weeks (until 1 July 2008). The final version of the survey contained 42 questions, which were grouped into the following seven themes: partnership with GFN; Ecological and Carbon Footprint activities; partners' thoughts on the network; network committees; suggestions on strengthening the network; GFN responses to partner issues and concerns; and communications and partners' involvement in other network activities.

Details of current partners of the network (as of June 2008), including the primary contact for each organisation, were provided by GFN. Partners were initially contacted by email explaining the purpose of the survey, who was conducting the research and how the results would be subsequently used. Due to the size of the network and also for reasons relating to commercial confidentiality, partners were also assured complete anonymity in their responses. To receive an organisational response to the survey, the online survey was completed by one representative.

Following the launch of the online survey, partners were also contacted directly by telephone, reminding them about the survey, and were given an opportunity to complete it there and then with the caller. Partners who wanted to take part in the survey but had difficulties in completing the survey in English were provided with a translator to assist them in completing the survey via the telephone. In addition to this, the survey was also publicised through direct emails to partners from GFN through list serve which contained a direct link to the online survey.

One week following the initial launch of the online survey, a reminder email was sent to all partners encouraging them to participate in the study. A further two email reminders were sent to partners before the planned closure of the online survey. Following the four-week period almost 20 per cent of partners had taken part in the survey. Given the size of the network, and the need to ensure that the survey responses were representative of the different types of partners in the network and from different regions, the deadline for the survey was extended for a further two weeks. Partners which had not already taken part in the survey were notified about this extended deadline by email and also through a direct email from GFN. Following the extended deadline period, the partner response rate increased to 58.9 per cent.

RESEARCH FINDINGS

The results from the partner questionnaire can be organised around a small number of key themes. These are: who is a partner of GFN and how long they have been a partner of GFN; what partners value most about the network; and partners' views on engagement and knowledge exchange.

Partnership and GFN

There are, of course, a number of key issues to establish with regard to GFN's partnership. Whilst our survey results provide only a snapshot in time (that is, partnership up to June 2008), and thus we can only track changes in partnership over a limited time, the results in Table 6.1 clearly demonstrate that at the time of conducting the online survey, GFN partners were drawn from three distinct groupings: social benefit and NGO bodies (such as WWF); consultancies (such as BFF); and research institutes (such as SEI–York). Together, these three groupings accounted for about 80 per cent of GFN partners. Other types of GFN partners included a variety of governmental bodies and corporations. One of the most interesting features of GFN as a network, and unlike a number of other networks, is that it is organisations which become partners and not individuals.

Table 6.1   Partner response to survey (by organisation type)

Type of organisation	% of current partners (June 2008) (n = 95)	% of responding partners (n = 56)
Corporation	6.3	1.8
Consultancy	21.1	23.2
Academic/research institution	17.9	17.9
National government	3.2	7.1
Regional government	6.3	5.4
Local government	4.2	7.1
Intergovernmental body/ government agency	1.1	3.6
Social benefit/NGO/ non-profit organisation	40.0	33.9
Total	100.0	100.0

From a network perspective, the partnership profile raises a number of interesting issues. First, social benefit and NGOs are the most popular type of organisation and may well have rather distinctive interests and resource capacity issues compared to other key partnership groupings. For example, social benefit and NGO bodies are likely to want to use the Ecological Footprint to communicate resource management issues to their stakeholders or to governments when engaged in lobbying activities. They are unlikely to have the capacity to engage in Footprint development work. Second, both consultancies and academic institutions are likely to have the capacity to engage in taking forward methodologies and applications of the Footprint. Third, as a result, it is quite possible that different types of GFN partners will be looking for the network to provide different, perhaps competing, types of values (for example, ease of communication versus academic rigour). A major challenge for the organisers of GFN is to promote positive partner experiences that utilise the diversity of member experiences and expectations, and this is discussed below.

A further source of diversity is the geographical background of partners (see Table 6.2). The majority of partners originate from Europe, where there has been much NGO, consultancy and academic interest in the Footprint. This is followed by North America and Australasia. Whilst there may be global interest in the Ecological Footprint, at the time of the survey GFN partners were rather more geographically selective. With the subsequent decline in GFN partners from 2010 onwards (see Chapter 1, Table 1A.1), the geographical dominance of Europe and North America has been further accentuated.

Table 6.2   Partner response to survey (by region)

Region	% of current partners (June 2008) (n = 95)	% of responding partners (n = 56)
Europe	51.8	49.5
North America	25.0	29.5
South America	3.6	4.2
Australasia	17.9	14.7
Africa	1.8	2.1
Total	100.0	100.0

As Table 6.3 shows, the most loyal network members are governments, especially national governments. This is likely to be because governments that are interested in the Ecological Footprint are looking for reassurance about its credibility. So, whilst government officials may not have an interest in participating in the work of GFN's Standards Committee they will have an interest in standardisation and the authority that stems from it.

Table 6.3 Duration of partnership (by organisation type)

Type of organisation	Number of years as partner (within organisation type) (%) (n = 56)		
	0–1 years	2–3 years	4 years or more
Corporation	100.0	0.0	0.0
Consultancy	61.5	15.4	23.1
Academic/research institution	20.0	60.0	20.0
National government	0.0	25.0	75.0
Regional government	0.0	66.7	33.3
Local government	50.0	50.0	0.0
Intergovernmental body/ government agency	0.0	50.0	50.0
Social benefit/NGO/ non-profit	5.3	63.2	31.6
Total (all organisation types)	25.0	26.4	28.6

Whilst a number of organisations have shown loyalty to GFN, it is important to note that the survey provides a snapshot of GFN partners at a time of high interest in the Ecological Footprint. As interest in the Ecological Footprint has waned, both private and governmental bodies have withdrawn from membership of GFN and in doing so have weakened the authority with which it can speak (see Chapter 7).

If we examine the duration of partnership by region (see Table 6.4) the results show, first, that interest in the Ecological Footprint has been longest and most sustained in Europe, Australasia and North America; and second, growth in partners in North America followed later.

Table 6.4   Duration of partnership (by region)

Region of organisation	Number of years as GFN partner (within region) (%) (n = 56)		
	0–1 years	2–3 years	4 years or more
Europe	13.8	48.3	37.9
North America	57.1	28.6	14.3
South America	100	0.0	0.0
Australasia	0.0	80.0	20.0
Africa	0.0	0.0	10.0
Total (all regions)	25.0	46.4	28.6

Valuing the Network

A good indication of what partners value most about GFN is provided in response to questions about the main reason why they joined the network (see Table 6.5) and reasons for renewing their partnership in subsequent years (see Table 6.6). The results in Tables 6.5 and 6.6 provide some interesting insights into partner expectations on joining GFN and how those may change over time as the benefits (or limitations) of their partnership become clearer. By far the most important reason for partners joining GFN initially is a rather vague one: to engage with the Footprint community. Three other reasons also emerge as important for partners in joining GFN. One is related to the work that GFN undertakes on standards. This is a key issue for GFN in establishing the credibility of the Ecological Footprint as a robust and replicable tool for resource measurement. The second and third reasons are closely related: opportunities for collaboration, and access to a national account licence. At the time of the survey there was a rapid growth of interest in academic and policy communities in the Ecological Footprint. Ecological Footprint studies became all the more credible if they had access to NFA data held by GFN and therefore the purchase of a licence became a highly desirable choice. Similarly the opportunities for collaboration provided by GFN appealed to those who were new to the Ecological Footprint community or who wished to gain a partner to apply the Ecological Footprint.

Table 6.5   Partners' main reason for joining the network

Main reason for joining the network	% response (n = 55)
Connect to the Footprint community	40.0
Support standards and/or methodological research	20.0
Gain credibility/exposure	3.6
Project collaboration opportunities	14.5
Obtain a national accounts licence	16.4
Other	5.5
Total	100.0

Table 6.6   Main reason for renewing partnership with the network

Reasons for renewing partnership	% response (n = 54)
Information and knowledge exchange	46.3
Engaging in Ecological Footprint projects	22.2
Assist with credibility	1.9
Sympathetic to Ecological Footprint concerns	18.5
Other	11.1
Total	100.0

By the time organisations are renewing their annual partnership there is a much clearer sense that a major benefit is in terms of information and knowledge exchange with other partners of the network. Table 6.6 highlights a number of interesting features relating to partner perceptions of GFN. Partners value GFN for the access that it provides to knowledge, such as the NFAs or engaging in thinking on standards development. The use of NFA data enables partners to undertake Ecological Footprint studies, and in this way the accounts can become a means of market entry as users may well expect national accounts to be used.

Finally, in relation to network expectations our online survey included questions about the values partners attached to professional networks and the values they attached to GFN (see Table 6.7). Here we wanted to explore whether partners believe there is something distinctive about GFN compared to other networks that they operate within or know of.

Table 6.7 *Values attached to the role of professional networks and GFN*

Roles of professional networks	Values attached to role of professional networks: partner priorities (%) (n = 38)			Values attached to the role of GFN: partner priorities (%) (n = 37)		
	Priority 1	Priority 2	Priority 3	Priority 1	Priority 2	Priority 3
Learning/ knowledge exchange	76.3	76.3	10.5	67.6	13.5	8.1
Capacity building for you or your organisation	7.9	7.9	26.3	5.4	32.4	16.2
Information dissemination	7.9	7.9	34.2	10.8	27.4	37.8
Participatory decision making	0.0	0.0	5.3	2.7	5.4	2.7
Market development	5.3	5.3	7.9	13.5	5.4	8.1
Collaboration between sectors	2.6	2.6	15.8	0	16.2	27.0
Total	100.0	100.0	100.0	100.0	100.0	100.0

Since individuals will normally have more than one reason for wanting to engage with a network, we asked survey respondents to identify the three issues they value most about a network. It is notable that respondents attached similar values to GFN and to other networks. Respondents placed most value on learning and knowledge exchange, and this factor was found to far outweigh any other. Other factors that score well as second- and third-level priorities are capacity building and information dissemination. In terms of governance, respondents place only limited value on being able to participate in decision making.

Partners, Engagement and Knowledge Exchange

Inevitably those who become active in a network are self-selecting; they will include individuals who have the resource capacity and commitment and/or such involvement is regarded as important by their organisation. For example, this may be for reasons of professional development, knowledge or market intelligence. Most network partners, though, are likely to play a more passive role. As Tables 6.8 and 6.9 demonstrate in terms of regions and types of organisations, participation in both GFN committees is limited to a minority of partners.

Table 6.8　　Partner involvement in network committees (by region)

Region	Involvement in network committees (%) (n = 54)			
	Yes, on the National Accounts Committee	Yes, currently on the Standards Committee	Served on a committee in the past	Never served on one of the committees
Europe	6.9	6.9	10.3	75.9
North America	0	7.7	15.4	76.9
South America	0	0	0	100
Australasia	0	22.2	0	77.8
Africa	0	0	0	100
Total (all regions)	3.7	9.3	9.3	77.8

Table 6.9 *Partner involvement in network committees (by organisation type)*

Organisation	Involvement in network committees (%) (n = 54)			
	Yes, on the National Accounts Committee	Yes, currently on the Standards Committee	Served on a committee in the past	Never served on one of the committees
Corporation	0.0	0.0	0.0	100.0
Consultancy	0.0	7.7	15.4	76.9
Academic/ research institution	10.0	10.0	10	70.0
National government	33.3	0.0	0.0	66.7
Regional government	0.0	33.3	0.0	66.7
Local government	0.0	0.0	0.0	100.0
Intergovernmental body/government agency	0.0	0.0	0.0	50.0
Social benefit/ NGO/non-profit organisation	0.0	0.0	11.1	83.3
Total (all organisation types)	3.7	9.3	9.3	77.8

Despite this, almost 70 per cent of responding partners still considered the role of committees as being either 'very valuable' or 'valuable'. The primary reason why partners value the committees (41 per cent) was in relation to the need to agree on Footprint Standards. The second most popular response (20.5 per cent), however, showed that partners had no knowledge or experience of GFN's committees. This would seem to indicate a significant difference of expertise amongst GFN partners between those who wish to participate in often technical discussions on national accounts and standards and those who are more passive. Additional responses received through the survey also indicated that the Communications Standards Committee in particular was perceived to have a relatively low profile, and more recently had been less active in terms of developing and agreeing on standards. Whilst limited involvement with GFN committees is no surprise, it does carry with it a number of consequences, two of which we wish to highlight here. First, since there is no notion of gaining representation from across GFN's different stakeholders, committee deliberations will be skewed. Second, the small numbers of active participants in GFN committee work means that there are risks associated to the work programmes of the committees if for any reason members should withdraw (for example as a result of changes in an individual's career plan or a shift in the focus of the organisation that they represent).

So far, we have mainly addressed the nature of communication and engagement within GFN. We now turn to consider how partners use the Ecological Footprint. What do partners believe to be the main purpose of the Ecological Footprint? Once again, in the Tables 6.10 and 6.11, we have distinguished between survey respondents by region and by type of organisation.

Table 6.10   Partners' main reason for using the Ecological Footprint (by region)

Region	Reasons for using the Ecological Footprint (%) (n = 56)				
	Communica-tions tool for addressing ecological limits/ sustainability	Accounting metric	Decision making and manage-ment tool	Research question	Other
Europe	41.4	17.2	20.7	17.2	3.4
North America	57.1	21.4	14.3	0.0	7.1
South America	50.0	0.0	50.0	0.0	0.0
Australasia	70.0	0.0	20.0	10.0	0.0
Africa	100.0	0.0	0.0	0.0	0.0
Total (all regions)	51.7	14.3	19.6	10.7	3.6

*Table 6.11   Partners' main reason for using the Ecological Footprint
(by organisation type)*

Organisation	Main reason for using the Ecological Footprint (%) (n = 56)				
	Communications tool for addressing ecological limits/ sustainability	Accounting metric	Decision making and management tool	Research question	Other
Corporation	100.0	0.0	0.0	0.0	0.0
Consultancy	38.5	15.4	38.5	0.0	7.7
Academic/ research institution	20.0	20.0	10.0	50.0	0.0
National government	50.0	0.0	25.0	25.0	0.0
Regional government	33.3	0.0	66.7	0.0	0.0
Local government	50.0	50.0	0.0	0.0	0.0
Intergovernmental body/ government agency	50.0	50.0	0.0	0.0	0.0
Social benefit/ NGO/ non-profit organisation	77.8	5.6	11.1	0.0	5.6
Total (all types of organisations)	50.9	14.5	20.0	10.9	3.6

Across all regions, the most important use of the Ecological Footprint by partners is as a communication tool. In North America and Europe there are a wider range of uses for the Footprint compared to other regions (though this finding may largely reflect the larger number of responses from these two areas).

With regard to organisational uses of the Ecological Footprint there is a much more diverse set of responses. For both corporations and NGOs the most important reason for using the Ecological Footprint is as a communication tool. Governments at all levels also rank communication as the most important, or second most important reason for using the Footprint. Equally interesting is that regional governments, consultancies and to a lesser extent national governments are also endeavouring to use the Ecological Footprint as an aid to decision making.

To further understand how organisations use the Ecological Footprint we asked GFN partners what use they made of it. Respondents were able to record multiple answers, as this recognised that a number of organisations would be using the Footprint in different ways. The results in Figure 6.1 show that there are a small number of applications that dominate (awareness raising, research and consultancy), followed by second-order uses (such as policy making and organisational engagement with the Ecological Footprint). These responses are clearly linked to the types of organisations that are partners of GFN (see Table 6.1).

Finally, Figure 6.2 shows who partners believe to be the target audiences for their use of the Ecological Footprint. Once again, respondents were able to record multiple responses to reflect the diverse Footprint work that they might undertake. The results show that there are two primary audiences for Ecological Footprint work: government and the public. Second-tier audiences include the media, clients and academics. The results are linked to the reasons for organisations using the Footprint: a key role for the Footprint is to communicate environmental information, and target audiences will be government and the public as these will be targeted to influence behaviour change.

Within conventional models of science and decision making, the assertion of authority (that is, knowledge) is partly based upon common standards of work and reputable databases. Establishing a rational scientific authority for the Ecological Footprint is at the heart of the work of GFN committees. Since bursting on to the public policy agenda, knowledge of the Ecological Footprint quickly became diffused amongst academics, consultancies and practitioners. One of the tasks of GFN has been to recognise that there are different methodologies for calculating the Ecological Footprint, and even the emergence of different types of Footprint (the Water Footprint and Carbon Footprint, for instance). In an environment when what counts as the (Ecological) Footprint is

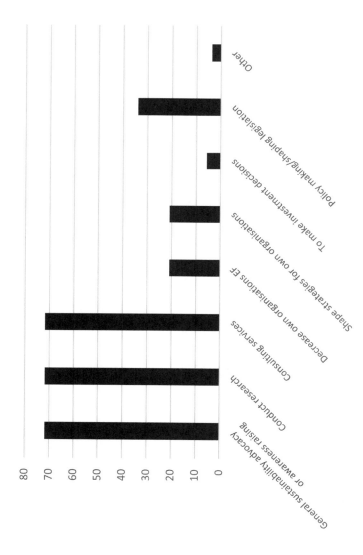

Figure 6.1 Partner applications of the Ecological Footprint

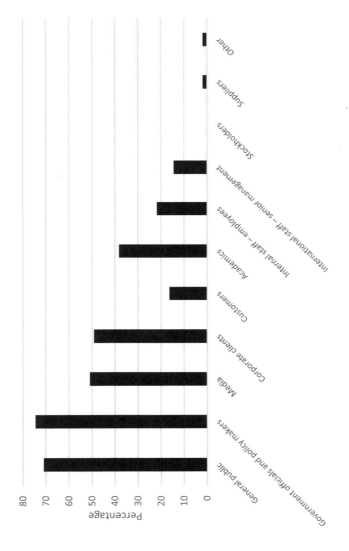

Figure 6.2 Partners target audiences in using the Ecological Footprint

contested, knowledge and skills have to be organised in a manner in which expertise can speak with authority to target audiences. In work that may have some relevance to GFN, Freidson (2001) has argued that the development of professional activity means bringing together knowledge and skills embedded in organisations and individuals. Freidson (2001, p. 208) notes that it 'is difficult to organize [such knowledge] in any other way than by some kind of protective monopoly and expert authority'. Once knowledge becomes part of a recognised professional community it becomes certified or endorsed. Professional knowledge is much more able to influence target audiences amongst government officials, for example, who will be facing a number of competing knowledge claims simultaneously.

CONCLUSIONS

The results of our survey indicate that GFN has been successful in recruiting and maintaining a wide range of stakeholders. GFN also has a number of other achievements. First, it has been an important actor in helping to give an identity to national and international Ecological Footprint activities. Second, GFN has acquired the authority to develop a standard (Brunsson et al. 2012), and the standard itself has been widely regarded as legitimate by both producers and users of the Ecological Footprint. However, we should recognise that the authority and legitimacy of the Ecological Footprint continually needs to be constructed, since it will be challenged by other environmental tools and by economic interests. The authority of the Ecological Footprint Standard, and of the Footprint, are likely to be at their height when there is a wide range of stakeholders who recognise the Footprint, as illustrated by our survey results in 2008 (see also Brunsson et al. 2012, p. 619). When there is an upsurge in academic and policy interest in the Ecological Footprint these arenas also bestow credibility on it, and when users make recourse to the national accounts and the standard it helps to further the trustworthiness of the Footprint.

On its own a robust standard is insufficient to guarantee the credibility of the Ecological Footprint. Once interest in the Eco-logical Footprint begins to wane, so its authority also begins to decline. The authority of a private environmental standard is fragile, and depends at least as much upon its acceptance within user groups as it does its technical sophistication. As a result, the environmental knowledge claims of the Ecological Footprint, its power to privilege one perspective over another, can also falter. Whilst a developing network can bring with it challenges of how to manage growth, which was an issue for the early years of GFN, as GFN enters a more mature phase it faces a different challenge of maintaining or coping with the gradual loss of partners. A growing partner base allows GFN to speak with greater authority on Ecological Footprint matters; a stable or falling membership, and greater competition from other environmental tools such as the Carbon Footprint, will inevitably have implications for the ability of the Ecological Footprint to influence policy debates. Like many networks, GFN has to continue to satisfy its partners' experience of being part of the network and of their changing needs. GFN has to ensure that it remains relevant to an ever-changing policy context, as do those who use and produce Ecological Footprint studies.

One challenge for GFN is how it accommodates the ever greater sophistication of Ecological Footprint methodologies within its standard so that it retains its relevance. There is always likely to be a tension between a standard constraining or facilitating methodological innovation. To retain their relevance, standards have to be used. Partners bring with them a diverse range of skills and knowledge in relation to the Ecological Footprint, and in the past GFN has proved adept at utilising that expertise in developing its standard. As partners begin to fall away and develop new interests, GFN has to ensure that it can continue to renew its expertise from practice and speak with the authority of its standard to policy audiences.

NOTES

1. The Ten-in-Ten campaign is concerned with engaging national governments to establish the Ecological Footprint as a prominent, globally accepted metric as ubiquitous as the gross domestic product (GDP). In 2005, GFN launched its Ten-in-Ten campaign with the goal of institutionalising the Ecological Footprint in at least ten key national governments by 2015. Progress in Ten-in-Ten is considered by GFN as an indicator of the success of the Footprint worldwide. In the first two years (2005–2007), projects were initiated in some 23 nations including Japan, the United Arab Emirates, Belgium and Switzerland.

2. The Sustainable Human Development Initiative is concerned with exploring and defining how ecological limits apply and relate to human development, and involves combining the Ecological Footprint with another indicator, the Human Development Index. In 2006, GFN and the Swiss Agency for Development and Cooperation launched a multi-phase Sustainable Human Development Initiative focusing on Africa.

3. Through programmes for cities and businesses GFN is extending the Ecological Footprint into new domains, developing new methodologies and tools and building the market for Ecological Footprinting. GFN has collaborated with a number of cities including Calgary (Canada) and London (UK), and businesses including the GPT Group (Australia) and the World Business Council for Sustainable Development.

4. NFAs are produced by GFN every two years and provide the Ecological Footprints and biocapacity figures for 150 nations worldwide. NFAs enable countries to understand their ecological balance sheet and gives them the data necessary to manage their resources and secure their future. The most recent NFAs were produced in 2009 for the year 2006.

5. The Ecological Footprint Standards are developed by GFN to ensure that Footprint assessments (including those for subnational populations, products and organisations) are produced consistently and according to the network's community-proposed best practices. They aim to ensure that assessments are conducted and communicated in a way that is accurate and transparent, by providing standards and guidelines on issues such as the use of source data, derivation of conversion factors, establishment of study boundaries, and communication of findings. Standards are developed by a Standards Committee drawn from partners including representatives from academia, government, NGOs and consulting firms. To promote the quality and integrity of Ecological Footprint accounting, all partners of GFN are asked to comply with these standards.

6. As of mid-2014.

7. Data correct as of July 2014.

8. Data from August 2014.

7. Footprinting futures

INTRODUCTION

In this book we have argued that the Ecological Footprint has been a significant development in academic debates on the measurement of environmental resource use. The Ecological Footprint has also made an equally significant policy contribution as it has assisted in confirming the status of the environment as a topic which local, national and supranational governments must take into account. We have also shown how interest in the Ecological Footprint quickly rose to prominence from the late 1990s as an environmental tool before declining a little more than a decade later (see also Boezman et al. 2010), but we have also been able to show how the Footprint continues to matter in organisations. The Ecological Footprint is able to gain traction as a concept because its power as a metaphor and way of communicating resource use means that it retains a direct relevance for its users. So, once an organisation has engaged with the Ecological Footprint there are likely to be those who remain sympathetic to it. Even when an organisation's commitment to the Ecological Footprint may not be apparent, there are those who continue to empathise with its ideas and are likely to use it when a more favourable context emerges to promote the Ecological Footprint. These organisational social carriers of the Footprint message are able to ensure that there remains an awareness of the idea which can, for example, be shown in a renewed commitment to the Ecological Footprint as an indicator or in policy developments. A good example of how this may happen is the One Planet Living commitment of Cardiff Council or the One Planet Economy project funded by the European Union (http://www.oneplanet economynetwork.org). It is important, though, not to overstate the importance of the Ecological Footprint or its contribution to policy development. For example, Global Footprint Network (GFN) has been highly successful in achieving its Ten-in-Ten campaign for ten national governments to commit to adopting the Ecological Footprint within a decade (2005–2015) (see Chapter 6). However, as we have shown in our detailed analysis of the way in which the Footprint works in practice (see Chapter 2), there can be a gap between a commitment to an indicator and the actual outcome (see also MacGillivray 1998). In this final chapter we take the opportunity to reflect upon the status of the Ecological Footprint, how it may fare against other members of the Footprint family – Carbon and Water Footprints – the role of environmental knowledge, and why the Ecological Footprint should continue to matter in academic and policy debates.

THE ECOLOGICAL FOOTPRINT: AN EVER-CHANGING STATUS

A key advantage of Kingdon's (1984) Multiple Streams Framework approach to policy change is that it recognises that the decision making process is not driven by a rational model. Policy making is a 'far messier social process' (Lancaster et al. 2014, p. 17) in which advocates of change can seek to match their perceptions of solutions to the way in which policy problems are framed. Inevitably, there is a connection between the people who shape the way a problem may be understood, and possible solutions (Bendor et al. 2001; Robinson and Eller 2010), as both are socially constructed (Zahariadis 2007). In the competition between solutions for measuring resource use, the Ecological Footprint has largely triumphed over alternatives such as Environmental Space (see also Boezman et al. 2010) (see also Chapter 1). The Footprint metaphor has emerged as a highly persuasive one, and so in turn the Ecological Footprint has faced challenges from the Carbon Footprint and Water Footprint. As discussed below, the latter is promoted as a complementary tool to the Ecological Footprint as it highlights the extent of water use in product development, and so stands alongside the Ecological Footprint which is a land-based measure. The Carbon Footprint, on the other hand, uses the increasingly dominant carbon currency and is a competitor indicator, partly because of the different metric (carbon) and partly because of the different interests which champion the two Footprints. The Carbon Footprint is increasingly linked to the business community and the International

Organization for Standardization (ISO), whilst the key champions for the Ecological Footprint are the GFN and small consultancies such as Best Foot Forward (BFF), and to a lesser extent local, regional and national governments.

The in-depth review of the Ecological Footprint study in Cardiff (Chapter 3) showed how the Footprint tool 'travelled' within the organisation. The Cardiff project developed a method to build capacity amongst local government officers so that they would be more confident in using the tool. Officers were able to validate the data collected for the Ecological Footprint study and help in the interpretation of the data. This process was sympathetic to the rational–technocratic sympathies of a number of the officers, and at the same time created opportunities for a more discursive model of decision making. Officers worked with a research team from Cardiff University and Stockholm Environment Institute – York (SEI–York) in Task and Finish groups to discuss what the Ecological Footprint measured and how it could be used within Cardiff Council. Officers were also involved in efforts to formulate policy problems, via policy scenarios, to which the Ecological Footprint could provide data on resource use. Again, the formulation of scenarios brought together both a technical and a discursive approach to decision making. The more technical side was the belief that the Ecological Footprint results would help to demonstrate the scale of resource use arising from policy alternatives, and so help to rule out some policy options and prioritise others. The more discursive element emerged from debates over the nature of policy options, the efficacy of policy analysis tools, the time scales over which thinking should take place, and how environmental knowledge could contribute to decision making when other considerations, such as economic development and short-term political calculations, also had to be recognised.

Many of the staff in Cardiff Council became aware of the Ecological Footprint and this marked a significant departure for the Council where environmental issues had traditionally tended to be concentrated in the Sustainable Development Unit (SDU). It is difficult, though, to detect any widespread discussion of the Ecological Footprint amongst officers. Discussions were largely limited to middle management – those who had to advise senior officials and political leaders on policy options and the means of delivery – and there is little evidence that senior management or politicians became involved in debates about the Ecological Footprint or the interpretation of data. Instead, high-level commitment to the Ecological Footprint was secured through corporate policy documents, and the status of the texts ensured the legitimacy of the Footprint within the Council. There is also an important legacy effect to note. A number of middle managers who became involved in the Ecological Footprint study have continued to work for the Council, and to some extent they have continued to be social carriers of the Footprint approach. Their imprint can now be seen in another high-level policy document in which the Council has committed itself to making Cardiff a One Planet City (Cardiff Council 2013).

In other countries too there has been a gradual process of change taking place. For example, Japan has long been interested in the Ecological Footprint, and the World Wide Fund for Nature (WWF) Japan an active promoter of the Footprint. Japan's Ministry of the Environment has incorporated the Ecological Footprint into its Basic Environment Plan (see Table 1A.1 in Chapter 1). Japan has one of the highest Ecological Footprints in the world, because its citizens are wealthy consumers and the country has a low biocapacity. Whilst this data makes a powerful case for a serious discussion on resource management, it has not tended to happen. Unless they relate to energy efficiency, environmental reforms have traditionally been difficult to promote in Japan because economic interests are so powerful (Hamasaki 2011). Japan's influential Ministry of Economy, Trade and Industry (METI) has discouraged discussion of environmental initiatives and so now much activity takes place outside of government and brings together the private sector and non-governmental organisations (NGOs). For example in 2014, Fujitsu Ltd and WWF Japan produced a set of educational materials for school children on 'One Planet Living – From the Perspective of the Ecological Footprint' (Japan for Sustainability 2014). The idea behind the project is for children to think about what One Planet Living might mean and what actions they can take to live within the Earth's carrying capacity.

The uptake of the Ecological Footprint in Japan illustrates the variable ways in which the Footprint can be adopted or marginalised in political systems. The UK was for a time at the forefront of methodological and policy initiatives as it benefited from funding of work on resource flows and specific Ecological Footprint projects (see Chapter 4). At the same time, there was a coincidence of interests between the major funder (Biffa Award), Ecological Foot-print practitioners such as Best Foot Forward (BFF) and SEI–York, and WWF UK to promote the Ecological Footprint as a method for better understanding resource consumption and a means of commu-nicating resource limits (see Chapter 4). Each partner gained from the enhanced credibility that together they were able to give to the Footprint. For example, WWF UK's profile rose and it found it easier to gain access to ministers and senior civil servants in Wales, though not necessarily the UK Government. BFF and SEI–York were able to speak with even greater authority about the Ecological Footprint data that they produced, so increasing their appeal as partners in projects with central and local government or with the private sector. During this time, the Welsh Government and local governments in Wales made commitments to use the Ecological Footprint to guide policy development, or as an indicator of environmental sustainability. The highpoint of Ecological Footprint-ing in the UK quickly passed. Once Biffa Award funding was no longer available, local and central governments showed much less interest in using their own resources to undertake Ecological Footprint studies. The decline in projects resulted in a dwindling enthusiasm for the Ecological Footprint, although as we have seen in Cardiff and elsewhere, despite the more difficult circumstances, there were those who retained sympathy for the approach. Australia presents another variation on the way in which the Ecological Footprint may become embedded in organisations and public pol-icy. Compared to the UK, there was much less funding available for work on the Ecological Footprint (see Chapter 4). Instead work was concentrated in a small number of academic institutions, such as the University of Sydney and government bodies, particularly the Environment Protection Authority Victoria (EPA Victoria). Greater use was also made of international networks and actors, notably GFN and Mathis Wackernagel, to add credibility to work being undertaken at the local level. The relatively fragile traction that the Ecological Footprint held in public and private bodies became increasingly apparent as environmental debates shifted towards climate change and the Carbon Footprint became a more important topic. In the section below we consider further the relationship between the Ecological, Carbon and Water Footprints.

ECOLOGICAL, CARBON AND WATER FOOTPRINTS

In recent years, the Ecological Footprint has been joined by the Carbon and Water Footprints. In this section, we briefly describe the methods and uses of the Carbon and Water Footprints when compared to the Ecological Footprint.

The methodology for calculating the Ecological Footprint draws on data for ecosystem services used in resource use, which are then linked to different types of bioproductive land (Galli et al. 2012a, p. 102; Wiedmann and Barrett 2010). These are crop land (land used for food and fibre), grazing land (animal-based food and other animal products), fishing grounds, forest land, carbon uptake land (absorption of carbon dioxide emissions), and built-up land (physical space used for shelter and other infrastructure). Each of these types of land is then assessed for its regenerative capacity and the resources that it is able to produce for human consumption. To make the calculation and help produce the Ecological Footprint, process-based life cycle analysis (LCA) data and information on the physical quantities of traded goods is needed (Galli et al. 2012a, p. 103). A similar data set is required to calculate the Water Footprint. What makes the Ecological Footprint a distinctive measure is that these resource flows are aggregated and then expressed as a fictive area of land, the global hectare (Monfreda et al. 2004), that is required to provide or regenerate the land area. Since the Ecological Footprint is used to highlight the demand for finite environmental resources and the dangers of overuse of resources for future human welfare, many studies including the *Living Planet Report* (LPR) and GFN's Earth Overshoot Day (the point during the year in which demand for environmental resources exceeds regenerative capacity; see Chapter 5) have pointed to the gap between current consumption and resource availability.

A Carbon Footprint draws upon the Footprint metaphor but is not a land-based measure (Galli et al. 2012a, p. 102). Instead the Carbon Footprint is expressed in terms of mass (for example, kilograms or tonnes). The Carbon Footprint measures the total amount of greenhouse gas (GHG) emissions that arise from an activity or are accumulated during the life of a product or service. Carbon Footprint accounts utilise a multiregional input–output

(MRIO) model to allocate emissions to consumption (Galli et al. 2012a, p. 103). When calculating Carbon Footprints, all direct (on-site, internal) and indirect (off-site, external) emissions are taken into account. The Carbon Footprint thus provides a measure of the link between consumption and the release of GHG emissions, and on to climate change. As carbon has become a new measure of environmental impact, the Carbon Footprint has become increasingly popular and could supplant the Ecological Footprint in public policy agendas.

The Carbon Trust has played a leading role in the certification of a Carbon Footprint for both organisations and products. The Trust's standard has been adopted by more than 1100 organisations since its launch in 2008 (Carbon Trust 2014a) and is aimed at reducing energy costs and carbon emissions. To meet the Carbon Trust Standard organisations need to meet three criteria: measure emissions, demonstrate an absolute or relative reduction in energy efficiency, and prove that carbon can be effectively managed. The Carbon Trust also certifies products and services over their whole life. Organisations can apply for either a carbon reduction label (showing that they are committed to and reducing carbon dioxide, CO_2), or a carbon measurement label (showing that they have undertaken a Carbon Footprint). The Carbon Trust has provided numerous examples of private companies and public sector organisations that have measured their Carbon Footprint and been able to improve their energy efficiency (see Carbon Trust 2008, 2014b). These include universities (Sheffield University, Cardiff Metropolitan University, King's College London), retailers (Marks & Spencer), the food and drink industry (Coca-Cola, Whitbread) and government (Oxford City Council, Foreign and Commonwealth Office). Throughout, the Carbon Trust provides a consistent message that carbon management makes business sense. As the Managing Director for Carbon Trust Certification explained:

> We believe that the market for carbon footprinting and carbon labelling will not be driven by top down regulation but by companies recognising the power and benefits of [carbon management] … in driving bottom line cost savings, new revenues and increased customer loyalty. After all if footprinting and labelling is to succeed it has to make business sense. (Messem 2012)

The Water Footprint is an indicator of freshwater use (Hoekstra 2003) and measures the volume of water required for current human consumption (Galli et al. 2012a, p. 102). The purpose of the Water Footprint is to demonstrate the link between consumption, water use and management, and global trade. The Water Footprint measures direct and indirect water use that will go into consumption or production. Water is divided into three components: blue water (surface and groundwater), green water (rainwater stored in the soil) and grey water (pollution). Water Footprints have been calculated for products and nations (Chapagain and Hoekstra 2004). For example, Ercina et al. (2011) have studied the Water Footprint of foodstuffs. They have been keen to compare water consumption in soy milk versus cow's milk, and soy burgers versus beef burgers, and found that the animal products use much more water than their soy equivalents.

In their review of the Ecological Footprint, Carbon Footprint and Water Footprint, Galli et al. (2012a) have pointed to the possibility of bringing together the three Footprint indicators to make more robust inter-industry analyses across multiple economies. Moreover, Galli et al. (2012a) argue that the three Footprint measures can make a valuable contribution to the evaluation of European Union (EU) environmental policy. Or as Galli et al. (2012, p. 110) put it, the Footprint suite 'represents a quantifiable and rational basis on which to begin discussions and develop answers on the limits to natural resource and freshwater consumption, greenhouse gas emissions, as well as on how to address the sustainability of natural capital use across the globe'. There is, though, another reading of these three Footprint indicators: the Ecological Footprint is on the wane in public policy circles, the Water Footprint remains a niche tool, and the most popular Footprint of all, that for Carbon, is increasingly becoming a communication tool for the business community, including in relation to carbon reductions (see Carbon Trust 2012), and is now contributing to debates on climate change where production-based models of carbon emissions dominate. It now appears that these are indicators in search of a policy problem to solve, and are looking for a policy window to open.

It is becoming increasingly difficult for decision makers to simply make rhetorical commitments to environmental protection or to assert that the environment will be integrated into policy development. There is now a growing expectation that senior officials, politicians and business leaders should be able to show how their organisations are making an impact on the environment and how that impact is being managed. The 'age of assessment' in policy making (Rayner 2003, p. 164) is being linked to an 'age of accountability'. In this age of accountability organisations seek to choose how they are held to account, what they are held to account over and who they account to. From the perspective of the Ecological Footprint (and environmental management more generally), measurement, reporting and accounting matter greatly, but they matter in different ways to different interests.

Many of those concerned with promoting the Ecological Footprint as a policy tool have sought to do so in a technical–rational manner and have regarded the Footprint as a technical tool, one whose results will enlighten decision makers to the environmental consequences of their choices. The reality is that the Ecological Footprint, like other policy tools, is used in a much more discursive manner (Cowell and Lennon 2014). What we have been able to show in this book is, first, how the Ecological Footprint can take root in different settings, from national to local governments; and second, how those different settings have been able to draw upon a common broader context in which Footprint debates takes place.

There are three specific features worth mentioning that have shaped the context in which policy debates have taken place. First, the rapid growth in the academic literature on Ecological Footprinting (see Chapter 5). Many of the papers were concerned to refine the Footprint methodology or provide examples of how the Footprint could be used. Together these papers help to provide a legitimacy and authority to Footprint practitioners. GFN, for example, has gone to great efforts to promote a science of the Ecological Footprint. Second, the standardisation of the Ecological Footprint method also adds to its credibility. As discussed in Chapter 6, standardisation is a powerful way to provide legitimacy to a process or tool. Third, the promotion of the Ecological Footprint by local and to a lesser extent national governments has provided a source of peer legitimacy (for example, Auckland Council made reference to the experience of Cardiff Council when it sought political approval for the use of the Ecological Footprint).

Cardiff Council's work on the Ecological Footprint, like that of a number of other public bodies, also demonstrates three other factors. First, that the prominence given to the Ecological Framework is temporary. Boezman et al. (2010, p. 1758) have pointed out that concepts which appear to be novel, attractive and promising are more likely to be widely accepted, but also to be equally quickly displaced by changing agendas or a newer tool. Second, for some professional groups, such as transport planners, there will always be other measurement or management tools to which they are more sympathetic. Third, the Ecological Footprint does not have a natural professional group within government which might champion it as a tool to measure resource use.

More generally, our work also demonstrates how the authority and legitimacy of the Ecological Footprint are co-constructed across multiple sites and arenas, from the local to the international. For example, in Australia, GFN and EPA Victoria worked together, each bringing with them an expertise and authority that together boosted the legitimacy of the Footprint (see Chapter 4). EPA Victoria had the authority of a government body and a reputation for thinking innovatively about environmental protection, whilst GFN brought with it its reputation for formulating Footprint standards and the prestige of its founder Mathis Wackernagel. Elsewhere, academic debates and interests fed off and contributed to a growing policy interest in the Footprint. Again, for example, Cardiff Council and Cardiff University gained mutual benefit from working with one another: the former gained access to the science of academia – a major card to be played when there were internal disputes surrounding the Footprint – and the latter to insights into how officials in an organisation dealt with new forms of environmental knowledge. This legitimacy and authority needed to be continually constructed and reconstructed in multiple arenas to retain its prominence as an environmental tool for any length of time.

One reason why it became difficult to sustain the authority of the Ecological Footprint over time is because of the highly variable way in which expertise was developed. Without a professional body that sought to develop expertise in the Ecological Footprint in public sector organisations (governments, environmental regulatory or advisory bodies), which were the key users of the Footprint, it meant that they were highly reliant on external bodies to undertake Footprint studies, interpret findings and update data sets. As long as the expertise remained external in bodies such as academic institutions, professional groups (for example, GFN) and consultancies it meant that they were the sources of innovation and creativity in methodology and applications (see Chapter 6). This gap between the producers and users of knowledge meant that once interest in the Ecological Footprint began to decline in public bodies, consultants had to seek new markets in the private sector, or revise their tools and attempt to create new markets for them in the public sector. Not surprisingly, therefore, once membership of GFN peaked in 2010 it then showed a continued decline (see Chapter 6). Similarly, for academics there was an agenda shift taking place, with less interest in applications of the Ecological Footprint and relatively more interest in methodological refinement. For example, for SEI–York almost 25 per cent of projects were related to methodological developments (see Chapter 5, Table 5.6).

As environmental debates moved on and as key actors gained new interests, it became more difficult to sustain the commitment to the Ecological Footprint. A vivid example is the decline in the number of published academic papers on the Ecological Footprint since 2007 (15 in 2007, to three in 2012). What we also have to recognise, therefore, is the fragility of voluntary environmental tools and knowledge. Lacking a legislative or regulatory base, public and private bodies can use the Ecological Footprint at times and in ways which are opportune for them. It also means that it is relatively easy to marginalise the Ecological Footprint. Moreover, for some professional groups the decline of the Footprint is an opportunity to reassert the authority of their favoured tools.

The relative decline of the Ecological Footprint is in marked contrast to another highly popular environmental tool, Environmental Impact Assessment (EIA). When first introduced in the early 1970s EIA, in rather similar ways to the Ecological Footprint, was heralded by its advocates as a major breakthrough in improving environmental protection. Whilst many of the early hopes of EIA have not been met, unlike the Ecological Footprint, EIA continues to flourish around the world. A key factor here is that although the use of the Ecological Footprint is a voluntary initiative by organisations, EIA is mandatory for specified land development projects. Within the EU there have been several pieces of legislation – notably in 1985, 1995, 1997, 2003 and 2009 – that require member states to have effective EIA procedures. EIA is also practised in most other countries of the world and nearly always has a legislative basis. This legislative base is important in at least two ways.

First, it provides a legitimacy and authority to those who carry out EIAs; and second, it has helped to create professionals who specialise in EIA and who also help to ensure a continuing commitment to EIA.

Voluntary or mandatory practices are, though, only part of the story of why particular forms of environmental knowledge may be more likely to contribute to decision making than others. Another highly popular environmental tool is an environmental management system (EMS) standard (such as ISO 14001). An EMS is a voluntary business-led initiative that has also been applied to the public sector, and which in marked contrast to the Ecological Footprint is continuing to flourish worldwide. Rather like EIA, EMSs have witnessed the development of professionals in companies and public sector organisations who can speak with authority on environmental matters. To understand why a voluntary measure like an EMS may flourish, there are four key points to briefly note. First, an EMS can help businesses to demonstrate their competence to manage their environmental affairs and so reduce need for further regulation. Second, businesses are under increasing external scrutiny from NGOs and regulators. An EMS allows companies to report on their environmental performance, so that reporting and accountability are largely on their terms. Third, environmental management becomes a competitive opportunity, for example the way in which one company may seek to distinguish itself in the market, or an EMS can be a supplier requirement. Fourth, EMS was developed by the business community for the business community. It makes much of how environmental improvements are gains in resource efficiency and thus savings to a company, which can help to improve its profits. Although an EMS can promote a weaker form of sustainable development which many business and political leaders may be comfortable with, at the heart of the Ecological Footprint is a much more challenging message: that there are ecological limits to development and these need to be recognised now.

THE ECOLOGICAL FOOTPRINT: A CONTINUING CONTRIBUTION

The Ecological Footprint has generated considerable academic and policy attention. The Footprint has largely been promoted by a small number of key individuals and organisations, such as Mathis Wackernagel, GFN, WWF, SEI–York, BFF and EPA Victoria. It is a tribute to their efforts that the Ecological Footprint has gained such credibility. It would be all too easy to forget that here is a voluntary measure that has gained serious consideration in a number of public bodies, and helped to stimulate internal debates on environmental protection. The Ecological Footprint, with its explicit recognition of resource limits and its message that consumption in Western countries needs to be curbed, has made a powerful point. Whilst One Planet Living is undoubtedly a challenge that political leaders and senior officials find difficult to embrace, the Ecological Footprint metaphor has shown itself to be a persuasive communicative tool and has brought into the political mainstream a stronger version of sustainable development.

Whilst the Ecological Footprint may well help to reshape thinking on resource use, it is important to remember that policy change and adoption of environmental knowledge on resource limits may take longer than expected. After all it was only in 2014, some ten years after the initiation of Cardiff's Ecological Footprint project, that the Council adopted the Footprint as a mainstream policy goal. Cardiff Council's commitment to One Planet Living is significant. It is rare to have the opportunity to study changes in the ideas of individuals over time, and what those mean for policy in an organisation. What is needed, though, is the prospect for others to be able to engage in similar long-term work so that we can have a better idea of how environmental knowledge travels through and over time within organisations.

We also need to know more about how standards can enhance the legitimacy of an environmental tool. The Ecological Footprint standard has been devised and promoted by the GFN. The Carbon Footprint has been standardised through the ISO (International Organization for Standardization). Here we have standardisation of process and methods through two different bodies, but what might this mean for the authority with which Carbon and Ecological

Footprints can speak to different audiences? Standardisation also privileges some forms of environmental knowledge and marginalises others. So, what perspective of environmental management is being constructed? For the Ecological Footprint it is resource constraints; for the Carbon Footprint it is resource efficiency. Once again, a business-oriented perspective on environmental protection is moving to the fore.

To understand more about why some environmental assessment tools may be more sympathetically received than others, we need to deepen and widen our analysis in a comparative manner, exploring how the legitimacy and authority of environmental knowledge differs in the public and private sectors, and how voluntary and mandatory environmental tools may lead to the development of variable levels of expertise and knowledge. In studying how environmental knowledge may contribute to decision making we need to, first, widen our observations when studying environmental knowledge and policy tools (not just focus on institutions); and second, lengthen our time horizons so that we can fully appreciate the way in which ideas may permeate professions and organisations.

Finally, it is worth highlighting that the Ecological Footprint has contributed in a very positive way to the vibrancy of environmental debates globally. It has also helped to develop thinking on the interactions between academia and practice. There is an ongoing debate as to how best to measure resource use, and the Ecological Footprint has become a valid measurement tool for a number of institutions, notably those who are part of the GFN's Ten-in-Ten campaign. There is also a major challenge of how to communicate a changing environment to citizens, and to political and organisational leaders. Once again, the Ecological Footprint has shown that it can make a valuable contribution. Whilst the Ecological Footprint may not regain the academic and political heights of the early to mid-2000s, it looks likely to remain a resonant metaphor in environmental policy debates for some considerable time.

References

Aall, C. and I.T. Norland (2005), 'The use of the ecological footprint in local politics and administration: results and implications from Norway', *Local Environment: The International Journal of Justice and Sustainability*, 10 (2), 159–172.

Aberdeen City Council (2006), *North East Scotland Global Footprint Reduction Report*, Aberdeen, UK: Aberdeen City Council.

ACF (2007), *Consuming Australia: Main Findings*, Melbourne, Australia: Australian Conservation Foundation.

Adelle, C., A. Jordan and J. Turnpenny (2012), 'Proceeding in parallel or drifting apart? A systematic review of policy appraisal research and practices', *Environment and Planning C: Government and Policy*, 30, 401–415.

Agrawal, M., J. Boland and J.A. Filar (2008), *The Ecological Footprint of Adelaide*, Adelaide, Australia: University of South Australia.

Amend, T., B. Barbeau, B. Beyers, S. Burns, S. Eißing, A. Fleischhauer, B. Kus and P. Poblete (2010), *A Big Foot on a Small Planet? Accounting with the Ecological Footprint. Succeeding in a World with Growing Resource Constraints.* Sustainability Has Many Faces, 10. Eschborn, Germany: Deutsche Gesellschaft für Technische Zusammenarbeit (GTZ).

Anderson, B. and M. M'Gonigle (2012), 'Does ecological economics have a future? Contradiction and reinvention in the age of climate change', *Ecological Economics*, 84, 37–48.

Andrew, R. and V. Forgie (2011), *An Analysis of New Zealand's Ecological Footprint as Estimated by the Global Footprint Network: An Update*, Oakland, CA, USA: GFN.

Anielski, M. (2010), 'Edmonton's Ecological Footprint', Discussion Paper 12, Edmonton, Canada: City of Edmonton.

Astleithner, F. and A. Hamedinger (2003), 'The analysis of sustainability indicators as socially constructed policy instruments: benefits and challenges of interactive research', *Local Environment*, 8 (6), 627–640.

Astleithner, F., A. Hamedinger, N. Holman and Y. Rydin (2004), 'Institutions and indicators – the discourse about indicators in the context of sustainability', *Journal of Housing and the Built Environment*, 19 (1), 7–24.

Ayres, R.U. (2000), 'Commentary on the utility of the Ecological Footprint concept', *Ecological Economics*, 32, 347–349.

Bagliani, M., A. Galli, V. Niccolucci and N. Marcgettini (2008), 'Ecological footprint analysis applied to a sub-national area: the case of the Province of Siena (Italy)', *Journal of Environmental Management*, 86, 354–364.

Barrett, J. (1998), *Sustainability Indicators and Ecological Footprints: The Case of Guernsey*, Liverpool, UK: Liverpool John Moores University.

Barrett, J. (2001), 'Component ecological footprint: developing sustainable scenarios', *Impact Assessment and Project Appraisal*, 19 (2), 107–118.

Barrett, J., R. Birch, N. Cherrett and T. Weidmann (2005a), *Reducing Wales' Ecological Footprint Main Report*, Cardiff, UK: WWF Cymru.

Barrett, J., R. Birch, N. Cherrett and T. Wiedmann (2005b), 'Exploring the application of the Ecological Footprint to sustainable consumption policy', *Journal of Environmental Policy and Planning*, 7, 303–316.

Barrett, J., R. Birch, N. Cherrett and T. Wiedmann (2005c), *Reducing Wales' Ecological Footprint: A Resource Accounting Tool for Sustainable Consumption*, Cardiff, UK: WWF Cymru.

Barrett, J., R. Birch, M. Thomas, M. Murray and M. Wackernagel (2003), *The Ecological Footprint of Hertfordshire: Results and Scenarios June 2006*, York, UK: SEI–York.

Barrett, J., N. Cherrett, N. Hutchinson, A. Jones, J. Ravetz, H. Vallack and T. Weidmann (2006b), *Taking Stock: A Material Flow Analysis and Ecological Footprint of the South East*, York, UK: SEI–York.

Barrett, J. and A. Scott (2001), *An Ecological Footprint of Liverpool: Developing Sustainable Scenarios. A Detailed Examination of Ecological Sustainability*, Liverpool, UK: Liverpool City Council.

Barrett, J. and A. Scott (2003), 'The application of the Ecological Footprint: a case of passenger transport in Merseyside', *Local Environment*, 8 (2), 167–183.

Barrett, J. and C. Simmons (2003), *An Ecological Footprint of the United Kingdom: Providing a Tool to Measure the Sustainability of Local Authorities*, York, UK: SEI–York.

Barrett, J., H. Vallack, A. Jones and G. Haq (2002), *A Material Flow Analysis and Ecological Footprint of York (Technical Report)*, York, UK: SEI–York.

Becken, S., C. Frampton and D. Simmons (2001), 'Energy consumption patterns in the accommodation sector – the New Zealand case', *Ecological Economics*, 39, 371–386.

Becker, M., T. da Silva Martins, F. de Campos and J. Mitchell (2012), *The Ecological Footprint of Camp Grande and its Family Footprint*, Brasilia, Brasil: WWF-Brasil.

Beder, S. (2011), 'Environmental economics and ecological economics: the contribution of interdisciplinarity to understanding, influence and effectiveness', *Environmental Conservation*, 38 (2), 140–150.

Bell, S. and S. Morse (1999), *Sustainability Indicators: Measuring the Immeasurable?*, London, UK: Earthscan.

Bell, S. and S. Morse (2001), 'Breaking through the glass ceiling: who really cares about sustainability indicators?', *Local Environment: The International Journal of Justice and Sustainability*, 6 (3), 291–309.

Bendor, J., T.M. Moe and K.W. Shotts (2001), 'Recycling the garbage can: an assessment of the research program', *American Political Science Review*, 5 (1), 169–190.

Best, A., S. Giljum, C. Simmons, D. Blobel, K. Lewis, M. Hammer, S. Cavalieri, S. Lutter and C. Maguire (2008), *Potential of the Ecological Footprint for Monitoring Environmental Impacts from Natural Resource Use: Analysis of the Potential of the Ecological Footprint and Related Assessment Tools for Use in the EU's Thematic Strategy on the Sustainable Use of Natural Resources*, Report to the European Commission, DG Environment, Brussels, Belgium: European Commission.

BFF (2001), *Herefordshire's Ecological Footprint*, Oxford, UK: BFF.

BFF (2002a), *Ol-troed Cymru / The Footprint of Wales. A Report to the Welsh Assembly Government by WWF Cymru*, Cardiff, UK: WWF-Cymru, available at http://www.wwf.org.uk/filelibrary/pdf/walesfootprint.pdf (accessed 7 July 2011).

BFF (2002b), *City Limits – A Resource Flow and Ecological Footprint Analysis of Greater London*, Oxford, UK: BFF.

BFF (2002c), *Five Cities Footprint: Estimating the Ecological Footprint of Aberdeen, Dundee, Edinburgh, Glasgow and Inverness*, Oxford, UK: BFF.

BFF and Imperial College (2000), *Island State: An Ecological Footprint Analysis of the Isle of Wight*, Oxford, UK: BFF.

BFF and Oxfordshire County Council (1999), *Oxfordshire's Ecological Footprint*, Oxford, UK: BFF.

Bicknell, K.B., R.J. Ball, R. Cullen and H.R. Bigsby (1998), 'New methodology for the ecological footprint with an application to the New Zealand economy', *Ecological Economics*, 27, 148–160.

Biffa Award (2006), *The Mass Balance Movement*, Newark, UK: Royal Society of Wildlife Trusts.

Biffa Award (2010), *Mass Balance United Kingdom Project*, available at http://www.massbalance.org/ (accessed 10 May 2011).

Birch, R., J. Barrett and T. Wiedmann (2004a), *Ecological Footprint of Inverness*, York, UK: SEI–York.

Birch, R., J. Ravetz and T. Wiedmann (2004b) *Footprint North West – An Ecological Footprint of the North West Region*, York, UK: SEI–York.

Birch, R., T. Wiedmann and J. Barrett (2005), *The Ecological Footprint of Greater Nottingham and Nottinghamshire – Results and Scenarios*, York, UK: SEI–York.

Birch, R., T. Wiedmann and J. Barrett (2006), *The Ecological Footprint of Kingston upon Thames*, York, UK: SEI–York.

Birch, R., T. Wiedmann, J. Barrett and C. Simmons (2004c), *Ecological Footprint of North Lincolnshire and North East Lincolnshire*, York, UK: SEI–York.

Boezman, D., P. Leroy, R. Maas and S. Kruitwagen (2010), 'The (limited) political influence of ecological economics: A case study on Dutch environmental policies', *Ecological Economics*, 69 (9), 1756–1764.

Bond, S. (2002), *Ecological Footprints: A Guide for Local Authorities*, Godalming, UK: WWF UK.

Bond, S. and P. Matthews (2006), *Ecological Footprints: Taking the First Step, A 'How to' Guide for Local Authorities*, Godalming, UK: WWF UK.

Borgatti, S.P. and P.C. Foster (2003), 'The network paradigm in organizational research: a review and typology', *Journal of Management*, 29 (6), 991–1013.

Borucke, M., D. Moore, G. Cranston, K. Gracey, K. Iha, J. Larson, E. Lazarus, J.C. Morales, M. Wackernagel and A. Galli (2013),

'Accounting for demand and supply of the biosphere's regenerative capacity: the NFAs' underlying methodology and framework', *Ecological Indicators*, 24, 518–533.

Boström, M. and K. Tamm Hallström (2010), 'NGO power in global social and environmental standard-setting', *Global Environmental Politics*, 10 (4), 36–59.

Brugmann, J. (1997), 'Is there a method in our measurement? The use of indicators in local sustainable development planning', *Local Environment*, 2 (1), 58–72.

Brunsson, N. and B. Jacobsson (2000a), 'The contemporary expansion of standardization', in N. Brunsson and B. Jacobsson (eds), *A World of Standards*, Oxford, UK and New York, USA: Oxford University Press, pp. 1–17.

Brunsson, N., A. Rasche and D. Seidl (2012), 'The dynamics of standardization: three perspectives on standards in organization studies', *Organization Studies*, 33 (5–6), 613–632.

Buhrs, T. (2004), 'Sharing environmental space: the role of law, economics and politics', *Journal of Environmental Planning and Management*, 47 (3), 429–447.

Buitenkamp, M., H. Venner and T. Warns (1992), *Sustainable Netherlands*, Amsterdam, The Netherlands: Vereniging Milieudefensie (Friends of the Earth Netherlands).

Bunting, S.W. (2001), 'Appropriation of environmental goods and services by aquaculture: a reassessment employing the ecological footprint methodology and implications for horizon integration', *Aquaculture Research*, 32, 605–609.

Burger, E., F. Hinterberger, S. Giljum and C. Manstein (2009), 'When carbon is not enough: comprehensive ecological rucksack indicators for products', paper presented at R'09 Twin World Congress in Davos.

Busch, L. (2000), 'The moral economy of grades and standards', *Journal of Rural Studies*, 16 (3), 273–283.

Calcott, A. and J. Bull (2007), *Ecological Footprint of British City Residents*, Godalming, UK: WWF UK.

Carbon Trust (2008), *Product Carbon Footprinting: The New Business Opportunity. Experience from Leading Companies*, London, UK: Carbon Trust.

Carbon Trust (2012), *Carbon Footprinting. The Next Steps to Reducing your Emissions*, London, UK: Carbon Trust.

Carbon Trust (2014a), 'Certification', available at http://www. carbontrust.com/client-services/footprinting/footprint-certification (accessed 22 September 2014).

Carbon Trust (2014b), 'Our clients', available at http://www. carbontrust.com/our-clients (accessed 22 September 2014).

Cardiff Council (2000), *Local Sustainability Strategy*, Cardiff, UK: Cardiff Council.

Cardiff Council (2002a), *Economic Development Plan 2003–2004*, Cardiff, UK: Cardiff Council.

Cardiff Council (2002b), *Cardiff Visitors Survey 2001*, Cardiff, UK: Cardiff Council.

Cardiff Council (2004), *Cardiff's Community Strategy 2004–2014: Better Communities, Brighter Lives*, Cardiff, UK: Cardiff Council.

Cardiff Council (2007), *Cardiff Economic Strategy 'Competitive Capital' 2007–2012*, Cardiff, UK: Cardiff Council.

Cardiff Council (2009), *Sustainable Development Action Plan Programme 2009–2012*, Cardiff, UK: Cardiff Council.

Cardiff Council (2013), *One Planet Cardiff*, report of Corporate Director Operations Agenda Item: 7, Cabinet Meeting, 11 July, Cardiff, UK: Cardiff Council.

Carley, M. and P. Spapens (1998), *Sharing the World*, London, UK: Earthscan.

Chambers, N., R. Child, N. Jenkin, K. Lewis, G. Vergoulas and M. Whiteley (2005), *Stepping Forward: A Resource Flow and Ecological Footprint Analysis of the South West of England*, Oxford, UK: BFF.

Chambers, N., P. Griffiths, K. Lewis and N. Jenkin (2004), *Scotland's Footprint – A Resource Flow and Ecological Footprint Analysis of Scotland*, Oxford, UK: BFF.

Chambers, N. and Lewis, K. (2001), *Ecological Footprint Analysis: Towards a Sustainability Indicator for Business*, London: ACCA.

Chambers, N., C. Simmons and M. Wackernagel (2000), *Sharing Nature's Interest: Ecological Footprints as an Indicator of Sustainability*, London, UK: Earthscan.

Chapagain, A.K. and A.Y. Hoekstra (2004), *Water Footprints of Nations*, Value of Water Research Report Series No. 16, Delft, The Netherlands: UNESCO-IHE, available at http://www.water footprint.org/Reports/Report16Vol1.pdf (accessed 22 September 2014).

Chen, B. and G.Q. Chen (2007), 'Modified ecological footprint accounting and analysis based on embodied exergy – a case study of the Chinese society 1981–2001', *Ecological Economics*, 61, 355–376.

Chen, B., G.Q. Chen, Z.F. Yang and M.M. Jiang (2007), 'Ecological footprint accounting for energy and resource in China', *Energy Policy*, 35, 1599–1609.

City of Calgary (2007), *Toward a Preferred Future – Understanding Calgary's Ecological Footprint*, Calgary, Canada: City of Calgary.

City of Cape Town (2007), *The Economic Imperatives of Environmental Sustainability*, Cape Town, South Africa: City of Cape Town.

Clark, W.C. and G. Majone (1985), 'The critical appraisal of scientific inquiries with policy implications', *Science, Technology and Human Values*, 10 (3), 6–19.

Cohen, M.J. (2011), 'Is the UK preparing for "war"? Military metaphors, personal carbon allowances, and consumption rationing in historical perspective', *Climatic Change*, 104, 199–222.

Cole, V. and A.J. Sinclair (2002), 'Measuring the Ecological Footprint of a Himalayan tourist centre', *Mountain Research and Development*, 22 (2), 132–141.

Collins, A., R. Cowell and A. Flynn (2009), 'Evaluation and environmental governance: the institutionalisation of ecological footprinting', *Environment and Planning A*, 41, 1707–1725.

Collins, A. and R. Fairchild (2007), 'Sustainable food consumption at a sub-national level: an Ecological Footprint, nutritional and economic analysis', *Journal of Environmental Planning and Policy*, 9 (1), 5–30.

Collins, A. and A. Flynn (2005), 'A new perspective on the environmental impacts of planning: a case study of Cardiff's International Sports Village', *Journal of Environmental Policy and Planning*, 7 (4), 277–302.

Collins, A. and A. Flynn (2007), 'Engaging with the Ecological Footprint as a decision-making tool: process and responses', *Local Environment*, 12 (3), 295–312.

Collins, A. and A. Flynn (2008), 'Measuring the environmental sustainability of a major sporting event: a case study of the FA Cup Final', *Tourism Economics*, 14 (4), 751–768.

Collins, A., A. Flynn, M. Munday and A. Roberts (2007), 'Assessing the environmental consequences of major sporting events: the 2003/04 FA Cup Final', *Urban Studies*, 44 (3), 457–476.

Collins, A., A. Flynn and A. Netherwood (2005), *Reducing Cardiff's Ecological Footprint: A Resource Accounting Tool for Sustainable Consumption*, Cardiff, UK: WWF Cymru.

Collins, A., C. Jones and M. Munday (2009), 'Assessing the environmental impacts of mega sporting events: two options?', *Tourism Management*, 30, 828–837.

Commissioner Environmental Sustainability Victoria (2008), *State of the Environment Victoria 2008 Summary*, Melbourne, Australia: Commissioner for Environmental Sustainability Melbourne, Victoria.

Cowell, R. and M. Lennon (2014) 'The utilisation of environmental knowledge in landuse planning: drawing lessons for an ecosystem services approach', *Environment and Planning C: Government and Policy*, 32, 263–282.

CSIRO (2005), *Balancing Act. A Triple Bottom Line Analysis of the Australian Economy*, 4 vols, Highett, Australia: CSIRO.

Curry, R., C. Simmons and C. McDaid (2004), *Northern Limits: A Resource Flow Analysis and Ecological Footprint for Northern Ireland*, Belfast, UK: ARENA Network.

Dawe, G.F.M., A. Vetter and S. Martin (2004), 'An overview of ecological footprinting and other tools and their application to the development of sustainability process', *International Journal of Sustainability in Higher Education*, 5 (4), 340–371.

Dawkins, E., A. Paul, J. Barrett, J. Minx and K. Scott (2008), *Wales' Ecological Footprint: Scenarios to 2020*, York, UK: SEI–York.

Dawkins, E., K. Roelich, and A. Owen (2010), *A Consumption Approach for Emissions Accounting – the REAP Tool and REAP Data for 2006*, York, UK: SEI–York.

Department of the Environment, Transport and the Regions (2000), *Local Quality of Life Counts*, available at http://www.sustainable-development.gov.uk/publications/pdf/localqolc.pdf (accessed 10 January 2009).

Dias De Oliveira, M.E., B.E. Vaughan and E.J. Rykiel (2005), 'Ethanol as fuel: energy, carbon dioxide balances, and Ecological Footprint', *Bioscience*, 55 (7), 593–602.

Dobson, A. (2003), *Citizenship and the Environment*, Oxford, UK: Oxford University Press.

Doughty, M.R.C. and G.P. Hammond (2004), 'Sustainability and the built environment at and beyond the city scale', *Building and Environment*, 39, 1223–1233.

Dunlop, C.A. (2014), 'The possible experts: how epistemic communities negotiate barriers to knowledge use in ecosystems services policy', *Environment and Planning C: Government and Policy*, 32, 208–228.

Eaton, R.L., G.P. Hammond and J. Laurie (2007), 'Footprints on the landscape: an environmental appraisal of urban and rural living in the developed world', *Landscape and Urban Planning*, 83, 13–28.

EPA Victoria (2005), *The Ecological Footprint of Victoria: Assessing Victoria's Demand on Nature*, report prepared for EPA Victoria by the Centre for Integrated Sustainability Analysis (ISA), University of Sydney and GFN, Sydney, Australia: University of Sydney.

EPA Victoria (2008a), *An Ecological Footprint of Consumption in Victoria*, report prepared by SEI at the University of York (UK) and the Centre for Integrated Sustainability Analysis (ISA), University of Sydney, Melbourne, Australia: EPA Victoria.

EPA Victoria (2008b), *Global Footprint Network Sustainability Covenant*, Melbourne, Australia: Environment Protection Authority Victoria.

EPA Victoria (2013), *Ecological Footprint Calculators*, available at http://www.epa.vic.gov.au/ecologicalfootprint/calculators/ (accessed 22 April 2013).

Erb, K-H (2004), 'Actual land demand of Austria 1926–2000: a variation on Ecological Footprint assessments', *Land Use Policy*, 21, 247–259.

Ercina, A.E., M.M. Aldayab and A.Y. Hoekstraa (2011), 'The water footprint of soy milk and soy burger and equivalent animal products', *Ecological Indicators*, 18, 392–402.

European Environment Agency (2005), *The European Environment – State and Outlook 2005*, Copenhagen, Denmark: Office for Official Publications of the European Communities (OPOCE).

EWS-WWF (2010), *UAE Ecological Footprint Initiative 'Al Basma Al Beeiyah Initiative'*, Abu Dhabi, UAE: EWS-WWF.

Fairchild, R. and A. Collins (2011), 'Serving up healthy and sustainable school meals? An analysis of school meal provision in Cardiff (UK)', *Journal of Environmental Policy and Planning*, 13 (1), 1–21.

Farrer, J. and J. Nason (2005), *Reducing Gwynedd's Ecological Footprint: A Resource Accounting Tool for Sustainable Consumption*, Cardiff, UK: WWF Cymru.

Feindt, P. and A. Flynn (2009), 'Review of current practices and criteria used to integrate environmental and social aspects into urban infrastructure development processes in cities in Europe', report prepared for the Expert Group Meeting on Developing Eco-efficient and Sustainable Urban Infrastructure in Asia and Latin America, Bangkok, 10–12 February.

Ferng, J.J. (2002), 'Toward a scenario analysis framework for energy footprints', *Ecological Economics*, 40, 53–69.

Ferng, J.J. (2005), 'Local sustainable yield and embodied resources in ecological footprint analysis – a case study on the required paddy field in Taiwan', *Ecological Economics*, 53, 415–430.

Fischer, F. and J. Forester (eds) (1993), *The Argumentative Turn in Policy Analysis and Planning*, London, UK: UCL Press.

Flint, K. (2001), 'Institutional ecological footprint analysis – a case study of the University of Newcastle, Australia', *International Journal of Sustainability in Higher Education*, 2 (1), 48–62.

Flynn, A. (2010), 'Environmental policy' in B. Jones and P. Norton (eds), *Politics UK*, 7th edn, Harlow, UK: Pearson Education, pp. 581–613.

Flyvbjerg, B. (1998), *Rationality and Power*, Chicago, IL, USA: University of Chicago Press.

Folke, C., N. Kautsky, H. Berg, A. Jansson and M. Troell (1998), 'The Ecological Footprint concept for sustainable seafood production: a review', *Ecological Applications*, 8 (1), 61–63.

Fraser, E.D.G., A.J. Dougill, W.E. Mabee, M. Reed and P. McAlpine (2006), 'Bottom up and top down: analysis of participatory processes for sustainability indicator identification as a pathway to community empowerment and sustainable environmental management', *Journal of Environmental Management*, 78 (2), 114–127.

Freidson, E. (2001), *Professionalism: The Third Logic*, Cambridge, UK: Polity.

Frey, S.D., D.J. Harrison and E.H. Billett (2006), 'Ecological Footprint analysis applied to mobile phones', *Journal of Industrial Ecology*, 10 (1–2), 199–216.

Fricker, A. (1998), 'The ecological footprint of New Zealand as a step towards sustainability', *Future*, 30 (6), 559–567.

Gahin, R., V. Veleva and M. Hart (2003), 'Do indicators help create sustainable communities?', *Local Environment*, 8 (6), 661–666.

Galli, A., J. Kitzes, P. Wermer, W. Wackernagel, V. Niccolucci and E. Tiezzi (2007), 'An exploration of the mathematics behind the Ecological Footprint', *International Journal of Ecodynamics*, 2 (4), 250–257.

Galli, A., D. Moore, N. Brooks, K. Iha and G. Cranston (2012b), *Mediterranean Ecological Footprint Trends*, Oakland, CA, USA: GFN.

Galli, A., T. Wiedmann, E. Ercinc, D. Knoblauch, B. Ewing and S. Giljum (2012a), 'Integrating Ecological, Carbon and Water Footprint into a "Footprint family" of indicators: definition and role in tracking human pressure on the planet', *Ecological Indicators*, 16, 100–112.

GFN (2004) *Global Footprint Network News*, 1 (1), available at http://www.footprintnetwork.org/newsletters/footprint_network_1-1-0.html (accessed 19 May 2010).

GFN (2006a), *Charter for Global Footprint Network Committees* (Revision 2), available at http://www.footprintnetwork.org/en/index.php/GFN/page/committees_charter/ (accessed 3 June 2010).

GFN (2006b), *Ecological Footprint Standards 2006*, Oakland, CA, USA: GFN.

GFN (2006c), *Africa's Ecological Footprint: Human Well-Being and Biological Capacity*, Oakland, CA, USA: GFN.

GFN (2008), *The Ecological Footprint Atlas 2008*, Oakland, CA, USA: GFN.

GFN (2009a), *Africa FactBook 2009*, Oakland, CA, USA: GFN.

GFN (2009b), *Ecological Footprint Standards 2009*, Oakland, CA, USA: GFN.

GFN (2009c), *The Ecological Footprint Atlas 2009*, Oakland, CA, USA: GFN.

GFN (2010a), *Pegada Ecologica Curitiba* (Curitiba's Ecological Footprint) (in Portuguese), Curitiba, Brazil: SENAI Empresas.

GFN (2010b), *The Ecological Footprint Atlas 2010*, Oakland, CA, USA: GFN.

GFN (2010c), *The Ecological Wealth of the Nations*, Oakland, CA, USA: GFN.

GFN (2011), *Resource Constraints and Economic Performance in Eastern Europe and Central Asia*, Report to UNDP Bratislava, Bratislava, Slovakia: United Nations Development Programme.

GFN (2012), *A Measure for Resilience 2012 Report on the Ecological Footprint of the Philippines*, Oakland, CA, USA: GFN.

GFN (2013a), *Earth Overshoot Day 2013, Around the World*, available at http://www.footprintnetwork.org/en/index.php/GFN/blog/earth_overshoot_day_2013_around_the_world (accessed 8 August 2013).

GFN (2013b), *Resorting Balance in Laguna Lake Region. 2013 Ecological Footprint Report*, Oakland, CA, USA: GFN.

GFN (2014), *Partnership Agreement, Updated July 18, 2014*, available at http://www.footprintnetwork.org/images/uploads/Partnership_Agreement_2014.pdf (accessed 22 August 2014).

GFN and Confederation of Indian Industry (2008), *India's Ecological Footprint: A Business Perspective*, Hyderabad, India: Confederation of Indian Industry.

Giljum, S., E. Burger, F. Hinterberger, S. Lutter and M. Bruckner (2011), 'A comprehensive set of resource use indicators from the micro to the macro level', *Resources, Conservation and Recycling*, 55 (3), 300–308.

Gismondi, M. (2000), *Dr. William Rees Interviewed By Dr. Michael Gismondi*, available at http://aurora.icaap.org/index.php/aurora (accessed 5 May 2012).

Glasson, J., R. Therivel and A. Chadwick (2012), *Introduction to Environmental Impact Assessment*, 4th edn, London, UK: Routledge, Taylor & Francis.

Gössling, S., C. Borgström, O. Hörstmeier and S. Saggel (2002), 'Ecological footprint analysis as a tool to assess tourism sustainability', *Ecological Economics*, 43, 199–211.

Gottlieb, D., M. Kissinger, E. Vigoda-Gadot and A. Haim (2012), 'Analyzing the ecological footprint at the institutional level – the case of an Israeli high school', *Ecological Indicators*, 18, 91–97.

Government Statisticians' Collective (1993 [1979]), 'How official statistics are produced: views from the inside', first published in M. Hammersley (ed.) (1979), *Social Research: Philosophy, Politics and Practice*, London, UK: Sage.

Haberl, H., K-H. Erb and K-H. Krausmann (2001), 'How to calculate and interpret ecological footprints for long periods of time: the case of Austria 1926–1995', *Ecological Economics*, 38, 25–45.

Haines-Young, R. and M. Potschin (2014), 'The ecosystem approach as a framework for understanding knowledge utilisation', *Environment and Planning C: Government and Policy*, 32, 301–319.

Hajer, Maarten. A. (1995), *The Politics of Environmental Discourse*, Oxford, UK: Oxford University Press.

Hamasaki, H. (2011), 'The politics and economics of climate change in Japan: an analysis of the Kyoto Protocol and towards a post-Kyoto framework', PhD thesis, Cardiff, UK: Cardiff University.

Hannigan, J.A. (2006), *Environmental Sociology*, 2nd edn, New York, USA: Routledge.

Haraldsson, H.V., U. Ranhagen and H. Sverdrup (2001), 'Is eco-living more sustainable than conventional living? Comparing sustainability performances between two townships in southern Sweden', *Journal of Environmental Planning and Management*, 44 (5), 663–679.

Hemphill, L., J. Berry and S. McGreal (2004), 'An indicator-based approach to measuring sustainable urban regeneration performance: Part 1, conceptual foundations and methodological framework', *Urban Studies*, 41 (4), 725–755.

Henson, S. and J. Humphrey (2009), 'The impacts of private food safety standards on the food chain and on public standard-setting processes', paper prepared for FAO/WHO, Codex Alimentarus Commission, ALINORM 09/32/9D-Part II, available at http://origin-www.fsis.usda.gov/shared/PDF/Codex_al32_09Dbe.pdf (accessed 11 August 2014).

Herendeen, R.A. (2000), 'Ecological Footprint is a vivid indicator of indirect effects', *Ecological Economics*, 32, 357–358.

Hertin, J., J. Turnpenny, A. Jordan, M. Nilsson, D. Russel and B. Nykvist (2009), 'Rationalising the policy mess? Ex ante policy assessment and the utilisation of knowledge in the policy process', *Environment and Planning A*, 41, 1185–1200.

Herva, M., A. Franco, S. Ferreiro, A. Alvarez and E. Roca (2008), 'An approach for the application of the Ecological Footprint as an environmental indicator in the textile industry', *Journal of Hazardous Material*, 156, 478–487.

Hezri, A.A. and S.R. Dovers (2006), 'Sustainability indicators, policy and governance: issues for ecological economics', *Ecological Economics*, 60 (1), 86–99.

Hille, J. (1997), *The Concept of Environmental Space. Implications for Policies*, Environmental Reporting and Assessments, Experts'

Corner No 1997/2, Copenhagen, Denmark: European Environment Agency.

Hixon, M.A. (2008), 'Carrying capacity', in S.E. Jørgensen and B.D. Fath (eds), *Encyclopaedia of Ecology*, Vol. 1, Oxford, UK: Elsevier Press, pp. 528–530.

Hoekstra, A.Y. (ed.) (2003) *Virtual Water Trade: Proceedings of the International Expert Meeting on Virtual Water Trade*, Delft, The Netherlands, 12–13 December 2002, Value of Water Research Report Series No. 12, Delft, The Netherlands: UNESCOIHE, available at www.waterfootprint.org/Reports/Report12.pdf (accessed 22 September 2014).

Holden, E. (2004), 'Ecological footprints and sustainable urban form', *Journal of Housing and the Built Environment*, 19, 91–109.

Holden, E. and K.G. Hoyer (2005), 'The ecological footprint of fuels', *Transportation Research Part D*, 10, 395–403.

Holland, L. (2003), 'Can the principle of the ecological footprint be applied to measure the environmental sustainability of business?', *Corporate Social Responsibility and Environmental Management*, 10, 224–232.

Hong, L., Z.P. Dong, H. Chunyu and W. Gang (2007), 'Evaluating the effects of embodied energy in international trade on ecological footprint in China', *Ecological Economics*, 62, 136–148.

Hooper, A. and J. Punter (eds) (2006), *Capital Cardiff 1975 –2020: Competitiveness, Boosterism and the Urban Environment*, Cardiff, UK: University of Wales Press.

Horne, R.E., T. Grant and K. Verghese (2009), *Life Cycle Assessment: Principles, Practice and Prospects*, Melbourne, Australia: CSIRO Publishing.

Hoyer, K.G. and E. Holden (2003), 'Household consumption and Ecological Footprints in Norway – does urban form matter?', *Journal of Consumer Policy*, 26, 327–349.

Huang, Q., R. Wang, Z. Ren, J. Li and H. Zhang (2007), 'Regional ecological security assessment based on long periods of ecological footprint analysis', *Resources, Conservation and Recycling*, 51, 24–41.

Hubacek, K. and S. Giljum (2003), 'Applying physical input–output analysis to estimate land appropriation (ecological footprints) of international trade activities', *Ecological Economics*, 44, 137–151.

Huijbregts, M.A.J., S. Hellweg, R. Frischknecht, K. Hungerbuhler and A.J. Hendriks (2008), 'Ecological footprint accounting in the life cycle assessment of products', *Ecological Economics*, 64, 798–807.

Hunter, C. (2002), 'Sustainable tourism and the touristic Ecological Footprint', *Environment, Development and Sustainability*, 4, 7–20.

Hunter, C. and J. Shaw (2007), 'The ecological footprint as a key indicator of sustainable tourism', *Tourism Management*, 28, 46–57.

Illge, L. and R. Schwarze (2009), 'A matter of opinion – how ecological and neoclassical environmental economists think about sustainability and economics', *Ecological Economics*, 69, 594–604.

Japan for Sustainability (2014), *Newsletter*, 2–8 September, available at http://www.japanfs.org/en/news/archives/news_id035041. html (accessed 22 September 2014).

Kingdon, J. (1984), *Agendas, Alternatives and Public Policies*, New York, USA: Harper Collins.

Kingdon, J. (1995), *Agendas, Alternatives and Public Policies*, 2nd edn, New York, USA: Harper Collins.

Krockenberger, M., P. Kinrade and R. Thorman (2000), *Natural Advantage: A Blueprint for a Sustainable Australia*, Melbourne, Australia: Australia Conservation Foundation (ACF).

Lancaster, K., A. Ritter and H. Colebatch (2014), 'Problems, policies and politics: making sense of Australia's "ide epidemic"', *Policy Studies*, 35 (2), 147–171.

Larson, B. (2011), *Metaphors for Environmental Sustainability: Redefining our Relationship with Nature*, New Haven, CT, USA: Yale University Press.

Lawrence, J.G. (1998), 'Getting the future that you want: the role of sustainability indicators', in D. Warburton (ed.), *Community and Sustainable Development*, London, UK: Earthscan, pp. 68–80.

Lenzen, M. (2008), *An Ecological Footprint Study of New South Wales and Sydney*, Report for the Department of Environment and Climate Change, New South Wales, Sydney, Australia: University of Sydney.

Lenzen, M., C. Borgström Hansson and S. Bond (2007), 'On the bioproductivity and land-disturbance metrics of the Ecological Footprint', *Ecological Economics*, 61, 6–10.

Lenzen, M., S. Lundie, G. Bransgrove, L. Charet and F. Sack (2003), 'Assessing the Ecological Footprint of a large metropolitan water supplier: lessons for water management and planning towards sustainability', *Journal of Environmental Planning and Management*, 46, 113–141.

Lenzen, M. and S. Murray (2001), 'A modified ecological footprint method and its application to Australia', *Ecological Economics*, 37, 229–255.

Li, G.J., Q. Wang, X.W. Gu, J.X. Liu, Y. Ding and G.Y. Liang (2008), 'Application of the componential method for ecological footprint calculation of a Chinese university campus', *Ecological Indicators*, 8, 75–78.

Low, G., Z. Todd, A. Deignam and L. Cameron (eds) (2010), *Researching and Applying Metaphor in the Real World*, Amsterdam, The Netherlands: John Benjamin Publishing Company.

MacGillivray, A. (1998), 'Turning the sustainability corner: how to indicate right', in D. Warburton (ed.), *Community and Sustainable Development*, London: Earthscan Publications with World Wide Fund for Nature (WWF UK), pp. 81–95.

Maclaren, V.W. (1996), 'Urban sustainability reporting', *Journal of the American Planning Association*, 62 (2), 184–202.

Mamouni Limnios, E.A., A. Ghadouani, S.G.M. Schilizzi and T. Mazzarol (2009), 'Giving the consumer the choice: a methodology for product Ecological Footprint calculation', *Ecological Economics*, 68, 2525–2534.

Marsden, T., R. Lee, A. Flynn and S. Thankappan (2010), *The New Regulation and Governance of Food: Beyond the Food Crisis?*, Routledge Studies in Human Geography, Vol. 29, Abingdon, UK: Routledge.

May, T. (2011), *Social Research: Issues, Methods and Processes*, 4th edn, Maidenhead, UK: Open University Press/McGraw-Hill Education.

McDonald, G.W. and M.G. Patterson (2004), 'Ecological Footprints and interdependencies of New Zealand regions', *Ecological Economics*, 50, 49–67.

McGann, J.G. (2013), *2012 Global Go To Think Tanks Report and Policy Advance*, Think Tanks and Civil Societies Program, Philadelphia, PA, USA: University of Pennsylvania.

McGregor, P.G., J.K. Swales and K.R. Turner (2004), 'The impact of Scottish consumption on the local environment: an alternative to the Ecological Footprint?', *Quarterly Economic Commentary – Economic Perspectives*, 29 (1), 29–34.

McLaren, D., S. Bullock and N. Yousuf (1998), *Tomorrow's World. Britain's Share in a Sustainable Future*, London, UK: Earthscan.

Medved, S. (2006), 'Present and future ecological footprint of Slovenia – the influence of energy demand scenarios', *Ecological Modelling*, 192, 25–36.

Messem, D. (2012), *Creating Change through Carbon Footprinting*, available at http://www.carbontrust.com/news/2012/02/creating-change-through-carbon-footprinting (accessed 26 March 2013).

Moffatt, I. (2000), 'Ecological Footprints and sustainable development', *Ecological Economics*, 32, 359–362.

Mol, A.P.J. (1995), *The Refinement of Production: Ecological Modernization Theory and the Chemical Industry*, Utrecht, The Netherlands: Van Arkel.

Mol, A.P.J. (2001), *Globalization and Environmental Reform: The Ecological Modernization of the Global Economy*. Cambridge, MA, USA: MIT Press.

Mol, A.P.J. and D.A. Sonnenfeld (eds) (2000), *Ecological Modernisation around the World: Perspectives and Critical Debates*, London, UK and Portland, OR, USA: Frank Cass.

Monfreda, C., M. Wackernagel and D. Deumling (2004), 'Establishing national natural capital accounts based on detailed ecological footprint and biological capacity assessments', *Land Use Policy*, 21, 231–246.

Moore, D. (2011), *Ecological Footprint Analysis: San Francisco – Oakland-Fremont, CA Metropolitan Statistical Area*, Oakland, CA, USA: GFN.

Moore, D., J. Larson, K. Iha, K. Gracey and M. Wackernagel (2013), *The Ecological Footprint and Biocapacity of California*, Oakland, CA, USA: GFN.

Moore, S., M. Nye and Y. Rydin (2007), 'Using ecological footprints as a policy driver: the case of sustainable construction planning policy in London', *Local Environment*, 12, 1–15.

Muniz, I. and A. Galindo (2005), 'Urban form and the ecological footprint of commuting: the case of Barcelona', *Ecological Economics*, 55, 499–514.

National Assembly for Wales (2000) *A Sustainable Wales – Measuring The Difference*, Consultation Paper, 8 September, Cardiff UK: National Assembly for Wales.

National Assembly for Wales (2000–2001), *Deciding to Live Differently*, The First Sustainable Development Report of National Assembly for Wales under Section 121(6) Government of Wales Act 1998, Cardiff, UK: National Assembly for Wales.

Niccolucci, V., A. Galli, J. Kitzes, R. Pulselli, S. Borsa and N. Marchettini (2008), 'Ecological Footprint analysis applied to the production of two Italian wines', *Agriculture, Ecosystems and Environment*, 128, 162–166.

North Lanarkshire Council (2006), *North Lanarkshire Partnership Global Footprint Project: Footprint Reduction Report*, Motherwell, UK: North Lanarkshire Council.

Onisto, L.J., E. Krause and M. Wackernagel (1998), *How Big is Toronto's Ecological Footprint? Using the Concept of Appropriated Carrying Capacity for Measuring Sustainability*, Toronto, Canada: Centre for Sustainable Studies.

ONS (2001), *Census 2001: The Most Comprehensive Survey of the Population*, London, UK: Office for National Statistics.

OPEN (2013), *OPEN: EU Project Background Information*, available at http://www.oneplaneteconomynetwork.org (accessed 11 July 2011).

Opschoor, H.J.B. and L. Reijnders (1991), 'Towards sustainable development indicators', in Kuick Onno and Harmen Verbruggen (eds), *Search of Indicators for Sustainable Development*, Dordrecht, The Netherlands: Kluwer Academic Publishers, pp. 7–27.

Opschoor, J.B. and R. Weterings (1994), 'Environmental utilisation space: an introduction', *Milieu*, 9 (5), 198–205.

Owens, S. and R. Cowell (2002), *Land and Limits: Interpreting Sustainability in the Planning Process*, London, UK: Routledge.

Owens, S., T. Rayner and O. Bina (2004), 'New agendas for appraisal: reflections on theory, practice, and research', *Environment and Planning A*, 36, 1943–1959.

Patterson, T.M., V. Niccolucci and S. Bastianoni (2007), 'Beyond "more is better": ecological footprint accounting for tourism and consumption in Val di Merse, Italy', *Ecological Economics*, 62, 747–756.

Patterson, T.M., V. Niccolucci and S. Bastianoni (2008), 'Adaptive environmental management of tourism in the Province of Siena, Italy using the ecological footprint', *Journal of Environmental Management*, 86, 407–418.

Paul, A., A. Welch, J. Barrett and J. Ravetz (2006), *Ecological Budget North East*, Godalming, UK: WWF UK.

Paul, A., T. Wiedmann, J. Barrett, J. Minx, K. Scott, E. Dawkins, A. Owen, J. Briggs and I. Gray (2010), 'The Resources and Energy Analysis Programme (REAP)', in Joy Murray and Richard Wood (eds), *The Sustainability Practitioner's Guide to Input–Output Analysis*, Champaign, IL, USA: Common Ground Publishing, pp. 133–144.

Pinfield, G. (1996), 'Beyond sustainability indicators', *Local Environment*, 1 (2), 151–163.

Poblete, P., D. Moor, Y. Wada, K. Iha and N. Okayasu (2012), *Japan Ecological Footprint Report 2012*, Tokyo, Japan: WWF Japan.

Ravetz, J., J. Barrett and T. Wiedmann (2006), *Ecological Budget West Midlands*, Godalming, UK: WWF UK.

Raymond, C.M., G. Singh, K. Benessaiah, J.R. Bernhardt, J. Levine, H. Nelson, N.J. Turner, B. Norton, J. Tam and K.M.A. Chan (2013), 'Ecosystem services and beyond: using multiple metaphors to understand human–environment relationships', *Biosciences*, 63 (7), 536–546.

Rayner, S. (2003), 'Democracy in the age of assessment: reflections on the roles of expertise and democracy in the public sector decision making', *Science and Public Policy*, 30, 163–170.

Rees, W. (1992), 'Ecological footprints and appropriated carrying capacity: what urban economics leaves out', *Environment and Urbanization*, 4, 121–130.

Retail Week (2008), *Top 20 Retail Towns and Cities*, 17 October, available at http://www.actsmart.biz/news/top-20-retail-towns-and-cities.php9 (accessed 30 June 2011).

Risk and Policy Analysis Ltd (2007), *A Review of Recent Developments in, and the Practical Use of, Ecological Footprinting Methodologies*, Report to the Department for Environment, Food and Rural Affairs, London, UK: Department for Environment, Food and Rural Affairs.

Robinson, S.E. and W.S. Eller (2010), 'Participation in policy streams: testing the separation of problems and solutions in subnational policy systems', *Policy Studies Journal*, 38, 199–215.

Ross, A. (2006), *Ecological Footprints: The Journey so Far, Lesson Sharing and Case Studies of Local Authorities in the United Kingdom*, Report prepared for WWF UK, Godalming, UK: WWF UK.

Roth, E., H. Rosenthal and P. Burbridge P (2000), 'A discussion of the use of the sustainability index: "ecological footprint" for aquaculture production', *Aquatic Living Resource*, 13, 461–469.

Saab, N. (2012), *Arab Environment: 5 Survival Options Ecological Footprint of Arab Countries*, Beirut, Lebanon: Arab Forum for Environment and Development.

Sanderson, E.W., J. Malanding, M.A. Levy, K.H. Reford, A.V. Wannebo and G. Woolmer (2002), 'The human footprint and the last of the wild', *Bioscience*, 52 (10), 891–904.

Scotti, M., C. Bonavalli and A. Bodini (2009), 'Ecological Footprint as a tool for local sustainability: the municipality of Piacenza (Italy) as a case study', *Environmental Impact Assessment Review*, 29, 39–50.

SEI (2007), *An Introduction to the Resources and Energy Analysis Programme*, York, UK: SEI–York.

SEI (2010), *SEI Strategy 2010–2014*, Stockholm, Sweden: SEI.

SEI–York (2007), *An Introduction to the Resources and Energy Analysis Programme*, York, UK: SEI–York.

Shove, E. (1998), 'Gaps, barriers and conceptual chasms: theories of technological transfer and energy in buildings', *Energy Policy*, 26, 1105–1112.

Simmons, C. (2002), *Five Cities Footprint – Estimating the Ecological Footprint of Aberdeen, Dundee, Edinburgh, Glasgow and Inverness*, Report prepared for the Scottish Executive, Oxford, UK: BFF.

Simmons, C. and N. Chambers (1998), 'Footprinting UK households: how big is your ecological garden?', *Local Environment*, 3 (3), 355–362.

Simmons, C., K. Lewis and J. Barrett (2000), 'Two feet – two approaches: a component-based model of Ecological Footprinting', *Ecological Economics*, 32, 375–380.

Sonesson, U., B. Mattsson, T. Nybrant and T. Ohlsson (2005), 'Industrial processing versus home cooking: an environmental comparison between three ways to prepare a meal', *Ambio*, 34 (4–5), 414–421.

Spangenberg, J.H. (ed.) (1995), *Towards Sustainable Europe*, Luton, UK and Brussels, Belgium: Friends of the Earth.

Stoeglehner, G. and M. Narodoslawshy (2009), 'How sustainable are biofuels? Answers and further questions arising from an ecological footprint perspective', *Bioresource Technology*, 100, 3825–3830.

Sustainable Development Commission (2008), *Indicators*, available at http://www.sd-commission.org.uk/pages/indicators.html (accessed 22 January 2009).

Sutton, P., S.J. Anderson, B.T. Tuttle and L. Morse (2012), 'The real wealth of nations: mapping and monetizing the human ecological footprint', *Ecological Indicators*, 1, 11–22.

Swansea Council (n.d.), 'Local Development Plan. Sustainability appraisal and strategic environmental assessment – draft scoping report', available at http://swansea.jdi-consult.net/ldp/readdoc.php?docid=220&chapter=19&docelemid=d37698#d37698 (accessed 4 May 2014).

Timmermans, S. and S. Epstein (2010), 'A world of standards but not a standard world: toward a sociology of standards and standardization', *Annual Review of Sociology*, 36, 69–89.

Torras, M. (2003), 'An Ecological Footprint approach to external debt relief', *World Development*, 31 (12), 2161–2171.

UK Cities (2011), *Largest Cities in the UK*, available at http://www.ukcities.co.uk/populations/ (accessed 30 June 2011).

UNFPA (2007), *State of the World Population 2007. Unleashing the Potential of Urban Growth*, New York, USA: UNFPA.

Van den Bergh, J. and F. Grazi (2010), 'On the policy relevance of Ecological Footprints', *Environmental Science and Technology Viewpoint*, 44, 4843–4844.

Van den Bergh, J.C.J.M. and H. Verbruggen (1999), 'Spatial sustainability, trade and indicators: an evaluation of the "Ecological Footprint"', *Ecological Economics*, 29, 61–72.

Van Kooten, G.C. and E.H. Bulte (1999), 'The Ecological Footprint: useful science or politics?'. Working Paper 1999–2005, University of Alberta, Alberta, Canada.

Van Vuuren, D.P. and E.M.W. Smeets (2000), 'Ecological footprints of Benin, Bhutan, Costa Rica and the Netherlands', *Ecological Economics*, 34 (234), 115–130.

Venetoulis, J. (2001), 'Assessing the ecological impact of a university: the ecological footprint for the University of Redlands', *International Journal of Sustainability in Higher Education*, 2 (2), 180–197.

Verghese, K. and D. Hes (2007), 'Qualitative and quantitative tool development to support environmentally responsible decisions', *Journal of Cleaner Production*, 15, 814–818.

Vergoulas, G. (2004), *An Ecological Footprint Analysis of Buckinghamshire – South East England*, Oxford, UK: BFF.

Vergoulas, G., K. Lewis and N. Jenkin (2003), *An Ecological Footprint Analysis of Angus, Scotland*, report prepared for Angus Council, Oxford, UK: BFF.

Vergoulas, G. and C. Simmons (2004), *An Ecological Footprint Analysis of Essex – East of England*, report prepared for Essex County Council, Oxford, UK: BFF.

Vienna City Administration (2009), *Der ökologische Fußabdruck der Stadt Wien / The Ecological Footprint of the City of Vienna*, Vienna, Austria: Vienna City Administration.

von Weizsacker, E., A.B. Lovins and L.L Hunter (1997), *Factor Four: Doubling Wealth, Halving Resource Use – The New Report to the Club of Rome*, London, UK: Earthscan.

Wackernagel, M. (1994), 'Ecological Footprint and appropriated carrying capacity: a tool for planning toward sustainability', PhD thesis, Vancouver, Canada: School of Community and Regional Planning, University of British Columbia. OCLC 41839429.

Wackernagel, M. (1998), 'The ecological footprint of Santiago de Chile', *Local Environment: the International Journal of Justice and Sustainability*, 3 (1), 7–25.

Wackernagel, M. and B. Beyers (2010), *Der Ecological Footprint: Die Walt neu Vermessen*, Hamburg, Germany: Europäische VA.

Wackernagel, M., J. Kitzes, D. Cheng, S. Goldfinger, J. Espinas, D. Moran, C. Monfreda, J. Loh, D. O'Gorman and I. Wong (2005a), *Asia-Pacific 2005: The Ecological Footprint and Natural Wealth*, Gland, Switzerland: WWF.

Wackernagel, M., J. Kitzes, D. Moran, S. Goldfinger and M. Thomas (2006), 'The Ecological Footprint of cities and regions: comparing resource availability with resource demand', *Environment and Urbanization*, 18, 103–112.

Wackernagel, M., C. Monfreda, K-H. Erb, H. Haberl and N.B. Schulz (2004a), 'Ecological footprint time series of Austria, the Philippines, and South Korea for 1961–1999: comparing the conventional approach to an "actual land area" approach', *Land Use Policy*, 21 (3), 261–269.

Wackernagel, M., C. Monfreda, N.B. Schulz, K.H. Erb, H. Haberl and F. Krausmann (2004b), 'Calculating national and global ecological footprint time series: resolving conceptual challenges', *Land Use Policy*, 21, 271–278.

Wackernagel, M., D. Moran, S. Goldfinger, C. Monfreda, A. Welch, M. Michael, S. Burns, C. Königel, J. Peck, P. King and M.

Ballesteros (2005b), *Europe 2005: The Ecological Footprint*, Brussels, Belgium: WWF.

Wackernagel, M., L. Onisto, P. Bello, A.C. Linares, L. Falfán, J.M. García, G.A.I. Suárez, G.M.G. Suárez (1999), 'National natural capital accounting with the ecological footprint concept', *Ecological Economics*, 29, 375–390.

Wackernagel, M. and W. Rees (1996), *Our Ecological Footprint: Reducing Human Impact on Earth*, Gabriola Island, BC, Canada: New Society Publishers.

Wada, Y., K. Iha, A. Oursler, M. Stechbart, A. Reed, S. Goldfinger, Y. Kuki, H. Kiyono, N. Okayasu and Y. Saotome (2009), *Japan Ecological Footprint Report 2009: Maintaining Well-being in a Resource Constrained World*, Tokyo, Japan: WWF Japan.

Waylen, K.A. and J. Young (2014), 'Expectations and experiences of diverse forms of knowledge use: the case of the UK National Ecosystem Assessment', *Environment and Planning C: Government and Policy*, 32, 229–246.

Weiss, C.H. (1995), 'The haphazard connection: social science and public policy', *International Journal of Educational Research*, 23, 137–150.

Welsh Assembly Government (2002), *Assembly's Statistical Bulletin*, Cardiff: Welsh Assembly Government.

Welsh Assembly Government (2010a), *Planning Policy Wales*, Edition 3 (July), Cardiff, UK: Welsh Assembly Government.

Welsh Assembly Government (2010b), 'UK–Cardiff: a strategic monitoring framework for the planning system in Wales', available at http://www.tendersdirect.co.uk/Search/Tenders/Expired.aspx?ID=%20000000002979697&sect=C059&cat=31&Source=Categories (accessed 10 February 2011).

White, T. (2000), 'Diet and the distribution of environmental impact', *Ecological Economics*, 34 (234), 145–153.

Whittlesea, E.R. and A. Owen (2009), *Stepping Towards a Low Carbon Future: Development and Application of a Tourism Footprinting Tool in the South West*, York, UK: SEI–York.

Whittlesea, E.R. and A. Owen (2012), 'Towards a low carbon future – the development and application of REAP Tourism, a destination footprint and scenario tool', *Journal of Sustainable Tourism*, 20 (6), 845–865.

Wiedmann, T. and J. Barrett (2005), *The Use of Input–Output Analysis in REAP to allocate Ecological Footprints and Material*

Flows to Final Consumption Categories REAP Report 2, York, UK: SEI–York.

Wiedmann, T. and J. Barrett (2010). 'A review of the ecological footprint indicator – perceptions and methods', *Sustainability*, 2 (6), 1645–1693.

Wiedmann, T., J. Barrett and N. Cherrett (2003), *Sustainability Rating for Homes – The Ecological Footprint Component*, York, UK: SEI–York.

Wiedmann, T., J. Minx, J. Barrett and M. Wackernagel (2006), 'Allocating ecological footprints to final consumption categories with input–output analysis', *Ecological Economics*, 56, 28–48.

Willi, V., J. Wachtl, A. de Montmollin, A. Boesch, A. Sauron, N. North, S. Schwab, J. Trageser, T. von Stocker and R. Zanonella (2011), *Sustainable Development Report 2012*, Neuchâtel, Switzerland: FSO.

Wood, R. and M. Lenzen (2003), 'An application of a modified Ecological Footprint method and structural path analysis in a comparative institutional study', *Local Environment*, 8 (4), 365–386.

WWF (2000), *Living Planet Report 2000*, Gland, Switzerland: WWF International.

WWF (2002), *Living Planet Report 2002*, Gland, Switzerland: WWF International.

WWF (2004), *Living Planet Report 2004*, Gland, Switzerland: WWF International.

WWF (2006), *Living Planet Report 2006*, Gland, Switzerland: WWF International.

WWF (2007), *Europe 2007: Gross Domestic Product and Ecological Footprint*, Brussels, Belgium: WWF European Office (EPO).

WWF (2008), *Living Planet Report 2008*, Gland, Switzerland: WWF International.

WWF (2010), *Living Planet Report 2010*, Gland, Switzerland: WWF International.

WWF (2012), *Living Planet Report 2012*, Gland, Switzerland: WWF International.

WWF (2014), *Living Planet Report 2012*, Gland, Switzerland: WWF International.

WWF Brazil (2012), *The Ecological Footprint of São Paulo – State and Capital and the Footprint Family*, Brasilia, Brasil: WWF Brasil.

WWF China (2010), *China Ecological Footprint Report 2010: Biocapacity, Cities and Development*, Beijing, China: WWF China.

WWF China (2012) *China Ecological Footprint Report 2012: Consumption, Production and Sustainable Development*, Beijing, China: WWF China.

WWF Hong Kong (2008), *Hong Kong Ecological Footprint Report 2008: Living Beyond our Means*, Hong Kong, China: WWF Hong Kong.

WWF Hong Kong (2010), *Hong Kong Ecological Footprint Report 2010: Paths to a Sustainable Future*, Hong Kong, China: WWF Hong Kong.

WWF Hong Kong (2013), *Hong Kong Ecological Footprint Report 2013*, Hong Kong, China: WWF Hong Kong.

WWF Scotland, Aberdeenshire Council, Aberdeen City Council and North Lanarkshire Partnership (2007), *Scotland's Global Footprint. Reducing Our Environmental Impact Final Report*, Dunkeld, UK: WWF Scotland.

WWF Türkiye (2012), *Türkiya'nin Ekolojik Ayak İzi Raporu* (Turkey Ecological Footprint Report), İstanbul, Türkiye: WWF Türkiye.

WWF UK (2006), *Ecological Budget United Kingdom Counting Consumption*, Godalming, UK: WWF UK.

WWF and GFN (eds) (2007), *Canadian Living Planet Report 2007*, Toronto, Canada: WWF Canada.

WWF and GFN (2008a), *2010 and Beyond: Rising to the Biodiversity Challenge*, Gland, Switzerland: WWF.

WWF and GFN (2008b), *Africa: Ecological Footprint: and Human Well-being*, Gland, Switzerland: WWF International.

WWF and GFN (2008c), *Report on the Ecological Footprint of China*, Beijing, China: WWF China.

Yearley, S. (1991), *The Green Case: A Sociology of Environmental Issues, Arguments and Politics*, London, UK: Harper Collins Academic.

Young, S. (1996), 'Promoting participation to community-based partnerships in the context of LA21: a report for practitioners', Paper 1/96, European Policy Research Unit, Department of Government, Manchester, UK: University of Manchester.

Yue, D., X. Xu, Z. Li, C. Hui, L. Wenlong, H. Yang and J. Ge (2006), 'Spatiotemporal analysis of ecological footprint and biological capacity of Gansu, China 1991–2015: down from the environmental cliff', *Ecological Economics*, 58, 393–406.

Zahariadis, N. (2007), 'The multiple streams framework', in P.A. Sabatier (ed.), *Theories of the Policy Process*, Boulder, CO, USA: Westview Press, pp. 73–96.

Index